1089

WHY WE WERE

IN VIETNAM

Norman Podhoretz

A TOUCHSTONE BOOK
Published by Simon and Schuster
NEW YORK

Copyright © 1982, 1983 by Norman Podhoretz
All rights reserved
including the right of reproduction
in whole or in part in any form
First Touchstone Edition, 1983
Published by Simon & Schuster, Inc.
Simon & Schuster Building
Rockefeller Center
1230 Avenue of the Americas
New York, New York 10020
TOUCHSTONE and colophon are registered trademarks of
Simon & Schuster, Inc.
Designed by Irving Perkins and Associates
Manufactured in the United States of America
10 9 8 7 6 5 4 3 2 1
10 9 8 7 6 5 4 3   Pbk.
Library of Congress Cataloging in Publication Data
Podhoretz, Norman.
    Why we were in Vietnam.
    Includes bibliographical references and index.
    1. Vietnamese Conflict, 1961-1975—United States.
2. United States—History—1945-   . I. Title.
DS558.P63   959.70433'73   81-21305
                                     AACR2
ISBN 0-671-44578-2
ISBN 0-671-47061-2 Pbk.

For
Jacob Abrams and Samuel Munson

"Woe to the statesman whose reasons for entering a war do not appear so plausible at its end as at its beginning."

—Bismarck

CONTENTS

ONE: DELIVERANCE FROM A DEBATE   9

TWO: WHY WE WENT IN   16

THREE: WHY WE STAYED IN   64

FOUR: WHY WE WITHDREW   133

FIVE: WHOSE IMMORALITY?   174

POSTSCRIPT TO THE TOUCHSTONE EDITION:
          THE ISSUE OF "FULL DISCLOSURE"   211

          NOTES   221

          INDEX   241

ONE:

DELIVERANCE FROM A DEBATE

ON April 30, 1975, when the last American helicopter scurried desperately off the roof of the American Embassy in Saigon as the city fell to the invading North Vietnamese army, the Washington *Post* said that it was a day of "deliverance" for the United States. In some sense, of course, it was. For nearly fifteen years, Americans had been working, fighting, and dying in Vietnam; and from this, surely, they were delivered on April 30, 1975.

They were also delivered from something else on that fateful day—something less bloody than the war itself but in some ways no less anguished and anguishing. This was the debate over the war that had been raging with an intensity that escalated along with American involvement, bursting from time to time out of the confines of words and ideas and arguments into the demonstrations, the skirmishes, and the more violent confrontations of what had come to be called "the war at home." Overnight, it

9

seemed, Vietnam, the great obsession of the past decade and more, disappeared from the national consciousness. The newspapers and magazines and television stations carried what were in effect obituary notices, and the debate, along with the war that had provoked it, was then hastily interred in the forensic equivalent of an unmarked grave.

But of course nothing in history ever really happens overnight. In the case of the debate over Vietnam, by the time it was buried, it had long since lost its right to be called a debate. For at least the last five years of American involvement in Vietnam, hardly any voices had been raised in defense of our continued participation in the war. The arguments all came from the other side, and for the most part they remained unanswered. Entering office in 1969, Richard Nixon, like Lyndon Johnson in the last phase of his Presidency, spoke mainly of how to get the United States out of Vietnam. Rarely did he, or anyone else in those days, attempt to justify the intervention itself. Nixon had supported the decision of John F. Kennedy's Administration to go into Vietnam; he had supported the deepening of American involvement under Johnson; and then, by resisting the temptation to withdraw immediately upon becoming President, he had taken the onus of Vietnam upon himself, turning it (in an act that many thought foolish from the point of view of his own political fortunes) into "his" war. Yet he never really made it "his" war in the sense of defending it politically and morally. There was no point, he and his people kept saying, in arguing over how and why we had got into Vietnam; the only question was how best to get out. Thus what Nixon mainly did was defend his strategy of gradual withdrawal against the demand for an immediate end to the American presence. The effect was to concede the moral and political arguments to the antiwar forces—by now a coalition that included people who had led the country into Vietnam in the first place and were eager to atone by leading it out.

Even before April 30, 1975, then, Vietnam had become perhaps the most negatively charged political symbol in American history, awaiting only the literal end of American involvement to achieve its full and final diabolization. From a narrowly political point of view, it had become to the generation that had experienced it what Munich had been to an earlier generation: the self-evident symbol of a policy that must never be followed again.

Indeed, for many people whose original support of American intervention in Vietnam had been based on memories of Munich, Vietnam not only replaced it but canceled it out. To such people the lesson of Munich had been that an expansionist totalitarian power could not be stopped by giving in to its demands and that limited resistance at an early stage was the only way to avoid full-scale war later on. Prime Minister Neville Chamberlain, returning to England from the conference in Munich at which Nazi Germany's claims over Czechoslovakia had been satisfied, triumphantly declared that he was bringing with him "peace in our time." But as almost everyone would later agree, what he had actually brought with him was the certainty of a world war to come—a war that Winston Churchill, the leading critic of the policy of appeasement consummated at Munich, would later call "unnecessary." According to Churchill, if a line had been drawn against Hitler from the beginning, he would have been forced to back away, and the sequence of events that led inexorably to the outbreak of war would have been interrupted.

Obviously, Vietnam differed in many significant ways from Central Europe in the late 1930s. But there was one great similarity that overrode these differences in the minds of many whose understanding of such matters had been shaped by the memory of Munich. "I'm not the village idiot," Dean Rusk, who was Secretary of State first under Kennedy and then under Johnson, once exploded. "I know Hitler was an Austrian and Mao is a Chinese. . . . But what is common between the two situations is the phenomenon of aggression."[1] In other words, in Vietnam now as in Central Europe then, a totalitarian political force— Nazism then, Communism now—was attempting to expand the area under its control. A relatively limited degree of resistance then would have precluded the need for massive resistance afterward. This was the lesson of Munich, and it had already been applied successfully in Western Europe in the forties and Korea in the fifties. Surely it was applicable to Vietnam as well.

When, however, it began to become evident that, in contrast to the cases of Western Europe and Korea, the differences between Vietnam now and Central Europe then were more decisive than the similarities, the relevance of Munich began to fade, and a new set of lessons—the lessons of Vietnam—began to take hold. The legacy of Munich had been a disposition, even a great readiness, to resist, by force if necessary, the expansion of totalitarianism; the legacy of Vietnam would obversely be a reluctance, even a refusal, to resist, especially if resistance required the use of force.

For some of the older generation who rejected the tutelage of Munich in favor of the tutelage of Vietnam, the new pedagogic dispensation was generally limited to lessons of a strictly political character. When they said, or (less given to being so explicit) nodded in agreement as others said, "No More Vietnams," they had in mind a new foreign policy that would base itself on more modest expectations of American power than had prevailed in the years of Kennedy and Johnson. For them the main lesson of Vietnam was that the United States no longer should or could play the role of "policeman of the world." We had certain core interests—Western Europe, Japan, Israel—that we were, and must remain, committed to defend. But however desirable it might ideally be to undertake more than that, we lacked the power, the will, and the wisdom to carry out a more ambitious strategy with any hope of success. In this view, Vietnam represented the great cautionary argument against the "arrogance of American power."

In addition to humility about the extent of American power, Vietnam persuaded many, or perhaps most, converts from the school of Munich that humility was also required in defining the purposes for which this limited American power could and should be used. Even assuming that it might be desirable to contain the spread of Communism—and many by now had lost their former conviction that it was desirable—Vietnam showed that the United States was unable (or indeed unqualified) to go on making the effort with any hope of success. On this issue Vietnam was taken to be an irrefutable piece of evidence showing the folly of an ideologically based foreign policy in general and of an anti-Communist "crusade" in particular.

But these were only the blandest of the lessons of Vietnam. For, unlike Munich, Vietnam became the symbol of something much broader than a mistaken foreign policy. Especially for younger people who had no personal memory of the Second World War, Vietnam did not so much reverse the legacy of Munich as it succeeded to the legacy of Auschwitz. Only the most extreme elements within the antiwar movement took to spelling the name of the country as "Amerika," but many who shied away from so open an identification of the United States under Johnson with Germany under Hitler tacitly acquiesced in (if only by failing to object to) the idea that American involvement in Vietnam was an evil fully comparable to the evils done by Nazi Germany.

Sometimes the evil was taken to be the American intervention itself: an act of aggression against a people fighting to liberate themselves from a corrupt and repressive regime. Far from resisting the spread of totalitarianism, we were propping it up. We were the counterrevolutionaries, we were the imperialists, we were the enemies of freedom and self-determination.

As time went on, however, the emphasis shifted from the original "Amerikan" sin, the evil of the intervention, to the atrocities and crimes we were said to be committing in the fighting of the war itself. Within South Vietnam, the country we were allegedly trying to defend, we were uprooting villages, indiscriminately bombing and bombarding areas populated by civilians, defoliating forests and destroying crops, setting women and children on fire with napalm and other incendiary weapons, and committing random atrocities like the massacre of My Lai; and when, after 1965, we extended the war to North Vietnam, we became guilty of terror-bombing aimed at harmless civilian targets. All this added up to the great crime of genocide. Some Americans agreed with Europeans like Jean-Paul Sartre and Bertrand Russell that the United States was deliberately "wiping out a whole people and imposing the Pax Americana on an uninhabited Vietnam";[2] others thought that the policy was not deliberate but that (in the words of the American writer Frances FitzGerald) it "had no other military logic" and that the results were in any case "indistinguishable" from genocide.[3]

So well and widely established did this view become, and so halfhearted and ineffective were the replies, that the word Vietnam became serviceable as a self-evident symbol of evil even outside the context of politics. (Here, for example, was how it would later seem natural for a member of the Vietnam generation to speak of himself: "Sometimes my life seems like my own personal Vietnam policy. A rap sheet so heinous that I wonder why those hooded judges of my conscience did not condemn me long ago. . . .")[4]

But within the context of politics, the idea that the American intervention into Vietnam had been a crime led, as we would expect, to sterner lessons than those that followed from the idea that the intervention had merely been a mistake. Instead of learning humility about the extent of their power, Americans were to learn renunciation. Until we could teach ourselves to intervene on the side of good—the side of revolutionary change—the best thing we could do both for ourselves and for the rest of the world was not to intervene at all. Oppressed peoples everywhere were rising and demanding their rights, and everywhere they encountered American opposition. The lesson of Vietnam was that the United States, not the Soviet Union and certainly not Communism, represented the greatest threat to the security and well-being of the peoples of the world.

Thus it was that by April 30, 1975, the debate over Vietnam had already been settled in favor of the moral and political position of the antiwar movement. At best Vietnam had been a blunder; at worst it had been a crime. At best it exposed the folly of trying to contain the spread of Communism anywhere outside Western Europe; at worst it demonstrated that we were and always had been on the wrong side of a worldwide struggle.

That the United States was defeated in Vietnam is certain. But did that defeat truly mean what the antiwar movement seems to have persuaded everyone it meant? Do the policies that led the United States into Vietnam deserve the discredit that has been attached to them? Does the United States deserve the moral contumely that Vietnam has brought upon it in the eyes of so many people both at home and abroad? Is it true, as the German novelist Guenter Grass has said, that America "lost in Vietnam its right to appeal to morals"?[5] The only way to answer these questions is to reopen the debate over Vietnam from which the United States was prematurely delivered in the closing years of the war. But before the political and moral issues can be properly engaged, it will be necessary to retell the story of how and why the United States went into Vietnam and how and why it was driven out.

TWO:

WHY WE WENT IN

SO much that has been written about Vietnam has come out of an antiwar perspective that reading through the literature leaves one with the impression that the men who made the decisions leading to an ever-deepening American involvement must all have been madmen and fools.

The truth, however, is that if they were not exactly "the best and the brightest," as David Halberstam half sarcastically and half seriously called them in the title of one of the most famous books published about the war while it was still going on, neither were they the worst and the most stupid. For Halberstam, the problem was to explain how so many of his own political heroes and friends should have taken so self-evidently wrong a turn. (His answer was irresistible pressure from the Right.) The same problem presented itself to former members of the Kennedy Administration—Arthur Schlesinger, Jr., Theodore Sorensen, and Richard N. Goodwin, for example—who later turned against the war. For such as these the problem was resolved in effect by

16

blaming, on the one hand, the Truman and Eisenhower Administrations, which had come before and left Kennedy a legacy of
commitment he had no choice but to honor; and on the other
hand, the Johnson Administration, which came after and escalated the American commitment beyond anything Kennedy himself allegedly would have done had he lived.

Yet as another critic of the war, Theodore Draper, asks, "If
President Kennedy's options were so limited in 1961 without
American combat troops in South Vietnam, why did they [his
former associates] think—as many did when they turned against
the war after 1965—that President Johnson's options were so
much less limited with 400,000 American troops there?" Kennedy, as Draper rightly says, emerges from the accounts of
Schlesinger and Sorensen as "a man who did what he did not
want to do, what he knew or felt he should not do, and what he
had little faith would come out right in the end."[1] And he
emerges in the same way from Halberstam's account: "Kennedy
had made the commitment without much enthusiasm and with a
good deal of misgivings. He had made it not so much because he
wanted to, but because he felt he could not do less, given the
time and the circumstances. But he was never in any deep sense
a believer. . . ."[2]

This reading of Kennedy is based on a highly selective and
even more highly tendentious use of the evidence bearing on his
ideas about the world in general and Vietnam in particular. Both
Schlesinger and Sorensen, for example, quote a speech Kennedy
made as a senator on April 6, 1954, warning against American
aid to the French in their losing struggle to maintain imperial
control over Vietnam. In that speech Kennedy said: "I am
frankly of the belief that no amount of American military assistance in Indochina can conquer . . . 'an enemy of the people'
which has the sympathy and covert support of the people. . ...
For the United States to intervene unilaterally and to send troops
into the most difficult terrain in the world, with the Chinese able
to pour in unlimited manpower, would mean that we would face
a situation which would be far more difficult than even that we
encountered in Korea."[3]

Schlesinger also quotes a sentence from the same speech in which Kennedy raised the question "whether all or part of Indochina is absolutely essential to the security of Asia and the free world." [4] He further tells us that Kennedy as President "used to mutter from time to time about our 'overcommitment' in Southeast Asia." "They want a force of American troops," Schlesinger reports Kennedy remarked to him one day. "They say it's necessary in order to restore confidence and maintain morale. . . . Then we will be told we have to send in more troops. It's like taking a drink. The effect wears off, and you have to take another." [5]

If these had really been Kennedy's sentiments, his decision to involve the United States militarily in Vietnam would indeed be easier to explain as the act of a madman or a fool than as the fatalistic submission Schlesinger sometimes makes it out to be, or as the act of a distracted President too busy with other crises (". . . Vietnam was still in these years a low-level crisis. It was far less urgent than Cuba, or Berlin, or Latin America, or nuclear testing, or preserving the European alliance, or fighting for civil rights in the United States; far less urgent than the neighboring Asian crisis in Laos"). [6]

Now, Schlesinger is certainly right in saying that Vietnam was a low-level crisis in the first two years of the Kennedy Administration. As late as April 1962, for example, a piece entitled "The Crisis in Ecuador" competed for attention on the editorial page of the New York *Times* with one called "The Root Cause in Vietnam." [7] A few months earlier, a long analysis in *Commentary* on "The Problem of South Vietnam" by Joseph J. Zasloff, a political scientist who had just returned from a teaching stint at the University of Saigon, began with the words: "While Laos and then Berlin and then Katanga have been dominating the front pages in recent months, a situation of equally critical proportions has been building up in South Vietnam, where the government of President Ngo Dinh Diem is struggling for survival against well-organized strongly sustained guerrilla forces—the Vietcong—inspired and supported by the Communist Vietminh government of the North." [8]

Nevertheless, it is misleading to suggest that Kennedy either as a senator or as President regarded Vietnam as unimportant to the United States. Kennedy as a senator made other statements which Schlesinger never mentions but which consort so naturally with what he did later as President that they have a far better claim to be taken as reflecting what he really thought.

Thus, on June 1, 1956, two years after delivering Schlesinger's favorite speech, Kennedy spoke before the American Friends of Vietnam on "America's Stake in Vietnam." By this time the French had been defeated, and Vietnam had been partitioned under a set of agreements negotiated in Geneva, with a Communist regime under Ho Chi Minh established in the North and a non-Communist government under Ngo Dinh Diem set up in the South. According to the Geneva agreements, Vietnam was to be unified under a government to be elected in 1956, but Kennedy declared that "neither the United States nor Free Vietnam [was] ever going to be a party to an election obviously stacked and subverted in advance" by the Communists of the North and their agents and allies in the South. To Kennedy, Vietnam represented "the cornerstone of the Free World in Southeast Asia, the keystone to the arch, the finger in the dike. Burma, Thailand, India, Japan, the Philippines and obviously Laos and Cambodia . . . would be threatened if the red tide of Communism overflowed into Vietnam."

This was the first of the four reasons Kennedy gave for "America's stake in Vietnam." The second was that Vietnam represented "a proving ground for democracy in Asia . . . the alternative to Communist dictatorship. If this democratic experience fails, if some one million refugees have fled the totalitarianism of the North only to find neither freedom nor security in the South, then weakness, not strength, will characterize the meaning of democracy in the minds of still more Asians." It was, Kennedy said, an experiment we could not "afford to permit . . . to fail."

The third reason was that Vietnam, in addition to representing a test of democracy in Asia, also represented "a test of American responsibility and determination" there. Characterizing the

United States as the "godparents" of "little Vietnam" and Vietnam as "our offspring" ("We presided at its birth, we gave assistance to its life, we have helped to shape its future"), Kennedy concluded that if Vietnam were to fall "victim to any of the perils that threaten its existence—Communism, political anarchy, poverty and the rest," we would be held responsible and our prestige in Asia would "sink to a new low."

Finally (and most prophetically), America's stake in Vietnam was "a very selfish one" in the sense that "American lives and American dollars" would inevitably have to be expended if "the apparent security which has increasingly characterized that area under the leadership of President Diem" were to be jeopardized.[9]

What Kennedy was saying in this speech was that the Geneva accords of 1954 had belatedly turned Vietnam into exactly the same kind of case that Germany and Korea had become in the immediate aftermath of World War II. As the eminent specialist on international affairs Hans J. Morgenthau, also writing in 1956, put it: "The provision for free elections which would solve ultimately the problem of Vietnam was a device to hide the incompatibility of the Communist and Western positions, neither of which can admit the domination of all of Vietnam by the other side. It was a device to disguise the fact that the line of military demarcation was bound to be a line of political division as well. In one word, what happened in Germany and Korea in the years immediately following 1945 has happened in Vietnam in the years following 1954."[10]

Like Germany and Korea before it, Vietnam had been divided into two different countries, one Communist and the other non-Communist. From the beginning, the United States had clearly and unambiguously committed itself to preventing the takeover of West Germany by the Communists. By 1947 there were alarming signs that the Soviet Union had no intention of surrendering control over the countries of Eastern Europe occupied by the Red armies in the course of their victorious westward sweep toward Germany at the end of World War II. Further, the Soviets were employing local Communist parties to subvert non-Communist countries like Greece and Turkey. In the face of all this,

President Harry Truman found himself declaring that "it must be the policy of the United States to support free peoples who are resisting attempted subjugation by armed minorities or by outside pressures." [11]

Thus was enunciated the policy that came to be known as the Truman Doctrine, or "containment." In calling for political and economic measures to strengthen the non-Communist societies of Europe against the threat of internal subversion (the reality of which was dramatically demonstrated by a Communist coup in Czechoslovakia and by the existence of huge Communist parties in France and Italy), containment gave birth to the Marshall Plan. And in calling for resistance to any attempt by Soviet troops to push beyond the boundaries of the empire they had already established, containment begat the North Atlantic Treaty Organization (NATO).

But if there was little or no doubt about the American commitment to hold the line against any further expansion of Communist rule in Europe, there remained uncertainty as to whether the same rule applied to Asia, and specifically to Korea. After 1949, when the Communists under Mao Zedong finally defeated the forces of Chiang Kai-shek and took over the mainland of China, the question of American policy toward the threat of spreading Communist rule in Asia assumed a new urgency.

In subsequent years much ridicule came to be heaped upon the idea of an international Communist movement or a monolithic Communist conspiracy, but there was nothing ridiculous or even overstated about this idea in 1949. With the single exception of Tito's Yugoslavia, a Communist country that (without renouncing Communism) had broken free of Soviet domination, all Communist parties everywhere, whether in power or in a minority, were controlled by the Soviet Union. That is, they all took orders from the Soviet Union, saying and doing only what they were told even if—as was often the case—following the Soviet line and subordinating themselves to Soviet interests damaged their own interests within the political systems in which they had to live. Local Communist leaders who could not bring themselves to obey orders handed down from Moscow either resigned or were expelled. This was as true of the Communist parties of the United States, France, and Italy as it was of the Communist parties of China, Korea, and Vietnam.

It was obvious, therefore, that the conquest of China represented a major victory for the Soviet Union and an enormous extension of its power. It was equally obvious that this victory would inspire and energize other Communist insurgencies throughout Asia. Was the United States prepared to extend the principles of the Truman Doctrine to cover such insurgencies as well?

The answer was unclear. On the one hand, the most authoritative and highly articulated public statement of the assumptions behind containment, the famous article by the then Director of the State Department's Policy Planning Staff, George F. Kennan (published in 1947 in *Foreign Affairs*, under the pseudonym "Mr. X"), could only be read to imply that in principle at least containment was global in scope. "The main element," said Kennan, "of any United States policy toward the Soviet Union must be that of a long-term, patient but firm and vigilant containment of Russian expansive tendencies . . . by the adroit and vigilant application of counter-force at a series of constantly shifting geographical and political points, corresponding to the shifts and maneuvers of Soviet policy. . . ." Nor did Kennan leave any doubt as to the relation between local Communist parties and the Soviet Union: the duty of "all good Communists" everywhere in the world, he wrote, "is the support and promotion of Soviet power, as defined in Moscow." [12]

Yet on the other hand, three years later, Kennan's boss, Truman's Secretary of State, Dean Acheson, seemed to suggest that the United States did not regard the independence of South Korea as a vital interest. [13] This the Soviet Union, the Chinese, and the North Koreans evidently all took as a signal that the forcible extension of Communist rule to the South would not be met by the application of American counterforce. It seems unlikely that Acheson, who as much as any one individual was the father of containment—"present," as he put it in the title of his memoirs, "at the creation"—really intended to send such a signal. But whether there was a misunderstanding here or a last-minute change of mind, the invasion of South Korea on June 25, 1950, triggered an immediate American response. Only two days after the outbreak of the war, President Truman declared that "the attack upon Korea makes it plain beyond all doubt that Communism has passed beyond the use of subversion to conquer independent nations and will now use armed invasion and war." [14]

Not only was the United States now extending the principles of containment from Europe to Asia, then; it was going even further in practice. In Europe the threat of war had so far been enough; in Korea war itself had become necessary. And so the United States went to war.

In explaining why he decided to go to war in Korea ("the toughest decision I had to make as President," although he had also had to make the decision to use the atomic bomb), Truman clearly linked it to the experience of the thirties: "This was," he wrote in his memoirs, "the same kind of challenge Hitler flaunted in the face of the rest of the world when he crossed the borders of Austria and Czechoslovakia. The free world failed then to meet that challenge, and World War II was the result." [15] The memory of Munich, then, came consciously and saliently into play.

Even more explicit was Truman's association of the decision with the policy of containment and the various actions previously taken under the aegis of that policy. No sooner had the decision to send American troops into Korea been made than "our allies and friends abroad were informed through our diplomatic representatives . . . that we considered the Korean situation vital as a symbol of the strength and determination of the West. Firmness now would be the only way to deter new actions in other portions of the world. Not only in Asia but in Europe, the Middle East, and elsewhere the confidence of peoples in countries adjacent to the Soviet Union would be very adversely affected . . . if we failed to take action to protect a country established under our auspices. . . . If, however, the threat to South Korea was met firmly and successfully, it would add . . . a fourth success in opposition to the aggressive moves of the Communists" to three earlier such successes—in Iran in 1946, when Soviet troops had been forced out of Azerbaijan; in Berlin in 1947, when a Soviet blockade had been defied through a massive American airlift; and then in Greece, where the threat of a Communist takeover had been averted with the help of the military aid provided by the Truman Doctrine. "And each success, we suggested to our allies, was likely to add to the caution of the Soviets in undertaking new efforts of this kind." [16]

The "allies and friends" of the United States abroad responded with relief and enthusiasm to this argument. Averell Harriman (a great supporter of containment until the war in Vietnam began going badly) reported to Truman after a trip to Europe that "the people there had been gravely concerned lest we fail to meet the challenge in Korea." After Truman's decision had been announced, Harriman said, ". . . there had been a general feeling of relief. . . ." [17]

The Security Council of the United Nations joined in on June 27 with a "resolution calling on all members of the U.N. to give assistance to South Korea," and before long troops from many countries had joined with those of the United States in the effort to repel the North Korean invasion. "By mid-October there were in Korea, besides United States and Republic of Korea troops, ground units of Australia, Great Britain, and the Philippines. A Swedish hospital field unit was in action. Infantry from Thailand and Turkey were being disembarked at Korean ports. . . . Naval assistance had come from Australia, Colombia, France, Great Britain, the Netherlands, New Zealand, and Norway. Furthermore, Belgium, Colombia, Canada, Ethiopia, France, and Greece were preparing ground units for movement to Korea. . . . All in all, considering monetary and supply contributions, forty-two nations had by then offered their aid to the United Nations." [18]

Within the United States itself, the response was no less forthcoming. Indeed, looking back on Korea from a perspective shaped by the experience of Vietnam, what seems most remarkable is the absence of any serious opposition to what Truman decided to do. After all, the United States had only yesterday brought "the boys back home" from four long years of war; and so little was any future military action on the American mind in 1945 that, as Truman put it, "the American people had chosen to scuttle their military might." He himself as President and General Dwight D. Eisenhower as Army Chief of Staff had both warned against "hasty and excessive demobilization," but their voices had been "drowned out" by Congress and the press.[19] Yet now, only five years later, there was scarcely a protest against the remobilization required by the decision to go into Korea: the activation of several National Guard divisions and the reinstitution of the draft (by unanimous vote in the Senate). This seems all the more remarkable when we consider that many veterans of World War II who were called back into service had only just begun establishing themselves in families and careers and now had to undergo yet another cruel interruption and delay, and that many of the younger draftees had only the faintest conception of why they were being asked to fight for a country halfway around the world, a country they had never even heard of before.

"What a nation can do or must do begins with the willingness and the ability of its people to shoulder the burden," wrote Truman,[20] and the fact remains that the American people were willing to shoulder the burden of Korea. There were still isolationists in the United States who saw no reason to fight in any distant place, but their ideas had been dealt so stunning a blow by the events of the past decade that they were reduced to surly and ineffectual mutterings. There were also groups in the United States opposed to the policy of containment, not because they were isolationists, but because they were either sympathetic to the Soviet Union or convinced that the Soviets were more sinned against than sinning and had more cause to defend themselves against us than we had to defend ourselves against them. But the influence of these groups had by 1950 been severely diminished by the refusal of the Soviet Union to behave in accordance with their interpretation of its intentions. The challenge they had mounted to Truman in the 1948 Presidential election had been exposed as politically shallow when their candidate, Henry Wallace, received not the ten million votes he had expected but only a million. And as if all this were not enough, they were further weakened by official harassment in the form of congressional investigations and all the other instrumentalities of what later came to be called McCarthyism.

Truman thus had next to no trouble with the isolationists or the Soviet apologists, and their ideas had next to no effect on the political culture that sanctioned his decision to intervene militarily in Korea and simultaneously shaped the response of the American people—including those who had to do the actual fighting. Where Truman did run into serious trouble, however, was with groups on the opposite end of the political spectrum who objected, not to the war itself, but to the way it was being fought.

In Europe the policy of containment called for the prevention of any further expansion of the Soviet empire beyond the lines drawn at the conclusion of the fighting in World War II. Given the fact that all Communist parties everywhere were in those days subservient to the Soviet Union, this rule applied, in theory at least, to internal subversion or insurrection no less than to invasion by the Red Army. Thus the great theorist of containment, George F. Kennan, who would later protest that his ideas had been misinterpreted as calling for a greater emphasis on the military over the political component than he had intended, "recommended outright military intervention should the Communists win" the elections in Italy in 1948.[21]

Nevertheless, the United States did not attempt to intervene when Czechoslovakia, which (in Truman's words) "had so long been the stronghold of democracy in Central Europe," fell to a Communist coup in 1948—foreshadowing in this the tacit agreement (which would be observed in Hungary in 1956 and again in Czechoslovakia in 1968) to allow the Soviet Union a free hand within its own sphere of influence. Italy, in other words, came under our protection; Czechoslovakia did not. Though it was a democratic country and therefore had a claim on an American policy aimed at defending the free world against Communist aggression, Czechoslovakia could not be saved without risking an all-out war between the United States and the Soviet Union. This risk the United States was not prepared to run. And so, to quote Truman again, "democratic Czechoslovakia, for the second time in less than nine years, fell under the heel of totalitarianism."[22] Having first been sacrificed to Nazism out of the fear of war, it was now sacrificed for the same reason to Communism (and would be again twenty years later).

But no such sacrifice was deemed necessary in the cases of Iran, Turkey, Greece, and of course Berlin. Nor, it appeared, was it deemed necessary in the Far East. Every effort short of direct American military intervention had been made to save China from being conquered by the Communists under Mao Zedong, but when the Communists nevertheless won, the United States refused to accept the result as final. We did not recognize the Communist government in "Peiping" (as we defiantly continued to call the capital which the Communists called Peking or Beijing), and our official stance was that the defeated Nationalist forces under Chiang Kai-shek, who had taken refuge on Formosa (Taiwan), represented the legal government of China; moreover, we endorsed the expectation that they would one day return to the mainland and liberate their country from Communism.

On the basis of the same reasoning, the United States—which had in general supported the dismantling of the European empires after World War II—sided with the French in their war against the Communist Vietminh in Indochina. In resisting the Vietminh, the French were not only trying to hold on to one of the colonies of their shrinking empire, they were also fighting to prevent the takeover of yet another country by the Communist movement. Thus in the same statement in which he committed American military forces to Korea, Truman "directed acceleration in the furnishing of military assistance to the forces of France and the Associated States in Indochina and the dispatch of a military mission to provide close working relations with those forces."[23] The invasion of South Korea, he thought, might be part of a coordinated offensive directed by the Soviet Union and executed by China. "The situation in Korea, it should be pointed out, was not the only instance of a new aggressiveness on the part of Communist China. There was evidence that the Communist rebel forces in Indochina were receiving increasing aid and advice from Peiping. Also, in the last days of October, Communist China had moved against the ancient theocracy of Tibet. We were seeing a pattern in Indochina and Tibet timed to coincide with the attack in Korea as a challenge to the Western world. It was a challenge by the Communists alone, aimed at intensifying the smoldering anti-foreign feeling among most Asian peoples."[24]

But even if Korea were only an isolated probe, it might well be followed by others if the weak spots in the Western position were left unfortified and "a minor incident could easily be created which would give the Russians an excuse for open intervention."[25]

If, however, the United States was prepared to pay a price in blood to save South Korea from Communism, was it prepared to go further? Was it prepared to drive the Communists out of North Korea and ultimately out of China? Was the policy to be containment or was it to be liberation?

According to his own account, Truman's answer to this question left no room for ambiguity. His objective was "to push the North Koreans back behind the 38th parallel." Military operations could be conducted above the thirty-eighth parallel—in, that is, North Korean territory—but they "should be designed only to destroy military supplies, for I wanted it clearly understood that our operations in Korea were designed to restore peace there and to restore the border." Truman also made it clear that such operations could only be conducted "provided that at the time . . . there had been no entry into North Korea by major Soviet or Chinese Communist forces, no announcement of an intended entry, and no threat by Russian or Chinese Communists to counter our operations militarily in North Korea."[26]

When, a few months later and despite the confident predictions to the contrary of the commanding general, Douglas MacArthur, a massive Chinese force did enter the war, Truman's policy was to do everything possible to prevent it from spreading any farther. MacArthur opposed this "tolerant effort to contain the war

to the area of Korea."[27] He wanted to carry the war to the mainland of China itself by blockading the coast and bombing the
interior, and he also suggested that Chiang Kai-shek's troops be
"introduced" not only into Korea but into South China as well.
Regarding all this as a prescription for the start of World War III,
Truman eventually fired MacArthur, setting off a storm of protest
both in the press and in Congress. Truman and Acheson were
charged with following a policy of appeasement, of fear and
timidity, and of cowardice in denying MacArthur the means to
victory.

But MacArthur's view did not prevail. "There is no substitute
for victory," he had declared, and Truman replied that the kind
of victory MacArthur had wished to pursue "would have been
the wrong kind of victory." (Truman then quoted General Omar
Bradley in support of his position: "To have extended the fighting to the mainland of Asia would have been the wrong war, at
the wrong time and in the wrong place.")[28]

To be sure, the dispute between MacArthur and Truman involved more than a conflict between two ideas of how to fight the
Korean War; it also involved a fundamental political question
that complicated and gave greater bite and urgency to the issue
of MacArthur's alleged insubordination and his challenge to the
constitutional principle of civilian control of the military. The
truth is that Truman was being disingenuous when he proclaimed
in his memoirs that his objective in Korea was merely to restore
the status quo ante. At one stage, and especially after the triumph
of MacArthur's landing at Inchon had turned the tide in our
favor, Truman and his advisers undoubtedly hoped to drive the
Communists out of the North as well as the South, thus achieving
(in the words of a Security Council Resolution which had been
drafted in the U.S. State Department) "the complete independence and unity of Korea."[29]

This was precisely MacArthur's own understanding of his mission, which was, as he put it after he was fired, "to clear out all
North Korea, to unify it and liberalize it."[30] Very likely Mac-
Arthur would have been allowed to follow through if the Chinese
had not intervened. Once they did, however, and in great and

terrifying force, the issue was settled (as it would be over and over again whenever the probable price was an all-out war with the Soviet Union or the Chinese) in favor of containment as against liberation. From that point on, whatever ambiguities there had been in American policy disappeared and MacArthur's persistent demands for permission to widen the war were just as persistently refused.

2.

But was this *American* policy or was it only the policy of the Democratic party? Running against Truman's hand-picked successor, Adlai Stevenson, in 1952, Eisenhower promised that if elected he would go to Korea personally, thereby suggesting that he would bring the war to an end through a negotiated settlement. At the same time, his running mate, Richard Nixon, played to the pro-MacArthur sentiment by attacking Stevenson as a graduate of Acheson's "Cowardly College of Communist Containment" whose ideas "had lost us China, much of Eastern Europe, and had invited the Communists to begin the Korean war." [31] Could an Eisenhower Administration, then, be expected to continue on the course of containment set by Truman, or would it go further and dedicate itself to recouping the losses to "international Communism," for which Truman's policies had, according to Nixon, been responsible?

In view of the fact that upon becoming President in 1953 Eisenhower appointed as his Secretary of State John Foster Dulles, a man clearly identified with the contemptuous Nixonian view of containment, the ambiguity of the campaign might have seemed on the way to a resolution in favor of "liberation" as against containment. But in the event no such change occurred. The Eisenhower Administration accepted a settlement of the Korean War on exactly the terms originally outlined by Truman. The North Koreans were driven back behind the thirty-eighth parallel, and the original division of the country into a Communist North and a non-Communist South was preserved against an armed effort to unify the two under Communist rule.

From the point of view of containment, this was a victory; from the point of view of liberation, it was a defeat. Nevertheless, Eisenhower sent Nixon himself to Korea with a letter to President Syngman Rhee, who—no less than the Communists of the North and no less than the party of liberation in the United States—"refused to accept the division of his country" and "still cherished hopes of ruling a united nation." The purpose of Nixon's mission was to make certain that Rhee understood that "the United States would not support any unilateral military attempt he might undertake to reunite his country." And on the same trip, Nixon, who in the past had spoken of "unleashing Chiang Kai-shek" against the mainland of China, gave the same message to Chiang on Formosa: "I could not tell Chiang outright that his chances of reuniting China under his rule were virtually nonexistent, but I made it clear that American military power would not be committed to support any invasion he might launch." [32]

Thus did containment become the policy not only of the Democrats but of the Republicans as well—which is to say, of the United States.

No sooner had this been established than the question of whether and how it applied to Indochina presented itself to the Eisenhower Administration. Here, to judge by the statements of all the leading figures in that Administration, the answer was entirely lacking in ambiguity. While in the spring of 1954 the French were making what would turn out for all practical purposes to be their last stand against the Vietminh at the fortress of Dien Bien Phu, Dulles warned that if the Communists won control of Vietnam "they would surely resume the same pattern of aggression against other free people in the area." [33] Nixon was "convinced . . . that unless the Communists knew that their so-called wars of liberation would be resisted by military means if necessary, they would not stop until they had taken over Southeast Asia, just as they had Eastern Europe." [34] Admiral Arthur W. Radford, Chairman of the Joint Chiefs of Staff, said that the loss of Indochina "would be the prelude to the loss of all Southeast Asia and a threat to a far wider area." [35] And Eisenhower himself, in what was to become one of the most famous and then notorious images of the American involvement in Vietnam, said it was necessary to prevent the fall of Indochina to Communism because "you have a row of dominoes set up, you knock over the first one, and what will happen to the last one is the certainty that it will go over very quickly."[36]

Given so high an estimate of the importance of preventing a Communist victory in Indochina, it would be astonishing—indeed inexplicable—if plans were not made by the United States to intervene militarily. And so they were. During the siege of Dien Bien Phu, which (according to Nixon) the press began to build up "as the first test since Korea of the free world's ability to resist Communist aggression,"[37] various forms and degrees of American intervention were proposed and considered. They ranged from Eisenhower's idea of a blockade of the Chinese mainland (to cut off the Vietminh's principal source of military supplies), to Nixon's of sending American ground forces, to Radford's of massive American air strikes and even the use (or perhaps only the threatened use) of tactical nuclear weapons.

Horribly extreme though Radford's proposal was, it can at least be said to have been commensurate with the seriousness of the situation as defined by Eisenhower and his chief advisers. And yet, far from threatening to use, let alone using, nuclear weapons to save Indochina from Communist rule in 1954, the United States did not go so far as to take even the mildest of the military measures under consideration. In fact, the United States did nothing as Dien Bien Phu fell. Eisenhower even pulled out two hundred American Army mechanics who had been sent there as technical advisers only a few months before.[38]

How can we account for this extraordinary behavior? How could the presumably responsible leaders of the most powerful nation on earth repeatedly tell themselves, their own people, and everyone else that (in the words of Truman's National Security Council) holding back the Communists in Vietnam was "essential to the security of the free world, not only in the Far East but in the Middle East and Europe as well"[39] and then stand passively by as this tremendous blow to "the security of the free world" was being delivered? Did the Americans perhaps not really mean what they had been saying about the importance of Indochina? Was it all rhetoric?

Even though this hypothesis is forced into consideration by the sheer weight that must be given to action (or in this case inaction) as against mere talk, I think it can be dismissed. It is impossible to read the documents and the memoirs of the period without being struck by the strength of the convictions that lay behind the alarmist view of the consequences of a Communist victory in Indochina. Fifteen years later, at the height of the antiwar fevers in the United States, there would be a good deal of talk about the silencing of dissent within the State Department during the McCarthyite period. There would be talk, too, about how different everything might have been if foreign-service officers like John Patton Davies, John Stewart Service, and John Carter Vincent—who disagreed with the strong anti-Communist orthodoxy of the period in general and who advocated a less hostile American policy toward the Chinese Communists in particular—had not been forced out of the department by charges of disloyalty. Yet unjust though the charges might have been in such cases, the very fact that diplomats as well connected as these men (Vincent was defended by Dean Acheson, for example, and Davies by Averell Harriman)[40] could be successfully attacked was not merely a tribute to the effectiveness of McCarthyism in suppressing dissent. It also testified to the power of the consensus on the issue of international Communism—on the nature of the danger it posed and on the kinds of measures that should be taken in order to cope with that danger. Absent McCarthyism, that is, Vincent and Davies and Service might all have kept their jobs, but it is extremely doubtful that their ideas would have prevailed.

Thus when, during the Korean War, the British Prime Minister, Clement Attlee, suggested to Truman and Acheson that a more sympathetic policy toward Communist China might encourage it to move in a Titoist direction, Truman held firm to the view that the Chinese were Soviet satellites. Acheson added that whether or not Communist China was a Soviet satellite, the American people could not be expected to support an interventionist policy in Europe and an isolationist policy in the Far East.[41]

Although in retrospect Attlee seems to have had the better of this argument with Truman, the truth is that they were both right. Communist China in those days *was* a Soviet satellite in the sense that it recognized the Soviet Union as the leader of the Communist world and looked to the Soviet Union for guidance and support. Ten years later, of course, China would break with the Soviet Union for reasons of its own. American hostility had nothing to do with this "Titoist" development one way or the other, and it may be doubted that American sympathy would have hastened it either.

Be all that as it may, however, Dulles was if anything a more devoted believer in the anti-Communist consensus as applied to Asia than his predecessor Acheson. (Once, reports Halberstam, "when Dulles was with Vincent, he pulled down a copy of Stalin's *Problems of Leninism* and asked if Vincent had read it. Vincent said he had not. 'If you had read it, you would not have advocated the policies you did in China,' Dulles said.")[42] If during the Truman Administration, as Guenter Lewy puts it in his authoritative history of the Vietnam War, "No serious discussion or questioning appears to have taken place of the importance of Southeast Asia to American security interests, of the correctness of the dire predictions regarding the consequences of the loss of the area,"[43] the Eisenhower Administration in its turn also took these judgments entirely for granted.

Again the contrast between the British and the American positions highlights the point. As Truman and Acheson had differed with Attlee over China, Eisenhower and Dulles now differed with Winston Churchill (who had succeeded Attlee in 1951 as Prime Minister) and his Foreign Secretary, Anthony Eden, over Indochina. Explaining to Eisenhower's emissary, Admiral Radford, why the British would not join the United States in a military intervention during the siege of Dien Bien Phu, "Churchill admitted that the rest of Indochina might fall if Vietnam were lost, but he did not foresee any threat to the rest of Southeast Asia, Japan, or Australia."[44] Eden similarly told Dulles that he "was not convinced" by Dulles's assertion "that the situation in Indochina was analogous to the Japanese invasion of Manchuria in 1931 and to Hitler's reoccupation of the Rhineland."[45] Yet so convinced were the Americans that not even Churchill and Eden, whose position at the time of Munich was the very model on which American policy now based itself, and who had also (in Nixon's words) "understood the Communist problem so well as early as 1946," could shake them. "Both Radford and I," wrote Nixon, "were astonished that Churchill . . . could have made this statement."[46]

The Americans, in short, unquestionably meant what they said about the importance of Indochina. Why then did they not take any action commensurate with what they said? One reason, surely, is that they had serious doubts about the willingness of the American people to get involved in another war in a faraway place so soon after Korea. Although there had been no opposition to speak of to the American intervention in Korea, the war had nevertheless grown increasingly unpopular as casualties mounted, and as it became clear that victory in the conventional sense—and the feelings of vindication and release which it brings —was ruled out as a matter of government policy. Thus, only a week after Nixon had said that he would support the sending of American troops if "it was the only way to save Indochina from being taken over by the Communists," a leading Republican congressman, Charles Halleck, told Eisenhower "that the suggestion that American boys might be sent to Indochina 'had really hurt,' and that he hoped there would be no more talk of that type."[47] Two highly influential Democratic senators, Richard B. Russell of Georgia and John Stennis of Mississippi, both of whom were hawkish in their views, also made it clear to Eisenhower that they were afraid of the "unwise introduction of American troops into that area."[48]

A second related reason had to do with what might be called the impurity of the cause for which the United States would be intervening. The Vietminh rebels were certainly Communists and they were clearly tied into the international Communist movement. Their leader, Ho Chi Minh, had actually founded the Communist party of Vietnam, he had been trained in Moscow, and his forces were now being supplied by the mainland Chinese. At the same time, however, Ho was fighting an anti-colonialist war to drive the French out of his country, so that in helping the French the United States found itself on the side of imperialism.

This was an uncomfortable and inconsistent position for the United States, which had, since the end of the Second World War, generally supported the breakup of the old European empires. Nixon and Dulles might sneer at "so-called wars of liberation" like the one being waged by the Vietminh against the French as a fraudulent cover for "Communist aggression" directed and supplied from the outside by the "Red masters of China" (who were in turn directed by the Soviet Union);[49] and they might wholeheartedly believe in this interpretation of what was going on. But they were also so uneasy about being ("for the first time in American history," says Theodore Draper)[50] on the side of a colonial power that as a condition for intervention they demanded "an unequivocal declaration by the French government of independence for the Associated States" (Vietnam, Laos, and Cambodia).[51] Eisenhower himself stressed this as "the strongest reason of all for the United States refusal" to intervene: ". . . among all the powerful nations of the world the United States is the only one with a tradition of anti-colonialism. . . . The standing of the United States as the most powerful of the anti-colonial powers is an asset of incalculable value to the Free World. . . . Thus it is that the moral position of the United States was more to be guarded than the Tonkin Delta, indeed than all of Indochina."[52]

To be sure, the Truman Administration had also pressured the French to move toward independence for Indochina on the theory that "in the long run, the security of Indochina against Communism will depend upon the development of native governments able to command the support of the masses of the people";[53] and in 1953, a year before Dien Bien Phu, Dulles had extracted a promise from the French government "to perfect the independence and sovereignty" of the Associated States.[54] The failure of the French to make good on this promise did not lead to a cutoff of American aid (which largely paid for the French war effort). But it does seem to have been decisive when the question of actual military intervention arose. Churchill told Admiral Radford that "if his people had not been willing to fight to save India for themselves, he did not think they would be willing to fight to save Indochina for the French." Eisenhower seems to have reached a similar conclusion about his people. It had been one thing to fight against Communism on the side of an independent South Korea governed by a solidly based nationalist leader; it was another to fight against Communism for the perpetuation of colonial rule. Eisenhower decided not to intervene. He could not, he said, "visualize a ground troop operation in Indochina that would be supported by the people of the United States." [55]

Yet Nixon was confident of the President's "ability to get the Congress and the country to follow his leadership" if he should decide to go in.[56] This judgment was confirmed by a contemporary observer, Chalmers M. Roberts, in a piece reconstructing the events that had led Eisenhower to the brink of intervention before drawing back and away: "Would Congress have approved intervention if the President had dared ask it? . . . On returning from Geneva in mid-May [1954], I asked that question of numerous Senators and Representatives. Their replies made clear that Congress would, in the end, have done what Eisenhower asked, provided he had asked for it forcefully and explained the facts and their relation to the national interest of the United States. . . . The fact emerges," Roberts concluded, "that President Eisenhower never did lay the intervention question on the line." [57]

To Nixon, this fact was predictable as early as April 6, a full month before the fall of Dien Bien Phu. In his diary note of a National Security Council meeting held that day, he wrote: ". . . it was quite apparent that the President had backed down considerably from the strong position he had taken on Indochina the latter part of the previous week. He seemed resigned to doing nothing at all unless we could get the allies and the country to go along with whatever was suggested and he did not seem inclined to put much pressure on to get them to come along." [58]

Eisenhower, then, could in all probability have intervened if he had chosen to do so. What restrained him was not any doubt about the importance of preventing a Communist victory in Indochina. He shared to the full the views of Truman, Acheson, Dulles, Nixon, and almost everyone else in Washington on this issue. But in his judgment the conditions for a successful intervention were simply not there. In addition to the palpable lack of enthusiasm in Congress, in the country generally, and in London, there was no clear consensus in the military as to whether Indochina could be held at a reasonable price.

Neither General James M. Gavin, then Chief of Plans and Development, nor General Matthew B. Ridgway, then the Army's Chief of Staff, thought that it could,[59] while the Joint Chiefs of Staff reported that "from the point of view of the United States, with reference to the Far East as a whole, Indochina is devoid of decisive military objectives and the allocation of more than token U.S. armed forces in Indochina would be a serious diversion of limited U.S. capabilities."[60] (Eisenhower had said much the same thing at an NSC meeting weeks before this memorandum was written.)[61] This left only air strikes and naval action, but, Eden told Dulles, there was little chance that "Allied intervention could be limited to the air and the sea."[62] And if it could not, then (as Eisenhower would later write) "the jungles of Indochina would have swallowed up division after division of United States troops, who, unaccustomed to this kind of warfare, would have sustained heavy casualties until they had learned to live in a new environment. Furthermore, the presence of ever more numbers of white men in uniform probably would have aggravated rather than assuaged Asiatic resentments." Eisenhower put it more succinctly at the time, in a diary note of March 1951: "I'm convinced that no military victory is possible in that kind of theater."[63]

For all the rhetorical anti-Communist extravagance for which he was famous, Dulles was no less prudent than Eisenhower. He pressed hard for intervention, but as Draper points out, he surrounded it with so many conditions that were unlikely to be met in the circumstances of the time that one might be forgiven for thinking that he never really wanted to make a military commitment. Dulles, said Georges Bidault, who was the French Foreign Minister at the time, "was always talking of 'calculated risks,' which in practice most often meant that he calculated a great deal and risked nothing."[64]

Again, this does not mean that Dulles was insincere in his

belief that a Communist victory in Indochina would be a disaster for the United States—any more than he was insincere in his belief that the Nationalist Chinese on Formosa were the legitimate government of China or that Eastern Europe should be liberated from Soviet domination. Yet the Administration in which he served as Secretary of State did not "unleash" Chiang Kai-shek against the mainland; and when—two years after the fall of Dien Bien Phu—the Soviet Union sent tanks and troops into Hungary to crush a rebellion against Communist domination, Eisenhower and Dulles did nothing. Instead of trying to force the Russians out of Hungary, they busied themselves with forcing the British, the French, and the Israelis—who had mounted a joint operation to take over the Suez Canal after Nasser had nationalized it—out of Egypt. In these contrasting responses to two acts of imperialism, one Soviet and the other Western, Dulles simultaneously demonstrated the depth of his prudence and the seriousness of his anti-colonialist convictions.

According to Nixon, "Dulles was infuriated and dispirited by the plan to surrender half of Vietnam to the Communists," which was negotiated at Geneva in July of 1954.[65] Nevertheless, with military action ruled out, there was little the United States could do beyond refusing to sign the Geneva accords and sending a team of CIA operatives under Colonel Edward Lansdale "to undertake paramilitary operations against the enemy and to wage political-psychological warfare."[66] Though covert, these operations were well enough known and colorful enough to inspire Graham Greene's novel *The Quiet American*. They ranged from the serious (sabotage, intelligence, and arms smuggling) to the comical (conducting English classes for mistresses of important Vietnamese personages, and hiring astrologers to predict misfortune for the Communists and good omens for the government of Diem). But the Landsale team, beginning while the Geneva conference was still in progress, did nothing to alter the outcome of that conference, and its subsequent activities in the post-Geneva period did little if anything to weaken the Communist position.

Unhappy though Eisenhower and Dulles were at the time with the Geneva agreements, and though the National Security Council pronounced the settlement a "disaster" that "completed a major forward stride of Communism which may lead to the loss of Southeast Asia,"[67] Eisenhower later took the position that the division of Vietnam (and the simultaneous granting of independence to Laos and Cambodia) had turned out to be a reasonably good bargain from the American point of view. Instead of a colonial regime, there was now an indigenous non-Communist government in South Vietnam, led by a man (Ngo Dinh Diem) who, though he had played no part in the war against the French, had solid credentials as a Vietnamese nationalist.* Dulles too eventually reconciled himself to Geneva, and he said something much more interesting and significant about it than Eisenhower. "We have a clean base there now without a taint of colonialism," he told the journalist Emmet John Hughes in 1956. "Dien Bien Phu was a blessing in disguise."[68]

In other words, the impurity that had made of Indochina so ambiguous a case for intervention had now been removed. A new situation had been created in which a new entity, South Vietnam (along with its immediately contiguous "dominoes," Laos and Cambodia), now became fully eligible for inclusion within the policy of containment. If despite all the concern expressed by the Truman and Eisenhower Administrations over the consequences of a spread of Communism to Indochina, the United States in the end announced that for all practical purposes French Indochina was not covered by the umbrella of containment, no such announcement could or would be made with regard to the new country of South Vietnam. This is what Dulles was saying in 1956, and it is what Senator John F. Kennedy in even more explicit terms was saying that same year in his speech to the American Friends of Vietnam. South Vietnam had the same claim to protection against "the red tide of Communism" as West Germany, Formosa, and South Korea.

* One of the ironic measures of the enormous change in American political culture since the 1950s, not only in general but in its constituent elements, is the fact that when Diem, a Roman Catholic, was in exile in the United States, he lived for two years with the Maryknolls, who would become famous (or perhaps notorious) thirty years later for their energetic support of Communist insurgencies in Central America.

With this objective in mind, the United States now set out to help Diem (as Eisenhower promised it would in a letter to him in October 1954 which would figure prominently in the debates ahead) "in developing and maintaining a strong, viable state, capable of resisting attempted subversion or aggression through military means."[69] This involved large-scale economic and military aid, including the equipping and training of a South Vietnamese army. It also involved acquiescing in Diem's refusal to honor the provision of the Geneva accords calling for national elections in 1956 to unify the country.

Acquiescing, not directing: the Pentagon Papers reveal that the United States did not, as was often alleged in the subsequent debates over the war, "connive with Diem to ignore the elections. U.S. State Department records indicate that Diem's refusal to be bound by the Geneva accords . . . were at his own initiative." Still, it is also clear from the Pentagon Papers that the United States was not eager for elections to be held. The NSC decided that in order "to give no impression of blocking elections while avoiding the possibility of losing them, Diem should insist on free elections by secret ballot with strict supervision. Communists in Korea and Germany had rejected these conditions; hopefully the Vietminh would follow suit."[70]

Of course, since neither the United States nor South Vietnam had signed the Geneva agreements, they were under no legal obligation to carry them out. Legalities aside, however, the main reason for opposing these elections was that they would in all probability have resulted in a victory for Ho Chi Minh. Some Americans, including Senator John F. Kennedy, professed to think, and perhaps really did think, that the elections would be "stacked and subverted in advance."[71] Others, including President Eisenhower himself, thought that "had elections been held as of the time of the fighting, possibly 80 percent of the population would have voted for the Communist Ho Chi Minh as their leader,"[72] and presumably he thought that Ho was still popular enough two years later, in 1956, to defeat Diem in a free and fair election.

In any case, the point was to prevent the Communists from taking over the whole of Vietnam. If in the name of democracy, elections had been forced on Diem and the Communists had won, the result would have been not the extension of democracy to the South but the destruction of any possibility of a development in the direction of democracy there. To quote Draper (no friend either of Diem or of American policy in Vietnam): "[Ho Chi Minh] might have taken power democratically, but he would not have kept power democratically, which is far more important. In 1960 the 'elections' in North Vietnam resulted in a 99.8 percent majority for the ruling Communist party and its two small satellite groups, with no one permitted to run on an opposition platform. For this reason it is fatuous to imagine that Vietnam would have been more 'democratic' if Ho Chi Minh had been permitted to get an 80-percent majority in a national election. . . ."[73]

There is no question, moreover, that the policy of the United States was to encourage Diem to establish South Vietnam as—in Kennedy's words—"a proving ground for democracy in Asia."[74] For one thing, the United States believed in democracy with a quasi-religious fervor. Compromises might be necessary at a given moment or in a set of given circumstances, but few Americans in those days doubted that democracy was superior to any other form of government and that it was the goal toward which all peoples truly aspired. There was also general agreement that democracy, in addition to being morally superior to Communism, provided the best protection against it. People living under a democratic government would not only fight to preserve it against external Communist aggression; even more to the point, they would rally behind efforts to resist internal subversion as well. And finally, where an American commitment was made that would certainly cost American dollars and might well cost American lives, it was important that (in Dulles's significant image) the "base" be "clean." In Vietnam the "taint of colonialism" had been removed, and now it was necessary to remove the taint of authoritarianism.

For all these reasons Eisenhower, in the same letter to Diem promising American aid, stipulated that "the Government of the United States expects that this aid will be met by performance on the part of the Government of Vietnam in undertaking needed reforms."[75] In the next two years, to the surprise of many (ap-

parently including the Communists, who had agreed to partition
on the assumption that Diem would never be able to establish a
solid regime in the South and that the prize would eventually fall
into their hands without too much trouble), South Vietnam
seemed well on its way to becoming a "free and independent
republic" taking its "first vital steps toward true democracy."[76]
Senator John F. Kennedy was not the only American to speak in
such terms. Senator Mike Mansfield—later to become a leading
critic of American military involvement in Vietnam—declared
after a visit to South Vietnam in 1956 that Diem "had taken what
was a lost cause of freedom and breathed new life into it."[77] And
even David Halberstam later acknowledged that "Diem acted
forthrightly and courageously in the early years of his government."[78]

The problem was that Diem's unquestionably positive and con-
structive achievements were offset by the wholesale suppression
of political opposition. Newspapers were shut down and tens of
thousands of people arrested. Such measures were justified as
necessary to the fight against Communist guerrillas who had remained in (or returned to) the South after partition, and to some
extent this was true. After the Geneva agreements, an exchange
of populations had been effected, with approximately a million
refugees from the North streaming into the South and perhaps
100,000 Vietminh troops and supporters going North. "The Communists," writes Lewy, "also left behind several thousand of
their best cadres as well as a large number of weapons caches."[79]

One of the things these cadres did was to engage in a systematic program of terrorism, called "the extermination of the traitors," whose aim was to assassinate "the most effective local
administrators, schoolteachers, medical personnel and social
workers who tried to improve the lives of the peasants."[80] It
was, says Schlesinger, "warfare in the shadows, ambush and
murder and torture, leaving behind a trail of burned villages,
shattered families, and weeping women."[81]

But Diem's campaign against the Communists also served as a
means of consolidating his own dictatorial power. To make matters worse, he followed policies in the countryside that alienated
the peasantry. This opened the way to greater Communist influ-

ence, while Diem's political authoritarianism was simultaneously increasing the range of his non-Communist opposition in the cities. Some elements of this non-Communist opposition would join the National Liberation Front (NLF) founded in 1960 not—as so many were fooled into believing—by indigenous South Vietnamese opponents of Diem but "at the instigation of the party in Hanoi."[82]

The reason for the pretense was that the Communists needed to represent the insurgency against Diem as an internal South Vietnamese rebellion—a civil war rather than an invasion from the North—just as they needed a front organization like the NLF to conceal the fact that they were in control. Diem's policies certainly fueled non-Communist opposition to his regime within South Vietnam itself; it is also true that the Communists within South Vietnam wanted to move more actively to "armed struggle" by 1959. But it is no less certain that the insurgency was (in the words used in 1976 by the French journalist Jean Lacouture, who had done so much to spread the impression that the NLF had been autonomous) "piloted, directed and inspired" by North Vietnam.[83] What was portrayed from the beginning as a civil war fought by an independent South Vietnamese guerrilla army (now called the Vietcong) would end fifteen years later with a massive invasion by the North Vietnamese army, and no Southerners—that is to say, no Southern Communists let alone non-Communists—would be given any important positions in the new government of a united Vietnam set up in the wake of those triumphant divisions from the North.

3.

This view of the situation as an attempt by North Vietnam to take over South Vietnam by force—ridiculed as it came to be by critics of the war and then vindicated by the eventual outcome of the war—was precisely the one held by official Washington when John F. Kennedy assumed office in 1961. As Kennedy himself put it later that year in a letter to Diem: ". . . the Communist

authorities in North Vietnam'' were resorting to ''force and subversion'' in ''their campaign to destroy the Republic of Vietnam.''[84] It was clear, moreover, that this campaign was making
progress. What still seemed unclear was whether the remedy was
internal political changes (up to and including the replacement of
Diem by another leader—''While no one can promise a safe tran-
sition,'' John Kenneth Galbraith, then ambassador to India, told
Kennedy, ''we are now married to failure. . . . It is a better rule
that nothing succeeds like successors'')[85]—or increased military
aid (up to and including the introduction of American combat
troops).

Those who saw the problem as primarily political later con-
trived to suggest that their view had been tantamount to opposing
American intervention. But an emphasis on the political aspect
of the problem would have required a greater degree of intervention than even the military emphasis required. It would have
meant forcing Diem to run his country in accordance with American ideas rather than his own, and getting rid of him if he remained recalcitrant; and this in turn would have led to an
increase in American involvement and in the concomitant American responsibility for carrying on the war.

Indeed it was precisely this reluctance to get involved in another land war in Asia (a reluctance expressed in what was called
in the Pentagon the ''Never Again Club'') that had weakened the
effect of American pressure on the French to grant independence
to Indochina and that now made the pressure on Diem for reform
so ineffective. In 1954, ''the overriding fear,'' writes Lewy,
''seemed to be that in the event of too much American pressure
the French would pull out of Indochina and put before the U.S.
the extremely undesirable choice of either abandoning Indochina
or dispatching American ground forces.''[86] The same problem
arose with Diem. First Eisenhower and then Kennedy were in-
hibited in exerting pressure on him, for fear that this would lead
to the same impossible dilemma.

Here another historical lesson—the lesson of China—came
into play. In January 1949 a young Democratic congressman
named John F. Kennedy, speaking on the floor of the House, did

an extraordinary thing: he denounced an administration run by his own party for its responsibility in the "disaster that has befallen China and the United States." "So concerned were our diplomats and their advisers, the Lattimores and the Fairbanks, with the imperfection of the democratic system in China after twenty years of war and the tales of corruption in high places that they lost sight of our tremendous stake in a non-Communist China."[87] No doubt Kennedy had changed a good deal in the ensuing twelve years, but not so much that he would have risked dealing the same "crippling blow" to the non-Communist government of South Vietnam that he charged the Truman Administration with having delivered to the Nationalist Chinese in threatening to cut off aid unless they broadened their political base (in that case by forming a coalition government with the Communists).

The truth is that the "political" approach was not an alternative to the "military" approach but rather a roundabout route to a complete Americanization of the war. All of this was to happen anyway, but it would have happened sooner if the group around Averell Harriman (which, according to Schlesinger, advocated subordinating the military to the political) had prevailed.

Nor was the political emphasis more modest or wiser than the military. It was, in fact, much more arrogant in assuming that Washington understood how to solve the political, social, and economic problems of South Vietnam—a faraway country of which Americans knew far less than Neville Chamberlain notoriously said the British knew about Czechoslovakia in 1939. The journalist Theodore H. White recognized this. In a letter to the White House from Saigon, he wrote: "If a defeat in South Vietnam is to be considered our defeat, if we *are* responsible for holding that area, then we must have authority to act. And that means intervention in Vietnam politics." But White wondered whether we had "the proper personnel, the proper instruments, the proper clarity of objectives to intervene successfully."[88] If he had spoken to Daniel Ellsberg, later to become one of the most extreme opponents of American policy but then working in the Defense Department, he would have had the answer. "It is fair to say," wrote Ellsberg in 1972, "that Americans in office read very few books, and none in French [the language of most of the literature then available on Vietnam]; and that there has never been an official of Deputy Assistant Secretary rank or higher (including myself) who could have passed in office a midterm freshman exam in modern Vietnamese history, if such a course existed in this country. (Until recently, there were two tenured professors in America who spoke Vietnamese . . .)."[89]

Even in saying that they understood how to win the war, the Americans turned out to be presuming too much; and yet this was at least a more limited claim and one to which experience and the historical record entitled them. For the war in Vietnam was a guerrilla war, and (in the words of the pseudonymous "Cincinnatus," a military analyst who is severely critical of the Army's performance in Vietnam) "it can fairly be said that the United States Army—at the beginning of the Vietnamese involvement—had had and should have learned by as much experience in the tactics of guerrilla warfare and counterinsurgency as the soldiery of any other modern nation."[90]

In any event, with the war going so badly, Kennedy—as Draper accurately puts it—was faced with the problem that had faced Eisenhower in 1954: "What should the United States do to stave off a complete collapse in Vietnam?" Draper, citing the contradictory speeches Kennedy had made in 1954 and 1956, goes on to say that he "came to the Vietnam problem . . . without a consistent position behind him."[91] But surely the preponderant weight of the evidence suggests that Kennedy never doubted for a moment that something military would have to be done "to stave off a complete collapse in Vietnam." Indeed, it would be amazing if this had not been so.

Kennedy (like most of the people around him) was of the generation for which the lessons of Munich remained the single most powerful force in the shaping of judgments on questions of war and peace. His first book, published in 1940 and entitled *While England Slept,* was an attempt to explain why the British had failed to heed Churchill's calls for rearmament in the face of the growing menace of Nazi Germany; and one of the reasons he gave was that democratic societies were "essentially peace-loving"—a quality that put them at a disadvantage in the struggle with totalitarian systems. Churchill, according to Schlesinger, "remained his greatest admiration." Did he know that his hero had disagreed when Eisenhower told him that the failure to stop the Communists in Indochina would be comparable to the failure to stop Hirohito, Mussolini, and Hitler in the thirties?[92] If so, he would probably have been as amazed as Nixon had been to hear Churchill take such a position.[93] Kennedy's Secretary of State, Dean Rusk, was equally influenced by the lessons of the thirties, as he would make clear in invoking the analogy on innumerable occasions in the years ahead. His National Security Adviser, McGeorge Bundy, had as a Harvard professor given a yearly lecture on Munich that had become legendary ("when it was on the day's schedule," writes Halberstam, himself a Harvard graduate, Bundy "played to standing room only").[94]

Nor is there any doubt that Kennedy and his people took it as virtually self-evident that the lesson of Munich was as applicable to the war in Vietnam as it had been to the war in Korea. No actual armies were crossing the border, as had been the case in Korea, but even if the means were different, the object was the same: North Vietnam was just as surely trying to conquer South Vietnam as North Korea had tried to conquer South Korea. Moreover, just as China had stood behind North Korea in this act of aggression, so China was standing behind North Vietnam now; and behind China, then as now, stood the Soviet Union. Thus the war in Vietnam was a variant, or a mutation, of the pattern of totalitarian aggression, and it called under the tutelage of Munich for the same response as its more conventional predecessor in Korea.

As it happens, the depth of the split between the Soviet Union and China was already becoming visible to such observers as Richard Lowenthal in 1961,[95] but it seems to have played little or no part in the calculations of Kennedy and his people where Vietnam was concerned. In fact, Kennedy expressed doubts to de Gaulle in June 1961 that "the split would become acute until the West was forced out" of Southeast Asia, and Schlesinger complains that the State Department refused to give up using the term "Sino-Soviet bloc" even as late as 1963.[96]

Yet when after Kennedy's death the seriousness of the split

became apparent to everyone, this only served to make Munich seem even more relevant. For the Chinese in those days were more militant about spreading Communism than the Soviet Union. Indeed, the doctrinal dispute between them turned precisely on the issue of the duty of Communist nations to foment and support revolutionary uprisings against the "imperialist bloc" led by the United States. While the Russians under Khrushchev were beginning to speak of "peaceful coexistence," the Chinese were stressing the need for an intensification of the revolutionary struggle. Consequently, the Chinese acting on their own seemed more dangerous than when under the presumably restraining influence of the Russians, whose own relative moderation on the issue of revolutionary violence was thought to stem from the fear that great-power involvement in "wars of national liberation" could escalate and ultimately lead to a nuclear exchange. The Chinese, as they often proclaimed, did not share the Russians' "cowardly" fear of nuclear war—a fear that served only to inhibit revolutionary zeal and to retard the victory of Communism throughout the world.

Thus in 1965, Averell Harriman (the leader of those who in the Kennedy days were urging a political rather than a military emphasis in American policy) would compare an article by Lin Piao, the Chinese Defense Minister, urging the underdeveloped nations to launch wars of national liberation, to Hitler's *Mein Kampf* as a blueprint for world revolution.[97] Thus, too, Lyndon Johnson had seen a special danger in the fact that "Red China's leaders preached the doctrine of violence and wars of 'national liberation.' "[98] There is no reason to suppose that Kennedy and his people (many of whom, including Rusk, Bundy, and Harriman, became Johnson's people after Kennedy's death) would have disagreed with this analysis.

If Munich supplied the broadest context for the decision to do something that might "stave off a complete collapse in Vietnam," containment provided the more immediately relevant premises. Adlai Stevenson, ambassador to the UN under Kennedy and then Johnson, brought the two themes of Munich and containment together in perhaps the most lucid and succinct statement of the case: "The period from 1947 to 1962 was largely

occupied in fixing the postwar line with the Soviet Union. . . .
We have no such line with the Chinese. Since they are in an
earlier, more radical stage in their revolution, it may be more
difficult to establish one. Should we try? And is the line we stand
on halfway across Vietnam a reasonable line? Should we hold
it?" The answer, Stevenson went on, depended on one's assumptions about Chinese power and Chinese intentions; in his judgment the Chinese were "very aggressive" and the war in
Vietnam was an instance of Chinese expansionism. "My hope in
Vietnam," Stevenson concluded, "is that relatively small-scale
resistance now may establish the fact that changes in Asia are
not to be precipitated by outside force." [99]

Kennedy's commitment to containment was as fervent as his
belief in the lessons of Munich. In his campaign against Nixon,
he had in effect charged the Republicans under Eisenhower and
Dulles with being "soft on Communism," and in adopting the
slogan "Let's get the country moving again," he held out the
promise of a more determined and aggressive foreign policy.
Upon assuming office, he delivered an inaugural address whose
most famous words reaffirmed the idea behind containment in
more ringing terms than either Truman or Eisenhower had ever
used: "Let every nation know, whether it wishes us well or ill,
that we shall pay any price, bear any burden, meet any hardship,
support any friend, oppose any foe, to assure the survival and
the success of liberty." [100]

Given this attitude, it was all but inevitable that he would approve the plan—already in formation during the Eisenhower Administration—for an invasion of Cuba by anti-Castro exiles. This
operation was what Draper describes as the rarest of all political-
military events, "a perfect failure," [101] but since its aim was to
overthrow an existing Communist regime rather than to prevent
the establishment of a new one, the failure was actually one of
"rollback" or "liberation" rather than of containment. Nevertheless, the damage it did in the eyes of the Soviet Union to his
credibility as an adversary was at least as much on Kennedy's
mind when he sent American troops to Vietnam as Korea had
been on Eisenhower's in making the opposite decision in 1954.

The "Never Again" rule of Korea (against getting involved in a land war in Asia), one might say, had been canceled out by the fresher and more recent "Never Again" rule of the Bay of Pigs (against another American defeat in the struggle against Communism).

When, only two months after the Bay of Pigs, Kennedy met with Khrushchev in Vienna, he was nearly traumatized by the Soviet leader's bellicosity over the issue of Berlin. He was also impressed by Khrushchev's vigorous defense of a pledge he had made a few months earlier—in January of that year—to support wars of national liberation, including the one in Vietnam; these were, Khrushchev now told Kennedy, "sacred" wars. According to Khrushchev's conception of "peaceful co-existence" (or what in the days of his successor Brezhnev would be called "détente"), the Soviet Union had a right to intervene in such wars, whereas the United States did not. "It will be a cold winter," said Kennedy upon leaving Vienna.[102] He was thinking of Berlin, but surely also of Vietnam. It was the terrible fiasco of the Bay of Pigs that had emboldened Khrushchev, and a show of effective resolve was now necessary to restrain him from acting as belligerently as he had talked.

But apart from the contrasting influences of Korea and Cuba, there was another significant difference between Indochina in 1954 and Vietnam in 1961 which helps account for Kennedy's decision to intervene militarily instead of staying out as Eisenhower had. The "taint of colonialism" had disqualified Indochina in 1954 for coverage by the umbrella of containment, and specifically of the imperative to use force if necessary to prevent the spread of Communism. But South Vietnam was now an independent non-Communist state and therefore no less qualified for inclusion than South Korea had been.

There was, to be sure, a new "taint" to worry about: the fact that South Vietnam had, after a promising beginning, failed to develop into the "proving ground for democracy" that Kennedy himself had called it in 1956. But the young congressman who in 1949 had denounced the Truman White House and the Acheson State Department for being so fastidious about the imperfections of Chiang Kai-shek that they lost sight of how much worse the actual alternative would be, remained alive and well enough in the President he had now become so that Kennedy could say of a politically analogous situation that developed in the Dominican Republic in 1961: "There are three possibilities in descending order of preference: a decent democratic regime, a continuation of the Trujillo regime or a Castro regime. We ought to aim at the first, but we really can't renounce the second until we are sure that we can avoid the third." [103]

More to the point, Kennedy in 1961 removed Elbridge Durbrow as ambassador to Saigon—a man, says Halberstam, whose "pleas to Diem about governmental reform, about improving the quality of commanders, about broadening the base of the government, resembled nothing so much as the pleas of General Stilwell to Chiang Kai-shek to do the same thing . . ."—and replaced him with Frederick E. Nolting, Jr., whose mission (as Halberstam not unreasonably describes it) was to inspire confidence in Diem by "being nice to him." [104] Kennedy, it is true, cabled Nolting that "a crucial element in USG willingness to move forward is concrete demonstration by Diem that he is now prepared to work in an orderly way on his subordinates and broaden the political base of his regime." [105] But in this period of what Homer Bigart, then of the New York *Times,* called "Sink or Swim with Ngo Dinh Diem," [106] the warning had no force behind it, and the United States did "move forward" without any significant reciprocal political concessions from Diem.

Finally, there was the matter of how to cope with "wars of national liberation"—those wars that were at once "sacred" to Khrushchev and the key to Mao Zedong's strategy for the triumph of Communism throughout what was then called the underdeveloped world. As early as 1954, Nixon had told Eisenhower that such wars, rather than "overt aggression" such as had occurred in Korea with "the Communists marching across a line" represented "the real future danger in Asia" and that it was necessary to find "a formula to resist this kind of aggression." [107]

Even earlier than that, in 1950, a group of professors from Harvard and MIT (including future members of the Kennedy Administration like McGeorge Bundy, Carl Kaysen, Jerome

Wiesner, Arthur Schlesinger, Jr., and John Kenneth Galbraith) had warned against an overemphasis in the American strategic posture on nuclear weapons. The doctrine of what in the Eisenhower Administration would come to be called "massive retaliation"—according to which the United States would respond to any act of Communist aggression with a nuclear strike against the Soviet Union—"provided the United States," said the Cambridge professors, "with no effective answer to limited aggression except the wholly disproportionate answer of atomic war. As a result, it invited Moscow to use the weapons of 'guerrilla warfare and internal revolt in marginal areas in the confidence that such local activity would incur only local risks.' " Kennedy himself picked up this theme eight years later in calling as a senator for a military posture that could respond to such threats as "limited brushfire wars, indirect non-overt aggression, intimidation and subversion, internal revolution." [108]

No wonder, then, that as President, Kennedy should have seen in Vietnam an opportunity to develop a new approach to the containment of this more subtle and insidious form of Communist aggression. As Nolting put it shortly after taking up his post as the new American ambassador to South Vietnam: "NATO was formed as a barrier against overt attack and it has held up for thirteen years. We haven't found a barrier yet against covert aggression. If we can find such a technique we'll have bottled up the Communists on another front." [109]

In the search for this technique, Kennedy began by approving a small number of additional military advisers and Special Forces personnel to train the South Vietnamese in the ways of counterinsurgency. He then sent his own military adviser, General Maxwell Taylor, to Vietnam on a fact-finding mission. Taylor returned with the recommendation that a task force of 8,000 American combat troops be dispatched to South Vietnam both to strengthen Diem's morale and to demonstrate our own seriousness of purpose. "The U.S. should become," Taylor wrote, "a limited partner in the war, avoiding formal advice on the one hand, trying to run the war on the other." [110]

The Joint Chiefs of Staff agreed with Taylor, and so did the Secretary of Defense, Robert S. McNamara. Said McNamara in a memorandum to the President: "We are inclined to recommend that we do commit the U.S. to the clear objective of preventing the fall of South Vietnam to Communism and that we support this commitment by the necessary military actions." [111]

Those military actions, according to McNamara and the Joint Chiefs of Staff, included the introduction of the 8,000-man task force Taylor had recommended. But this would certainly not be enough to "tip the scale decisively." The struggle might well be prolonged; Hanoi and "Peiping" might intervene; as many as 205,000 American troops might be required. And again, McNamara (this time writing in conjunction with Dean Rusk, the Secretary of State) asserted that "We should be prepared to introduce United States combat forces if that should become necessary for success. Dependent upon the circumstances, it may also be necessary for United States forces to strike at the source of the aggression in North Vietnam." [112]

Here, then, was another major difference between 1954 and 1961. Whereas Eisenhower's military advisers were very reluctant to intervene in 1954, Kennedy's favored intervention. ("The fall of South Vietnam to Communism," McNamara told Kennedy in his own name and in the name of the Joint Chiefs of Staff, "would lead to the fairly rapid extension of Communist control, or complete accommodation to Communism, in the rest of mainland Southeast Asia, and in Indonesia. The strategic implications worldwide, particularly in the Orient, would be extremely serious.") Since the chances were "against, probably sharply against, preventing that fall by any measures short of the introduction of U.S. forces on a substantial scale," those measures simply had to be taken—and taken, moreover, with the clear understanding that they would in all probability be only "the first steps" toward fulfilling our commitment "to the clear objective of preventing the fall of South Vietnam to Communism." [113] The situation, in Taylor's judgment, was "serious but not hopeless," and everyone else agreed that with the right mix of military and political measures, victory could be achieved.

Finally, there was the factor of public opinion. "The challenge we faced in 1954," wrote Nixon in his memoirs, "was to convince the American people of the importance of Dien Bien Phu

—that much more was at stake than the defense of some French troops besieged at a colonial outpost."[114] In 1961 the challenge was much easier. Though no one in America seemed eager to get involved militarily in Vietnam, neither did there seem to be any serious opposition. So far as the commitment to saving South Vietnam from Communism was concerned, the view, in such institutions as the Council on Foreign Relations, and in periodicals like the New York *Times,* the Washington *Post, Time,* and *Newsweek,* was consistent with the position expressed by officials of the government. The general tone was nicely caught in a *Times* editorial entitled "Prospects in Vietnam." It began by speaking of "Communist aggression" against South Vietnam that had been "launched as a calculated and deliberate operation by the Communist leaders of the North," and ended as follows: "The outlook in South Vietnam certainly gives no basis for optimism. . . . Free World forces, however, still have a chance in South Vietnam, and every effort should be made to save the situation. President Diem's call for additional financial help to build up his military forces, which has the support in Senator Mike Mansfield of one of the best-informed individuals in Congress on Vietnam affairs, should not go unheeded."[115]

Of course, only "additional financial help" was in the balance here. But when, eight months later, the State Department issued a White Paper charging North Vietnam with violating the Geneva accords and preparing the legal ground for an increase in American military involvement, the *Times* uncritically accepted its exaggerated claims of infiltration from the North;[116] and when, shortly thereafter, word began to leak out of "the expanded program of American participation in South Vietnam's anti-Communist struggle," the *Times* registered no protest. All it did was warn that "the increased American stake and American risk in South Vietnam now needs, more than ever, to be accompanied by a fresh, resilient and imaginative effort by President Ngo to mobilize resources for a fight that is certain to get harder before it gets easier."[117]

As for the literary world and the intellectual community generally, which were later to become two of the great centers of antiwar sentiment, in the early sixties they exhibited very little interest in Vietnam one way or the other. For example, the poet Robert Lowell and the critic Dwight Macdonald, who would hit the front page of the New York *Times* in 1965 for their vigorous opposition to the war (Lowell having refused President Lyndon Johnson's invitation to a reception and Macdonald having accepted and used the occasion to circulate a petition against American policy among the guests on the White House lawn), had both professed themselves bored by the issue of Vietnam only a few years earlier. And if among those who would later regard Vietnam as the most important event of the age, there were more than a few who found it as boring in the pre-1965 period as Lowell and Macdonald had, there were others who did pay attention but who were by no means as convinced as they would later be of the rights and wrongs of the situation.[118] (I remember, for example, being asked to participate in a panel discussion of Vietnam at a meeting sponsored by a radical group that would later figure prominently in the antiwar movement and being told in the letter of invitation that the meeting had been called because Vietnam was so "difficult an issue.")

Those who have tried to show that Kennedy's decision to step up the degree of involvement in Vietnam was made with great misgivings or unwillingly or against his own better judgment place a heavy emphasis on how limited were the measures he actually approved "to stave off a complete collapse of Vietnam." "All his principal advisers on Vietnam," writes Sorensen, favored the commitment of American combat troops. "But the President *in effect* voted 'no'—and only his vote counted."[119] I have italicized the words "in effect" because they give the game away. It is true that Kennedy rejected the recommendation to send combat troops, but especially in retrospect the practical distinction between what he rejected and what he approved (changing, as Taylor would later put it, the number but not the "quality" of our military advisers) seems metaphysical.[120] Sorensen sums up: "Formally Kennedy never made a final negative decision on troops. In typical Kennedy fashion, he made it difficult for any of the prointervention advocates to charge him privately with weakness. He ordered the departments to be prepared for the introduction of combat troops, should they prove to be necessary. He steadily expanded the size of the military assistance mission (2,000 at the end of 1961, 15,500 at the end of 1963)* by sending in combat support units, air combat and helicopter teams, still more military advisers and instructors and 600 of the green-hatted Special Forces to train and lead the South Vietnamese in anti-guerrilla tactics." [121]

According to Schlesinger and other apologists for Kennedy, he took this relatively small step on the basis of an assurance by his military advisers that it would be enough to turn the tide in Vietnam. But as we have already seen, Kennedy's advisers had told him in unmistakable terms that committing even the 8,000 combat troops recommended by Taylor would be insufficient to "tip the scales decisively"—that as many as 200,000 troops might have to be deployed and air strikes might have to be launched against North Vietnam.

Success was certainly possible in the judgment of Kennedy's people (William P. Bundy, then in the Pentagon, and soon to become Assistant Secretary of State for Far East Affairs, estimated that "an early and hard-hitting operation" involving the immediate commitment of 20,000 to 40,000 American troops, had a 70 percent chance of "*arresting* things and giving Diem a chance to do better and clean up"). [123] But just as certainly, they thought, the small-scale intervention Kennedy decided on would be ineffective. Moreover, the longer he waited to raise the degree of involvement to the necessary levels, the worse the chances of success would become (so said William Bundy). McNamara even warned of the domestic political dangers of a gradual buildup: "It is our feeling," he told the President, "that the country will respond better to a firm initial position than to courses of action that lead us in only gradually, and that in the meantime are sure to involve casualties." [124]

This was not, in short, a case of "the politics of inadvertence," as Schlesinger called it, or of being pushed step by small step

---

* These figures are not quite accurate. There were actually 3,164 U.S. military personnel in Vietnam at the end of 1961 and 16,263 at the end of 1963, when Kennedy was assassinated. [122]

into a "quagmire" (in Halberstam's image) by deceitful military men eager to make war. Kennedy had his own deepest convictions, the backing of "all his principal advisers," civilian as well as military, and the reasonable expectation of political support in the country working toward the decision to intervene militarily in Vietnam. The difficult question is not why he decided to intervene but why he acted so timidly. Daniel Ellsberg, who has puzzled over this question in the light of the evidence in the Pentagon Papers that makes tendentious nonsense of the "quagmire" and "inadvertence" theories of how the United States got into the Vietnam War, thinks that Kennedy was trying simultaneously to avoid both the "loss of Vietnam" in the short run and involvement in a land war in Asia. Going "slow and small" was a long shot, but he hoped against hope that it would pay off.[125] ("We are going to win in Vietnam," declared the President's brother Robert, then Attorney General, during a trip to Saigon in February 1962. "We will remain here until we do win.")[126]

Another way of describing Kennedy's approach is that he was trying to accomplish a very large objective—very large both in being intrinsically difficult and in being by his own lights of major importance—on the cheap. "In typical Kennedy fashion," to borrow Sorensen's phrase, he willed the end but not the means —just as he had done before with the Bay of Pigs in authorizing an invasion while forbidding the air cover without which the invasion was doomed to failure.

Nor was this habit confined to foreign affairs. Thinking mainly of domestic programs, the economist Oscar Gass wrote at the conclusion of Kennedy's first year in office: "Always and running through everything, there is the characteristic New Frontier polarity of a portentous general language and modest specifics. Only let a speech begin, 'The trumpet summons us again,' and we can be sure we are being called to wash our hands. The White House does not escape the tone of café society, yet it strikes for the demeanor of Churchill during the Battle of Britain. . . . Listen carefully, with ears tuned to the American language . . . and you will hear an old message: 'Put your nickel on the drum, and save your soul. . . .' How often we Americans have wished to be saved, for a nickel."[127]

So far as Vietnam in particular was concerned, of course, this effort to save it on the cheap did not originate with Kennedy. As Halberstam rightly points out, the same pattern could be traced in Eisenhower's policy: "Instead of intervening directly in the French Indochina war, the United States had decided that the benefits were not worth the risks; then, later, after the Geneva agreement in 1954, the United States had tried to get the same end result, an anti-Communist nation on the border of Asian Communism, again with others doing the real work for us." [128] Yet timid and hesitant though Kennedy was about "intervening directly" in the Vietnam War, unlike Eisenhower he did in fact wind up sending 16,000 American troops there. He did so in "typical Kennedy fashion," by which I mean not only trying to purchase salvation for a nickel but with the same arrogant disregard of the difficulties which he had demonstrated in other areas (for example, promising to eradicate discrimination against blacks in housing "by the stroke of a pen").

This cavalier attitude toward difficulty was not confined to Kennedy alone; it pervaded his Administration and was indeed more visible in some of his people than in the President himself. His National Security Adviser, McGeorge Bundy, was perhaps the most salient example: a man whose arrogance had been legendary at Harvard (where he had served as a dean before being summoned to the White House by Kennedy) and was so unshakable that it would survive the debacle of his ideas about Vietnam to shape policies on race relations in his future career as president of the Ford Foundation which would be equally disrespectful of local conditions and difficulties.

If Bundy's arrogance was an attribute of his personality, Walt W. Rostow's was mainly located in his intellect. Rostow, who held a variety of important positions in the Kennedy Administration, was confident that he knew everything: from how to fight and win a guerrilla war (about which he delivered a highly influential address in June 1961 to the graduating class of the U.S. Army Special Warfare School at Fort Bragg, where he said unequivocally, "I am confident that we can deal with the kind of operation now under way in Vietnam"),[129] to the laws of economic development (about which he had written a famous book entitled *The Stages of Economic Growth* in whose subtitle, *A Non-Communist Manifesto,* he implicitly claimed to be superseding Marx).

Then there was Robert McNamara, the Secretary of Defense, whose arrogance was a function of his belief that he could devise a system for dealing efficiently and successfully with any enterprise, whether an automobile company (he had been president of Ford in the days when Detroit was still a symbol of the awesome brilliance of American industry), a government bureau (he became instantly famous in the Kennedy Administration for the way he was bringing the Pentagon "under control"), or a guerrilla war.

McNamara, Rostow, and Bundy were all what would later be called "hawks," but Kennedy's "doves" (including those who when the going got rough in the late sixties would convert to dovishness or claim a dovish past for themselves) were not noticeably less arrogant. John Kenneth Galbraith, as he himself once put it, was not famous for being humble, nor was George Ball (who as a high official in the State Department played devil's advocate in the internal debates over Vietnam), nor were Arthur Schlesinger, Jr., and Richard N. Goodwin (neither of whom had much influence over policy but both of whom would later exert a great deal of influence in the public debates over Vietnam). As I have already suggested, to the extent that these men really pressed for a "political" rather than a "military" approach to the Vietnam War, they were advocating a kind and degree of American involvement that implied more, not less, disregard of the local difficulties. But in any case, none of them ever advised Kennedy to give up on Vietnam altogether. What they really seemed to want of him was to abandon Diem and find a replacement.

In this—thanks to Diem's increasing intransigence and especially to the ruthlessness with which he suppressed a Buddhist protest against his policies—they eventually had their wish. On November 1, 1963, Diem was ousted by a group of generals in a coup encouraged by the United States, and he and his family (in an act the United States neither instigated nor sanctioned) were murdered.[130] Three weeks later, John F. Kennedy himself was murdered. Lyndon Johnson, who only a few years earlier had called Diem "the Winston Churchill of Southeast Asia,"[131] now became President of the United States.

"Nothing succeeds like successors," John Kenneth Galbraith had told Kennedy around the same time Johnson had been saying that Diem was "the only boy we got out there." Now Johnson as President had the bitter satisfaction of discovering that he had been right and Galbraith had been wrong. Instead of leading to successful successors, the coup was followed by seven different governments in Saigon within the space of twelve months, none of them an improvement over Diem's, "none of them genuinely popular or competent."[132]

Thus in getting what they had for so long wanted, the "politicals" around Kennedy found themselves faced (not for the last time in the 1960s nor only in the realm of foreign affairs) with unintended consequences: less rather than more political stability in South Vietnam; and more rather than less American responsibility for a war that Kennedy and everyone around him had always made a point of saying was "their war and not ours to win or lose." From that point on, wrote a British scholar, "the question was not going to be how to encourage a regime in South Vietnam that America could support but of finding one that would support her in keeping up the struggle against the jubilant Communists."[133]

In retrospect it is hard to disagree with those, like Lewy, who believe that the United States would in all probability have lost in Vietnam with Diem just as surely as it lost with his successors. But would it have made any difference if Kennedy had taken McNamara's advice and gone in fast and big instead of "slow and small"?

Judging from what was to happen later, the answer is almost certainly no. In 1961, McNamara and the Joint Chiefs estimated that the "maximum U.S. forces required on the ground in Southeast Asia will not exceed 6 divisions, or about 205,000 men"— *provided* that both Hanoi and "Peiping" intervened overtly.[134] Seven years later, writes Ellsberg, "without facing any Chinese, General Westmoreland was requesting almost that identical force —206,000 troops—as an *addition* to the 520,000 already under his command," and despite the fact that North Vietnam had been bombed steadily for the past four years.[135]

Of course these numbers represented going in big and slow, not big and fast; they were achieved by precisely the kind of gradual escalation McNamara and the Joint Chiefs had warned against in 1961. Yet even if Kennedy had taken their advice and gone in fast as well as big, the chances are that the result would have been futility. According to Sir Robert Thompson, the British expert on guerrilla warfare, what was required in Vietnam was "a small elite army, highly mobile and capable of being deployed and switched to operations anywhere in the country." Yet for all the interest Kennedy and his people showed in counterinsurgency techniques, the United States (even before going in with its own forces) concentrated on creating a large conventional South Vietnamese army, which Thompson regarded as "the basic cause of the failure to defeat Communist insurgency there."[136] Faced with a guerrilla war, the United States responded by preparing the South Vietnamese (in the words of the well-known strategic analyst Albert Wohlstetter) for "another conventional invasion across a parallel separating a Communist north from a non-Communist south," such as had occurred in Korea.[137] Then, when American troops were introduced into the picture, the Army (as "Cincinnatus" says) "chose not to adapt to the unique environment of Vietnam," instead conducting "big-unit operations against bands of guerrillas," and relying "too heavily on technology and the lavish use of firepower."[138]

In short, it seems reasonable to conclude that the only way the United States could have avoided defeat in Vietnam was by staying out of the war altogether. Kennedy, facing as Eisenhower had before him the possibility of a complete collapse in Vietnam, would have had to follow Eisenhower's example and do nothing. To have made that decision would not have implied that his repeated assertions of the importance of preventing a takeover of South Vietnam by the Communists had been insincere or unserious. As we have seen, no such inference could legitimately have been drawn from Eisenhower's decision in 1954. Eisenhower *had* been serious, but he had also concluded that the possibilities of success were too small and the risks of failure too high. His decision to stay out had been a prudential decision against getting involved in "the wrong war at the wrong time in the wrong place." Kennedy was also acting prudently when he decided to go in "slow and small," but like the war itself, it was the wrong prudence at the wrong time and in the wrong place. The prudence itself was wrong because it did not go far enough; the time was wrong because, as Draper says, "some of the best opportunities to re-examine and reshape the war were lost in 1961";[139] and the place was wrong because a halfhearted and gradual intervention was bound to cause more political trouble (both in the United States and in Vietnam) than either the course of going in fast and big recommended by McNamara or the alternative of no intervention at all.

To have stayed out obviously would have meant conceding South Vietnam to the Communists, and it would obviously have been a defeat for the United States (although just as obviously a lesser defeat than we eventually suffered). But what Dean Acheson had said in his White Paper of 1949 on the loss of China would have been equally applicable to Vietnam in 1961: "The unfortunate but inescapable fact is that the ominous result of the civil war in China was beyond the control of the government of the United States. Nothing that this country did or could have done within the reasonable limits of its capabilities could have changed that result; nothing that was left undone by this country has contributed to it."[140]

It seems doubtful that Kennedy, who himself had attacked Acheson for the loss of China, and who was the kind of man he was and not the kind of man Eisenhower was, would have been willing or able to say such a thing about the loss of Vietnam. In any event, he did not. And so, failing to take the measure of the local obstacles both political and military, refusing to face up squarely to the dimensions of the commitment that would inevitably be required, and ignoring "the reasonable limits of its capabilities," the United States under Kennedy, for all practical purposes and in all but name, went to war in Vietnam.

THREE:

WHY WE STAYED IN

MINUTES after Lyndon Johnson was sworn in as President of the United States he "made a solemn private vow": he would devote himself to "seeing things through in Vietnam." He made "this promise not out of blind loyalty" to Kennedy but rather because he "was convinced that the broad lines of his [Kennedy's] policy in Southeast Asia . . . had been right." Accordingly, four days later, in what he described as his "first important decision on Vietnam," Johnson signed National Security Action Memorandum 273, affirming that "it remains the central objective of the United States in South Vietnam to assist the people and Government of that country to win their contest against the externally directed and supported Communist conspiracy." [1]

There is nothing surprising in Johnson's unhesitating and even enthusiastic assumption of the burden of the American commitment in Vietnam. Like Kennedy, he was a member of the generation whose first formative experience where issues of war and peace were concerned had been the politics associated with and symbolized by Munich. Indeed, even more than Kennedy (who as a young man had been sufficiently influenced by the isolationist views of his father, then the American ambassador in London, to mute the implicit call for American intervention in his book *While England Slept*), Johnson "felt strongly that World War II might have been avoided if the United States in the 1930s had not given such an uncertain signal of its likely response to aggression in Europe and Asia."

"I could not forget," Johnson would write in his memoirs, "the long and difficult fight over the Selective Service Act in 1940, when major wars were already being fought in both Europe and China";[2] and anyone who had ever heard him talk about how a bill extending the draft passed the House by only one vote (cast to break a tie by Speaker Sam Rayburn of Texas, his own political mentor) only four months before Pearl Harbor, could testify to his obsession with the dangers of American isolationism and the follies of appeasement in general.

These dangers continued to preoccupy him after the end of World War II. When he was a young congressman in 1947, it became clear to him during the legislative battle over the Truman Doctrine "that the voices of isolationism and appeasement had not been completely stilled, despite the painful lessons of the past," and in his own contribution to the debate on the floor of the House he made a scornful reference to "the words of one great appeaser . . . 'peace in our time.' " Another milestone was "the day President Truman decided that American military force would be used to resist aggression in Korea."[3] Johnson, by then a United States Senator, supported this decision with characteristic exuberance as an "inspired act of leadership [which] will be remembered as the finest moment of American maturity."[4]

If Johnson, like Kennedy before him, saw containment as flowing by negative example out of Munich, and Korea as an expression of the seriousness of containment, he also shared with Kennedy the view that containment applied no less clearly to Vietnam than to Korea. "The leaders of North Korea had demonstrated that they were willing to use force to get what they wanted. We had defeated them in the early 1950s, but they were still dangerous. Ho Chi Minh was another leader willing to use force to realize his dreams: Communist control over all of Vietnam as well as Laos and Cambodia. Peking had helped North Korea and was helping Ho Chi Minh.''[5]

Johnson also placed much greater emphasis than Kennedy had on the Southeast Asia Treaty Organization (SEATO), which Dulles had hastily put together shortly after the Geneva conference of 1954 on the rough model of NATO. "The spirit that motivated us to give our support to the defense of Western Europe in the 1940's," he said, "led us in the 1950's to make a similar promise to Southeast Asia."[6] The implication was that the SEATO treaty required the United States to intervene militarily in Vietnam, and although this claim would be convincingly challenged by critics later on, the point is that Johnson himself saw no essential difference, whether legal or political or moral, between the American commitment to the defense of Western Europe against "direct aggression" by the Soviet Union and the defense of the countries of Southeast Asia, including South Vietnam, against (in the words of the SEATO treaty) "armed attack and . . . subversive activities directed from without against their territorial integrity and political stability."[7]

Although Johnson, as Minority Leader of the Senate in 1954, had refused to go along with unilateral American military intervention to save Dien Bien Phu,[8] he described the fall of the fortress only a month later as the most "stunning reversal" ever suffered by American foreign policy "in all its history," putting the United States "in clear danger of being left naked and alone in a hostile world."[9] No doubt Draper is right in seeing this as partisan hyperbole, a turning of the tables on the Republicans, who had so often attacked the Democrats for losing China to Communism and one of whose most prominent spokesmen, Senator Joseph McCarthy, had only recently denounced the Democrats as "the party of treason." But hyperbolic or not, such language leaves no doubt that Johnson took the American interest in Vietnam very seriously from very early on. Thus when seven years later as Vice President he was sent to Southeast Asia by Kennedy to report on the situation and to make recommendations for policy, he might well have been expected to return with precisely the assessment he did bring back to the President.

"The fundamental decision required of the United States," he told Kennedy, "is whether we are to attempt to meet the challenge of Communist expansion now in Southeast Asia by a major effort in support of the forces of freedom in the area or throw in the towel." [10] At this point, in Johnson's judgment, the United States should mainly "help these countries defend themselves." [11] But the decision to do so "must be made in a full realization of the very heavy and continuing costs involved in terms of money, of effort and of United States prestige." What was most significant of all in this report was Johnson's warning that the effort he was recommending also "must be made with the knowledge that at some point we may be faced with the further decision of whether we commit major United States forces to the area or cut our losses and withdraw should our other efforts fail." [12] To "throw in the towel in the area" meant to "pull back our defenses to San Francisco and a 'Fortress America' concept. More important, we would say to the world in this case that we don't live up to our treaties and don't stand by our friends." This, said Johnson, "is not my concept." [13]

Not much time passed before Johnson, as President, was put to the test of his own "concept." Although McNamara had been optimistic only six weeks earlier—predicting in October 1963 that American forces could be withdrawn from Vietnam within two years—by December 21, within a month of Johnson's accession to the Presidency, McNamara was very disturbed by the deterioration, both political and military, of the situation. In fact, as McNamara himself acknowledged, it had not really deteriorated but had been worse all along than he had realized "because of our undue dependence on distorted Vietnamese reporting." [14] But as Johnson himself would admit in his memoirs, it was not only the Vietnamese who had been issuing overly optimistic assessments. The Americans too had been guilty of what Johnson would euphemistically call "an excess of wishful thinking" and of telling Washington what they thought it wanted to hear. [15]

It was on this issue that the famous "credibility gap" had first developed, when reporters in Vietnam (who were being sent there in increasing numbers as the American involvement grew) had begun questioning the validity of official statistics and progress reports and were finding their doubts vindicated. Despite Johnson's avowed intent, the practice, initiated under Kennedy (in the period of "sink or swim with Ngo Dinh Diem"), of reporting only progress and minimizing failure, continued into Johnson's own Administration, evoking criticism even from a hawkish correspondent like Hanson Baldwin of the New York *Times,* who attacked the Administration for giving a "misleading and sometimes distorted picture" of conditions in South Vietnam.[16] Thanks to Johnson's flamboyant personality and the rhetorically hyperbolic style so evident in his 1954 speech about Indochina and still there ten years later in private interviews and conversations about Vietnam, the credibility gap would widen to the point where charges of outright lying would replace the more delicate allegations of self-deception and subtle misrepresentation. Thus did the language in which the war was discussed escalate in violence along with the war itself.

The first and most serious episode in the history of the widening credibility gap was the Gulf of Tonkin resolution passed by Congress on August 7, 1964. This resolution—the closest the United States ever came to an actual declaration of war in what would prove to be the longest and costliest war in its history—spoke of "a deliberate and systematic campaign of aggression that the Communist regime in North Vietnam has been waging against its neighbors and the nations joined with them in the collective defense of their freedom" and authorized the President "to take all necessary measures to repel any armed attack against the forces of the United States and to prevent further aggression."[17]

One of Johnson's most fervent future opponents, Senator J. William Fulbright, Chairman of the Foreign Relations Committee, steered this resolution through the Senate. He did so, moreover, with open eyes. In answer to anxious questions from other senators, for example, he pointed out that the resolution would indeed empower the President to involve the United States in a major land war in Asia (although he also expressed the hope that the use of American air and sea power would make such a decision unnecessary). Other future opponents of Johnson's policies were not only clear about what they were doing in voting for the resolution; they were enthusiastic. "There is a time to question the route of the flag, and there is a time to rally around it, lest it be routed," said Senator Frank Church. "This is the time for the latter course, and in our pursuit of it, a time for all of us to unify." [18]

When, several years later, Fulbright, Church, and many others who had voted for the resolution changed their minds about the wisdom of the course they had originally supported, they did so, not with expressions of repentance over having been wrong, but with angry denunciations of Johnson and his people for having deceived them into going along with a previously planned escalation of the war. Johnson was charged with having either provoked or fabricated the incident which had served as the occasion for the resolution (an attack by North Vietnamese torpedo boats on two American destroyers followed by a one-shot American reprisal in the form of air strikes against North Vietnamese naval bases). As was so often the case with criticism of the war in the post-1965 period, these charges were themselves instances of an obvious credibility gap. For the evidence (including material turned up in the Pentagon Papers) is that the attack did take place and that it was not deliberately provoked by the United States. [19]

This does not mean that the attack was not seized upon by Johnson as a good excuse for doing what he had already been thinking of doing; it was. For just as there is little doubt that the attack took place, so there is no question that by the time it did Johnson was seriously considering an expansion of the war through military action against North Vietnam. Indeed, it would have been incomprehensible if this had not been the case.

The idea of taking such action had been in the air for a very long time; as we have already seen, the possibility was raised by almost everyone—Taylor, McNamara, Rusk, and the Joint

Chiefs of Staff—in the course of recommending that Kennedy
commit American troops in 1961. In the months before the incident in the Gulf of Tonkin, Johnson was already being pressured
—by the new American commander in Vietnam, General William
C. Westmoreland; by the American ambassador, Henry Cabot
Lodge; by one of the many short-lived successors to Diem, Pre-
mier Khanh; and by the Joint Chiefs of Staff in Washington—to
begin bombing the North and the Communist sanctuaries in Laos
from which men and supplies were infiltrated into South Vietnam.

Johnson also had what amounted to a draft of the Tonkin Gulf
resolution which, according to Tom Wicker of the New York
Times, "he had been carrying . . . around in his pocket for
weeks" by the time the attack occurred.[20] It was this fact—interpreted, as everything about Johnson later would be, in the worst
possible light (he would even be accused in a much-praised and
celebrated parody of *Macbeth* of having arranged for the assassination of Kennedy)[21]—that gave credence to the charge that
the Tonkin Gulf attack had been a fabricated pretext. But Johnson's own explanation is entirely plausible. "Concerning Vietnam, I repeatedly told Secretaries Rusk and McNamara that I
never wanted to receive any recommendation for actions we
might have to take unless it was accompanied by a proposal for
assuring the backing of Congress." Accordingly, "As we considered the possibility of having to expand our efforts in Vietnam,
proposals for seeking a congressional resolution became part of
the normal contingency planning effort. But I never adopted
these proposals, for I continued to hope that we could keep our
role in Vietnam limited."[22]

Even after the Tonkin Gulf resolution was adopted, this "hope
that we could keep our role in Vietnam limited" served as the
theme of Johnson's campaign promises in running for reelection
against Barry Goldwater in 1964. Looking back at this campaign
from the perspective of what was to follow, one is amazed to
discover that Vietnam played a relatively minor role in it. "In the
election of 1964," writes Richard N. Goodwin, then one of Johnson's chief speech writers, "although Vietnam was occasionally

mentioned, not a single complete speech of President Johnson's was devoted to that conflict. (We did not then refer to it as a war.)" The reason, it seems, is that "opinion polls commissioned by local candidates and the national Democratic party showed that as few as four or five percent of the people in many states considered it an issue of major concern."[23] In the press, too, Vietnam was what Peter Braestrup, then of the New York *Times,* calls "a neglected war." Vietnam, he says, "in terms of permanent assignment of U.S. correspondents, remained a backwater even after the fall of Diem and the commitment of 23,000 U.S. advisers," with only a handful of American reporters there and virtually no television coverage.[24]

To the extent that the war (or the "conflict") became an issue between Goldwater and Johnson, it turned into a subliminal replay of the debate between the Truman Democrats and the MacArthur Republicans over Korea. Goldwater represented the same strain of conservative Republican thought that had denounced the limits placed on the military in Korea, that had supported MacArthur in pressing for an extension of the war to the mainland of China, and that had then accused Eisenhower of accepting a "strategic defeat" in agreeing to a settlement on the terms previously outlined by Truman. Faced with such an opponent, Johnson in effect donned the mantle of Truman and attacked Goldwater exactly as Truman had attacked MacArthur.

Goldwater, he said or insinuated, was advocating measures that carried with them the danger of World War III. In addition to suggesting that Goldwater might authorize the use of nuclear weapons (which Goldwater indeed sometimes sounded as though he might do), Johnson—speaking after the Gulf of Tonkin resolution—excoriated the Republicans for their belief in the "wisdom of going North in Vietnam." He for his part would launch an offensive "only as a last resort"; he would be "very cautious and careful" before he started "dropping bombs around that are likely to involve American boys in a war in Asia with 700 million Chinese."[25]

In summing up his policy Johnson came close to linking it explicitly with Truman's policy in Korea: "So we are not going

North and drop bombs at this stage of the game, and we are not going South and run out and leave it for the Communists to take over. . . . So we are trying somehow to evolve a way, as we have in some other places, where the North Vietnamese and the Chinese Communists finally, after getting worn down, conclude that they will leave their neighbors alone.''[26] The echoes of Truman and Korea were audible for anyone with ears to hear.

Was Johnson lying when he said these things? Was he lying when he also said that he was "not ready for American boys to do the fighting for Asian boys"?[27] In thinking about that question, one has to remind oneself that the very use of the word "lying" to describe such statements is a legacy of the Vietnam War. Neither Woodrow Wilson nor Franklin Roosevelt, who made similar promises while running for the Presidency which they then proceeded to break by sending "American boys" to fight in foreign wars, was generally called a liar. Yet that is exactly what Lyndon Johnson would be called for following the example of predecessors whom some of his own critics, including a few who branded him a liar, admired for their acumen in foiling the forces of isolationism and appeasement through the clever deployment of just such political rhetoric.

That consideration apart, it is not at all self-evident that Johnson was consciously and deliberately deceiving the American people when he made those statements. It is true that shortly before delivering the speech from which I have just quoted he had authorized the drawing up of contingency plans for "going North." But it is also true that he would on two occasions—one just before the election and one after it—veto recommendations by Maxwell Taylor (at that point ambassador to Vietnam) to execute those plans.

The fact is that Johnson at this stage was still hoping against hope that the collapse of South Vietnam could be averted without deepening the American military involvement. Why would he not hold onto this hope as long as he possibly could? To suppose that he wanted to deepen the American involvement, or that he would decide on so serious a course unless and until he had seen no easier alternative, is to misread both Johnson's character and the political temper of the time. Unlike Kennedy, who admired the martial virtues so much that the sociologist David Riesman could discern in him a contemporary representative of those American patricians "who since Teddy Roosevelt's day have seen war and preparation for war as the condition of national health,"[28] Johnson was by nature a negotiator and a conciliator. His entire political career had been constructed on the foundation of his great skills as a "wheeler-dealer," and one of his favorite quotations was the biblical "Come now, let us reason together." In addition, the very fact that he himself thought it the better part of political wisdom to run as the "peace" candidate against the openly war-like Goldwater testifies to his awareness of the great risk he would incur by escalating the American commitment.

At the same time, and despite his talk of not sending "American boys to do the fighting for Asian boys," it is hard to disagree with Johnson's own response to the charge that he deceived the American people as to his intentions in the 1964 campaign: "On several occasions I insisted that American boys should not do the fighting that Asian boys should do for themselves. I was answering those who proposed, or implied, that we should take charge of the war or carry out actions that would risk a war with Communist China. I did not mean that we were not going to do any fighting, for we had already lost many good men in Vietnam. . . . Certainly I wanted peace. . . . But I made it clear from the day I took office that I was not a 'peace at any price' man. . . . The American people knew what they were voting for in 1964. They knew Lyndon Johnson was not going to pull up stakes and run. . . . They knew too that I was not going to wipe out Hanoi or use atom bombs to defoliate the Vietnamese jungles."[29]

In other words, Johnson was saying, they knew that he was neither Henry Wallace nor Douglas MacArthur—that he was committed without reservation to the policy of containment set and defined by Truman in going to war in Korea, accepted by Eisenhower in settling that war on the basis of the status quo ante instead of by liberating the North, and reaffirmed by Kennedy in sending more than 16,000 Americans into Vietnam. What Johnson did not say was that MacArthur himself, who had been so intent on victory in Korea, had advised both him (and Kennedy before him) against sending ground forces into Vietnam.[30] On the other hand, Eisenhower, who had decided against doing just that during his own term of office, nevertheless told Johnson in 1964 that "we could not let the Indochina peninsula fall. He hoped that it would not be necessary to use the six or eight divisions mentioned in some speculation. But if it should prove necessary, he said, 'so be it.' "[31]

Another indication that Johnson was still trying to avoid the large-scale deployment of ground troops was the very decision that would outrage the same people who would later call him a liar—the decision in early 1965 to begin bombing North Vietnam on a regular basis. Like everything else Johnson (and Kennedy before him) did, the bombing of the North was undertaken to save South Vietnam from Communism at the lowest possible cost to the United States. Obvious and even self-evident though this point ought to be, it has been obscured by so much of what has been said and written about the war that one has to keep reminding oneself of it. In the case of "Rolling Thunder" (as the bombing campaign was code-named), the hope was that it would preclude the need for a major commitment of combat troops.

Again like everything else about Vietnam (at least from 1965 on), the bombing of the North gave rise to a tremendous controversy. The theory behind the bombing was that the war was being directed and supplied by the North—that it was an invasion, albeit disguised, rather than a civil war—and that it could therefore be ended by inflicting damage on the real aggressor who had so far been fighting with relative impunity. But if that were the case, why had the United States waited so long before bombing the North? The official answer given to this question was that while the aggression against South Vietnam had from the beginning been directed and controlled by Hanoi, the pace of infiltration had recently increased.[32] In other words, the American escalation—so the Johnson Administration claimed—was a response to an escalation by the North Vietnamese.

This claim was, and has continued to be, hotly contested. It was the United States, more and more critics began charging with more and more vehemence, that had escalated the war, using the excuse of increased participation by the North Vietnamese when in fact there had been no evidence of any such increase. Indeed it was the very bombing itself that provoked the North Vietnamese to send their regular troops South in the first place.

Such is the contention of writers ranging from I. F. Stone (whose sympathies were with the Communists) [33] to Roger Hilsman (who had under Kennedy participated in the decision to step up American participation but who later resigned in protest against the bombing) [34] to Theodore Draper (whose powerful anti-Communist convictions did not prevent him from opposing the effort to save South Vietnam from Communism by military means). [35] Yet, according to Guenter Lewy, evidence not available at the time proves that "the initial escalation, through the introduction of North Vietnamese combat forces . . . was carried out by the Communists, well before the American decision to bomb North Vietnam." [36]

Although this evidence has failed to convince Draper, [37] it is hard to see how anyone can still maintain that a civil war was going on in Vietnam and that it was only the United States that provoked the North into intervening. Whether there were 400 North Vietnamese regulars in the South at the time the bombing began, as Draper maintained, or 5,800 (Lewy's estimate), the fact remains that Hanoi had been directing and supplying the insurgency in the South from the very beginning. Not only had the North Vietnamese been sending help in the form of weapons; between 1958 and 1964 they also infiltrated at least 28,000 regrouped Southerners who had been trained in the North and who, as Lewy says, "replaced battlefield casualties and often assumed command positions in the NLF." Lewy does concede that for the years 1965–67 "it is possible to maintain that the North Vietnamese merely matched the massive American buildup"; [38] or, as Draper scathingly puts it, "The Northern troops began to come down, and the more we bombed, the more they came." As of early 1967, when North Vietnamese regulars had jumped to about 20 percent of the total enemy force in the South, Draper wondered "how much more the enemy forces would have increased if we had bombed even more to reduce them."[39] Only a year later, he had his answer: the figure had skyrocketed to 71 percent.[40]

These figures certainly tell us that if the purpose of the bombing had been to prevent the North Vietnamese from going South, it was a complete failure. But the figures are irrelevant to the issue of whether the war in the South was a case of "foreign aggression." To the Communists and those who accepted their view of the situation, Vietnam was a single country and therefore no degree of Northern involvement in the South could be seen as a foreign aggression. Nevertheless, because it suited the purposes of their propaganda, the North Vietnamese continued to deny that they had any forces in the South and encouraged the world to believe that the war was a popular revolutionary uprising against the oppressions of an imperialist puppet government. This was not true in the beginning; and as for the end, this civil war conducted (according to the Committee of Concerned Asian Scholars) by "the largely peasant forces of South Vietnam" was won when North Vietnam, finally dropping all pretense, sent a huge regular army into the South and then proceeded to impose its rule without so much as a nod in the direction, let alone the participation, of the Southerners, whose struggle it had presumably been all along and to which Hanoi had supposedly started giving "meaningful support . . . only when the American assault intensified beyond where they could resist by their own means."[41]

But to return to Johnson's decision to begin bombing the North in early 1965, the hope that it would make the dispatch of very large numbers of American ground forces unnecessary turned out to be short-lived. Within a few months, it had become clear that inflicting damage on the North was not resulting in a diminution of Vietcong activity in the South. In July, McNamara, returning from a trip to Saigon, told Johnson that the situation was worse than it had been a year earlier "when it was worse than a year before that." He continued: "After a few months of stalemate, the tempo of the war has quickened. A hard VC push is now on to dismember the nation and to maul the army." The Communists, he concluded, "seem to believe that South Vietnam is on the run and near collapse." [42]

If the bombing was not succeeding in its military objective, neither was it achieving the political objective of bolstering the morale of the South by showing the people there, in Johnson's words, "that the North was paying a price in its own territory for its aggression." [43] Only a few months after the bombing began, there was yet another political crisis in Saigon which resulted in the overthrow of a civilian government and the coming to power of two military men, Marshal Ky and General Thieu, who immediately requested additional American combat troops up to an estimated total of 200,000.

By this point, what with one thing and another, the number of American forces in Vietnam had risen to about 75,000, but thus far they had been restricted mainly to a limited combat role. Large as this number was, moreover, it still did not represent—not in the eyes of Johnson—an answer to the "crucial question" of whether the United States was prepared to "use substantial U.S. forces on the ground to prevent the loss of that region to aggressive forces moving illegally across international frontiers." In the opinion of McNamara the only way to "stave off defeat in the short run and offer a good chance of producing a favorable settlement in the longer run" was to send another 100,000 troops to Vietnam immediately, with the understanding "that the deployment of more men (perhaps 100,000) may be necessary early in 1966, and that the deployment of additional forces thereafter is possible. . . ." [44]

Here, then, the moment of truth that Kennedy and then Johnson had been trying to postpone had finally arrived. Determined to save South Vietnam from Communism, they had tried desperately to do it on the cheap. Kennedy had gone in "slow and small," and when it became clear that this would not suffice, Johnson had resorted to bombing, again in the hope that the dreaded prospect of a land war in Asia could be avoided. When it became apparent, as it almost immediately did, that bombing the North could not prevent the Communists from winning the war in the South, Johnson found himself with no alternative to defeat and withdrawal other than the commitment of very large numbers of American combat troops.

Johnson consulted and pondered, but he did not hesitate for long. The consequences of an American withdrawal and the fall of South Vietnam to Hanoi would, he told himself, be catastrophic. "All of Southeast Asia would pass under Communist control, slowly or quickly, but inevitably." In addition, "Those who had counted so long for their security on American commitments would be deeply shaken and vulnerable." Then, into the power vacuum the United States would leave behind it, Moscow and Peking, whether independently or together, and "whether through nuclear blackmail, through subversion, with regular armed forces, or in some other manner," would move.[45]

At that point the United States would bestir itself and try to head off the full consequences of its withdrawal, just as it had done in reaction to German submarine warfare in April 1917, just as it had done again in switching from isolationism to collective security in 1940–41, and again in swerving in 1946–47 "from the unilateral dismantling of our armed forces to President Truman's effort to protect Western Europe," and yet again in 1950 in reacting to the invasion of South Korea after having taken its forces out. "As I looked ahead, I could see us repeating the same sharp reversal once again in Asia, or elsewhere—but this time in a nuclear world with all the dangers and possible horrors that go with it." Only a very few of his advisers opposed the decision, Johnson said, and none of them "gave me facts or arguments that broke or even weakened this chain of conclusions."[46]

Accordingly, on July 28, 1965, Johnson ordered another 50,000 men to Vietnam and announced that additional forces would be sent as requested by the commanding general, William Westmoreland. "Now," he wrote in his memoirs, "we were committed to major combat in Vietnam. We had determined not to let that country fall under Communist rule as long as we could prevent it. . . ."[47] This was not empty rhetoric: by the time Lyndon Johnson left office three years later, the number of American forces in Vietnam had risen to over half a million. Except for an occasional pause, moreover, the bombing also went relentlessly on. A total of 222,351 Americans were killed or wounded in the course of those years.[48]

Expensive in terms of blood and treasure though this effort undoubtedly was, however, the paradox is that Johnson was still trying to save South Vietnam on the cheap. Unlike Kennedy, he was willing to take the military measures that his advisers told him were necessary to avert a Communist victory. But he was no more willing than Kennedy had been to take the political measures that he of all men might have been expected to see as the indispensable foundation for so ambitious a military operation.

Only a little while earlier, he had insisted on securing the consent of Congress for everything he meant to do in Vietnam. Yet now he proposed "to send the flower of our youth, our finest young men, into battle,"[49] without asking Congress for a declaration of war. He also decided against calling up the reserves or increasing the draft or going on a war footing or declaring a state of emergency. "I don't want to be overly dramatic and cause tensions," he told a meeting of the National Security Council. "I think we can get our people to support us without having to be too provocative and warlike."[50] So intent was he on this low-keyed approach that he forced his Vice President, Hubert Humphrey, to remove a passage from a speech in which "Humphrey made an emotional appeal to the flag" and spoke of "the grief and anguish of war in quest of preserving freedom." Johnson's own speech of July 28 was televised in the afternoon rather than the evening when the audience would have been much larger, and it gave as the reason for going to war in Vietnam the less than stirring need to maintain "confidence in American promise or in American protection."[51]

In addition to thus forgoing—on this and other occasions—the "opportunity to galvanize the American people and arouse their support for the war,"[52] Johnson refused to finance the war either by increasing income taxes or by cutting back on the social programs that were collectively known as the Great Society. His emphasis had been on the Great Society from the beginning, and he would not permit the war in Vietnam to detract from the attention or to subtract from the resources he was determined to devote to the war that commanded his deepest passions—the war on poverty.

In his first State of the Union Message, in 1964, he had mentioned Vietnam only twice in passing; a year later, in his 1965 message, only 126 words had been given over to Vietnam; and even in his 1966 message—delivered six months after he had committed the nation "to major combat in Vietnam"—he did not get around to the subject until he had spent thirty-six minutes proposing new Great Society programs. Then, instead of asking for sacrifices of a wartime nature and dimension, he said: "There are men who cry out: We must sacrifice. Let us rather ask them: whom will they sacrifice? Will they sacrifice the children who seek learning—the sick who need care—the families who dwell in squalor now brightened by hope of a home? Will they sacrifice opportunity for the distressed—the beauty of our land—the hope of the poor? . . . I believe we can continue the Great Society while we fight in Vietnam." [53]

As Johnson would later tell his biographer Doris Kearns in explaining why he decided not to mobilize the American people: ". . . History provided too many cases where the sound of the bugle put an immediate end to the hopes and dreams of the best reformers: The Spanish-American War drowned the populist spirit; World War I ended Woodrow Wilson's New Freedom; World War II brought the New Deal to a close. Once the war began, then all those conservatives in the Congress would use it as a weapon against the Great Society. . . ." [54] As he often indicated, moreover, Johnson was proud of the fact that he never tried to generate a war fever in the country. So were many of his people. Thus, for example, McNamara: "The greatest contribution Vietnam is making—right or wrong is beside the point—is that it is developing an ability in the United States to fight a limited war, to go to war without the necessity of arousing the public ire." [55]

Johnson, then, was trying to save Vietnam on the political cheap—going in politically slow and small—just as Kennedy had done in trying to save it on the military cheap. But there was another similarity between these two otherwise so different Presidents reflected in the attitude each took toward Vietnam. For Johnson in his own way was no less cavalier about the difficulties of this war than Kennedy had been. The difference was that whereas Kennedy had mainly failed to take the measure of the obstacles within Vietnam to a successful intervention, Johnson failed to see that the conditions for a successful prosecution of the war were lacking in the United States.

The first and most important such condition was the one he himself might have created if he had gone in politically big and fast: enthusiastic popular support. I say *might* have created because there was very little opposition to the war in 1965; and indeed, as measured by the polls that Johnson obsessively studied and that he carried around with him to show to visitors, public opinion continued to back his conduct of the war even when his popularity began to plummet. This attitude was echoed and reflected in the positions taken by most politicians, very few of whom were yet willing to risk going public with whatever doubts they might have had about the wisdom of Johnson's policies. Congress continued to vote the appropriations without which the war could not have been fought, and when Senator Wayne Morse (who had said, "If American boys are killed in an undeclared war, it is murder")[56] introduced an amendment in March 1966 to repeal the Tonkin Gulf resolution, it was defeated by a vote of 92–5.

In the major newspapers and magazines too—the New York *Times*, the Washington *Post, Time,* and *Newsweek*—the importance of preventing the fall of South Vietnam to Communism was still taken almost entirely for granted even when doubts were expressed about the escalation of the war and the relation of the military tactics being employed to the political objectives being sought. Thus, for example, a New York *Times* editorial of April 1965 entitled "Vietnam's 'Wider War' " declared flatly that "no one except a few pacifists here and the North Vietnamese and Chinese Communists are asking for a precipitate withdrawal. Virtually all Americans understand that we must stay in South Vietnam at least for the near future. . . ."[57] As late as 1965,

David Halberstam, who had been the *Times* correspondent in Vietnam in the days of Diem and would subsequently write in derisive and contemptuous terms about the American involvement there, still believed "that Vietnam is a legitimate part of that [U.S.] global commitment . . . perhaps one of only five or six nations in the world that is truly vital to U.S. interests. If it *is* this important," he continued, "it may be worth a larger commitment on our part. . . ."[58]

As for the Washington *Post*—a much less important paper in those days than the *Times* and less influential than it would later become—it was edited by J. Russell Wiggins, who was a close personal friend of Johnson's and who "generally backed Administration war policy, albeit not without criticism."[59] Moreover, some of the most widely read syndicated columnists of the day—including Joseph Alsop and the team of Rowland Evans and Robert Novak—were among Johnson's strongest supporters.

Up until 1967, the two major news magazines were also on Johnson's side. *Time,* indeed (like its sister magazine *Life*), was hawkish to the point of what Peter Braestrup would call euphoria: "It's the right war in the right place at the right time," one editor said. *Newsweek* was less enthusiastic, blowing "hot, cold, and lukewarm, depending on the writers and editors involved," but its editors nevertheless tended toward support of Johnson's war policy.[60]

On the other hand, and even in the midst of all this support, portents of what was to come in the way of opposition to the war could already be easily discerned. In Congress, some of Johnson's closest associates began breaking ranks with him on Vietnam after regular bombing of the North was inaugurated. Previously only two senators—Wayne Morse of Oregon and Ernest Gruening of Alaska—had opposed him, but now liberals like George McGovern of South Dakota, Frank Church of Idaho, Eugene McCarthy of Minnesota, Gaylord Nelson of Wisconsin, and Stephen Young of Ohio (all of whom had voted for the Tonkin Gulf resolution) went public with criticism of Johnson for failing to work hard enough toward a negotiated settlement of the war. Soon old friends like Fulbright and Mansfield, and even a Johnson protégé like Vance Hartke of Indiana, would also make their misgivings public.

According to Evans & Novak, "What had started in 1964 with the two-man opposition of Wayne Morse and Ernest Gruening and then grew to a half dozen or more in 1965, now had mushroomed to perhaps half the sixty-six Democratic senators in 1966." [61] If George McGovern could be believed, this estimate was much too conservative. Speaking in February 1966, McGovern claimed that a clear majority of the entire Senate was opposed to any further escalation of the war and that "perhaps ninety out of one hundred senators think that we made a mistake in ever becoming involved in the first place. There are," he added, "a good many senators who will say that privately, but who will then say, 'Here we are, so mistake or no mistake, we have to see it through as best we can.' " Among these he included "some of those senators who have been advertised in the press as great hawks." [62]

The press too—again including papers and magazines that generally supported the objective of saving South Vietnam from Communism—began expressing more and more misgivings as the war escalated, and especially after the bombing of the North had become a regular feature of the American strategy. "A major task for President Johnson," said the *Times*, "is to explain to the American people and to the world . . . that the methods the United States is employing to defend South Vietnam are the wisest and the most effective." [63] Or again: "The Americans went into Vietnam . . . to contain the advance of Communism in that part of Southeast Asia. The motives are exemplary and every American can be proud of them, but the crucial questions are: Can it be done? Is the price too high? Was the military decision in the Kennedy Administration to increase American forces in Vietnam mistaken? Are the dangers of escalation too great? Is this a good battleground of the cold war on which to fight? Is the United States losing more than it is gaining? All lead up to the basic question that some senators are asking: Is this war necessary?" [64]

As with the *Times,* so with the Washington *Post,* where the editorial-page editor, Philip Geyelin, was increasingly at odds with the chief editor, Wiggins, over the prospects for victory in Vietnam. A similar split was evident in *Time,* whose skeptical reporters in Saigon were outraged by the editing of their stories in New York to conform to the magazine's hawkish line, and at *Newsweek* where in any case support for the war was (in Braestrup's term) "tepid."[65]

It is important to stress yet again, however, that the opposition to Johnson both in Congress and in the major newspapers and magazines was up to this point based mainly on tactical considerations rather than on any fundamental disagreement over objectives. What the skeptical reporters in Saigon were skeptical about was whether the war could be won, not whether it was worth winning. So, too, with those in Congress who were becoming known as the doves. As of 1965, no one in Congress—not even Senators Morse and Gruening—openly challenged the desirability of trying "to contain the advance of Communism in that part of Southeast Asia"; and when the future leader of the antiwar movement, George McGovern, criticized the bombing of the North in February of that year, he did so only on the narrow tactical ground that it would not bring Hanoi to the negotiating table.[66] Other doves, with memories of the Chinese intervention in Korea, expressed similarly tactical anxieties over whether the same thing would happen again if the United States went on bombing the North.

No wonder, then, that Johnson—who as majority leader of the Senate had become one of the great masters in the art of creating consensus by manipulating, cajoling, and pressuring his fellow senators—thought that he could deal in the same way with the critics of his conduct of the war. Elaborate White House briefings were arranged in which small groups of congressmen and senators were subjected to the famous Johnson "Treatment." Using all his considerable powers of charm and persuasion, the President tried to reassure those who doubted that his policies would work, or that he was less than fully serious about the desire for negotiations, or that he was on a collision course with the Chinese ("I won't let those Air Force generals bomb the smallest

outhouse north of the 17th parallel without checking with me,"
he told one such group).[67]

2.

The problem, however, was that another and more far-reach-
ing form of opposition to Johnson now began to show itself more
and more clearly in a sector of American society—the universities and the intellectual community generally—to which neither
Johnson's arguments nor the "Treatment" was an adequate response. This opposition had existed even in Kennedy's day, but
with the bombing of the North and the subsequent escalation of
American involvement in combat in the South, it too escalated
both in numbers and intensity. Having enjoyed only scattered
and marginal support even among intellectuals before 1965, it
now began to spread into something resembling a movement.

Unlike the Senate doves or their counterparts on the editorial
page of the New York *Times* and other such liberal periodicals,
the people making up this movement were not asking whether
the war was necessary. The question they were asking—and answering negatively in the very asking—was whether the United
States had any right to be fighting in Vietnam at all. Nor did they
restrict themselves to criticizing the bombing of the North and
the conduct of the war in the South as unwise or ineffective; they
attacked what the United States was doing as immoral and even
criminal. What worried them, moreover, was not that American
military intervention into Vietnam would fail but that it might
succeed.

Normally to side with the enemy in wartime is considered an
act of treason. But it was one of the many bizarre features of the
Vietnam War that Americans were able to side with the enemy
with complete impunity. Demonstrators marched under Vietcong
flags, organizations urged soldiers to throw down their arms and
desert, and Americans even visited North Vietnam and made
broadcasts from there endorsing enemy propaganda—all without
being subjected to any legal penalty or even much public cen-

sure. On the contrary, in the intellectual community the people who did these things were often treated as heroes and even patriots, while those who criticized them were excoriated and ridiculed.

To Johnson and his supporters the emergence of a serious opposition on the Left evidently came as a great surprise. They were well aware that the isolationism against which they had been contending all their political lives had never quite died; indeed, Johnson himself seems to have attributed the dovishness of midwestern senators like McGovern, Church, Young, and McCarthy at least in part to the fact that they all came from the traditional stronghold of isolationist sentiment, and (as we have already seen) it was the very possibility of its resurgence that supplied the main reason for his decision to commit large numbers of combat troops.

Johnson and his people were no less keenly aware of the opposition they faced on the Right. Although he had defeated Barry Goldwater in 1964 by one of the great landslides in American history, he had a "continuing conviction that the more dangerous threat to him lay not in peace-minded doves but in war-courting hawks."[68] Of the two sets of critics, the doves centered in the Senate Foreign Relations Committee and the hawks in the Senate Armed Services Committee, "the congressional hawks struck more fear in Johnson's heart."[69]

One wonders why. Was he perhaps afraid that General Curtis LeMay—who had retired as Air Force Chief of Staff in February 1965, just before the regular bombing of the North began, and who had reportedly said that "we ought to nuke the Chinks"[70] (and would later allegedly advocate bombing North Vietnam "back to the stone age")—might give him the same kind of political trouble that Douglas MacArthur had given Truman in the Korean War? If so, he could not have been more mistaken about the political climate of the country. Unlike MacArthur, to whom millions had rallied when he declared that "there is no substitute for victory," LeMay found no substantial following and was treated as a cross between a madman and a clown.

Yet even with so little opposition coming from the Right and so much becoming visible from the Left—"peace marches," teach-ins, draft-card burnings, and the like—the Johnson Administration still refused to take it with full seriousness. On October 15, 1965, for example, demonstrations were held all across the country to protest "the continuing United States involvement in the Vietnam War." In Berkeley, a "peace march" drew ten thousand people. In Ann Arbor about two hundred people tore down the American flag from a float and stamped on it. In Chicago, a marcher carried a placard reading "I Only Followed Orders: Adolf Eichmann," and in New York, where another ten thousand gathered, a young pacifist burned his draft card while several FBI agents looked on passively (even though a law had recently been passed making such action a federal crime). Asked to comment on all this, the press officer of the State Department said, "We are naturally aware of various noisy demonstrations that have taken place and are scheduled to take place, but I would like to point out that these groups constitute an infinitesimal fraction of the American people, the vast majority of whom have indicated their strong support of President Johnson's policies in Vietnam." [71]

No doubt the State Department was right so far as the sheer numbers were concerned. In the fall of 1965, a Gallup survey showed 64 percent of the American people supporting greater involvement. A few months later, in early 1966, 61 percent favored escalation if the bombing pause that had just been announced should fail to produce a response from the North Vietnamese. Around the same time, "with polls at his fingertips, the President cited figures: 10 percent 'want to go hot-headed–Goldwater types,' 10 percent 'are ready to run,' 20 percent favored more bombing, and 60 percent believed 'we are doing right.' " [72]

No doubt also the radicals who openly supported the Communists and compared the United States to Nazi Germany were in a minority even within the leftist opposition. Certainly the more moderate opponents of the war were embarrassed both by the language of the radicals and by their tactics. "We can't have any coordination in the movement as long as these kids keep shouting and waving Vietcong flags. They're rowdy and disorderly and they give the movement a bad name," an antiwar activist told a reporter after the first march on Washington in 1965.[73] Refusing to participate in that same march, Norman Thomas—the leader of the Socialist party and himself a pacifist and one of the earliest opponents of American intervention in Vietnam—explained that he could not work politically with people who "love the Vietcong more than they love peace."[74]

Nevertheless, it was the radicals who gave the antiwar movement its dynamism, its energy, and most of all its visibility. Even many who dissociated themselves from the view that the Communists deserved to win and that "Amerika"—as the radicals took to spelling the name in order to suggest an association with Nazi Germany—was waging a criminal war, generally did so because it "gave the movement a bad name" and not because they were outraged by such ideas. Those within the movement —individuals like Norman Thomas and groups like Negotiation Now—who believed neither that the Communists were a benevolent force nor that the United States was an evil one soon found themselves overwhelmed by a rising tide of pro-Communism, anti-anti-Communism, and anti-Americanism that swept everything before it.

Each of these three currents flowed, sometimes imperceptibly, into the other, and they were not always easy to tell apart. Nevertheless, there were distinctions of emphasis and nuance.

The pro-Communists—to begin with them—included actual Communists, that is, members of the Moscow-oriented Communist party and groups intimately associated with it (like the DuBois Clubs), as well as members of the Maoist Progressive Labor party and the Trotskyist Socialist Workers party. The number of actual Communists was by the sixties very much smaller than it had been in the thirties, thanks to the combined efforts of inner demoralization and harassment from without. Moreover, the fact that the Communists were now split into a party loyal to the Soviet Union, a party loyal to China, and a party loyal to the memory of Leon Trotsky obviously meant that they could not command the kind of influence they had enjoyed in the 1930s, when almost all Communists had been concentrated into a single body and subject to strict political discipline. Yet where Vietnam was concerned, these splits counted for very little: all American Communists (and indeed Communists everywhere in the world, including the Soviet Union and China) were united in supporting the Vietcong and the North Vietnamese against the South Vietnamese and the Americans.

In addition, all the Communist groups worked on increasingly close terms with the non-Communist radicals who made up the ever-swelling constituency of what had only recently become known as the New Left or the Movement. The New Left prided itself on its freedom from the ideological rigidity of the Old (or Marxist) Left, but on the issue of Vietnam such differences as divided New from Old were no more visible to the naked eye than they were in the case of various Communist factions. They all worked together in what was called the antiwar movement but their participation turned it more and more into a movement opposing not the war but only the side fighting the Communists.

Not only did many New Leftists march in demonstrations waving Vietcong flags; they also did everything they could to propagate a view of the war according to which the Vietcong and Hanoi represented good, and the South Vietnamese and the United States represented evil. Thus when a leaflet circulated by a typical New Left group, the Berkeley Vietnam Day Committee (VDC), declared: "We believe that the entire war in Vietnam is criminal and immoral," it was immediately made clear that this condemnation extended not to the entire war but only to the American role. "We are supposed to be fighting to protect democracy in Vietnam," but "as far as the Vietnamese are concerned, we are fighting on the side of Hitlerism"; we were also "supposed to be fighting to save the Vietnamese people from Communism. Yet . . . most Vietnamese think of the NLF leaders as their country's outstanding patriots." [75]

Similarly, the predominantly black Student Non-Violent Coordinating Committee (SNCC), which had up to this point been devoting all its energies to the fight for desegregation in the South, justified an extension of its concerns to Vietnam by drawing a parallel between the civil-rights workers in the American South and the peasants in the South of Vietnam, both of whom were struggling for "liberation and self-determination" against the United States government. Just as "we ourselves have often been victims of violence and confinement executed by United States government officials," so "Vietnamese are murdered because the United States is pursuing an aggressive policy in violation of international laws." In short, "our country's cry of 'preserve freedom in the world' is a hypocritical mask behind which it squashes liberation movements which are not bound, and refuse to be bound, by the expediencies of United States cold war policies." [76]

If the pro-Communists, whether of Old or New Left vintage, had been entirely on their own, the chances are that they would have made very little impact. Their numbers were relatively small, and the brazenness of their position probably put off more people than their clarity and forcefulness influenced. But their open support for the Vietcong and Hanoi was given a great push toward respectability by another group with greater intellectual credibility. This group was made up of writers not previously known for their sympathy with Communism—and some even with a history of highly visible opposition to Communism—who began in the mid- and late sixties traveling to Hanoi and writing articles and books about North Vietnam the like of which had not been seen since the rosy accounts of sympathetic Western travelers to the Soviet Union in the 1930s.

One of these, Susan Sontag, then at the height of her fame and influence as a critic of the arts, was even conscious of the comparison, but insisted that it did not discredit her own picture of North Vietnam: "If some of what I've written evokes the very cliché of the Western left-wing intellectual idealizing an agrarian revolution . . . I must reply that a cliché is a cliché, truth is truth, and direct experience is—well—something one repudiates at one's peril. In the end I can only avow that, armed with these very self-suspicions, I found, through direct experience, North Vietnam to be a place which, in many respects, *deserves* to be idealized." [77] (The italics are hers.)

True to her word, she described one of the most Stalinist regimes in the Communist world as an "ethical society"—indeed "a society tremendously overextended ethically," one that had been "democratized" by the war. "Incorporation into such a society [would] greatly improve the lives of most people in the world." As for the government, it "loves the people," and believes (had not Ho Chi Minh himself said this?) that "nothing is more precious than independence and liberty." [78]

How then account for the fact that "there are still quite a few pictures of Stalin in North Vietnam, hanging on the wall in some but hardly all government offices, factories, and schools"? The question troubled Sontag, but she had a ready answer. It was the Vietnamese abhorrence of waste, "the principle of getting maximal use from everything," "the Vietnamese lack of both time and incentive for symbolic controversy," and "a polite tribute to the *idea* of unity and solidarity among Communist countries": [79] anything, in short, but an open declaration of admiration for the creator of the model Communist regime.

Apart from expressing certain reservations about the puritanical sexual mores of North Vietnam, Susan Sontag could find only one great fault there: the "defect that the North Vietnamese aren't good enough haters." For example: "The North Vietnamese genuinely care about the welfare of the hundreds of captured American pilots and give them bigger rations than the Vietnamese population gets, 'because they're bigger than we are,' as a Vietnamese army officer told me, 'and they're used to more meat than we are.' People in North Vietnam really do believe in the goodness of man . . . and in the perennial possibility of rehabilitating the morally fallen, among whom they include implacable enemies, even the Americans." [80]

How could Sontag not suspect what we now know for certain —that those captured pilots were being abused and tortured? And how could she not suspect that North Vietnam was a totalitarian society? The answer is that such suspicions did enter her mind. Even while writing about "the moral beauty of the Vietnamese," she asked herself whether she might be succumbing to "phony sentimentality" and credulity; after all, the present government had committed "notorious crimes" in the past, and one might conclude from the monopoly of power held by the Communist party that even today "The Vietnamese must be regimented and deprived of personal liberty." But no: "For the Vietnamese, 'the Party' simply means the effective leadership of the country . . . a vast corps of skilled, ethically impeccable, mostly underpaid public servants, tutoring and working alongside people in all their activities, sharing their hardships . . ." While there may be "terrible abuses" under this system, "neither does it preclude the possibility that the present system functions humanely, with genuine substantive democracy, much of the time."[81]

In short, her suspicions were unworthy of respect: "Though it's second nature for me to suspect the government of a Communist country of being oppressive and rigid, if not worse, most of my preconceptions about the misuses of state power in North Vietnam were really an abstraction. Against the abstract suspiciousness I must set (and be overruled by) what I actually saw when I was there—that the North Vietnamese genuinely love and admire their leaders; and, even more inconceivable to us, that the government loves the people."[82]

Like Susan Sontag, Mary McCarthy went to North Vietnam at the invitation of Hanoi. A generation older than Sontag, she had (by her own account) "been an anti-Stalinist ever since the Moscow Trials," and she too, wanting to approve of North Vietnam, was bothered by the ubiquitous portraits of Stalin she found there. "Once, in a village cooperative I thought I saw Marx, Engels, Lenin, and Ho, and no Stalin—which made a joyful impression on me—but when I got up from my chair, I found that Stalin had been behind me all along, chuckling." (Sontag, in her earnest fashion, searched for possible exculpatory explanations; McCarthy, "reluctant to ask," let the question hang.)[83]

Like Sontag too, McCarthy was bothered by the incessant drumming of propaganda into her sensitive writer's ear. At first "the vocabulary repelled" her,[84] just as it did Sontag. But like her younger colleague (who had to learn to use words like "imperialism" and "capitalism" again because, as against what she had mistakenly come to believe in the past, "the political and moral reality is as simple as the Communist rhetoric would have it"),[85] McCarthy proved adept at finding the fault in herself as an American and in turning the tables on the United States: "In the Stalinist days," McCarthy said, "we used to detest a vocabulary that had to be read in terms of antonyms—'volunteers,' denoting conscripts, 'democracy,' tyranny, and so on. Insensibly, in Vietnam, . . . we have adopted this slippery Aesopian language ourselves, whereas the North Vietnamese, in their stiff phraseology, persist in speaking quite plainly. . . . Although we complain of the monotony, the truth, renamed by us 'propaganda,' has shifted to the other side."[86]

Less credulous and sentimental by temperament than Sontag, more acerbic and skeptical, McCarthy chided herself for relying on her "detachment and novelistic powers of observation," which "after a few days with those single-minded North Vietnamese" began to seem "not only inappropriate but also a sort of alibi."[87] She need not have worried: her description of North Vietnam was only slightly less rosy than Sontag's.

Despite American bombing, and "in glaring contrast to Saigon, Hanoi is clean. . . . The sidewalks are swept, there is no refuse piled up, and a matinal sprinkler truck comes through, washing down the streets." There are no prostitutes on the streets, "no ragged children with sores"—indeed, one hardly even sees "a child with a dirty face," and "wherever you go, you are met with smiles, cheers, hand clapping. Passers-by stop and wave to your car on the road."[88]

In the countryside too (where "you see the lyrical aspect of the struggle") everything is wonderful, especially as compared with South Vietnam: "Last year I saw the filthy hamlets there and the refugee camps. Here everything I am shown is clean." Is this, she asks herself, because they are hiding the bad sights from her? She doubts it. "In the South, they cannot hide the dirt, disease, and misery. They would not know where to begin. . . . At any rate, in the North I saw no children with sores and scalp diseases, no trachoma . . . , no rotten teeth or wasted consumptive-looking frames. . . . In the countryside, children and young people were radiant with health; as far as I could judge, everybody under forty was in peak physical condition." At this point it occurs to her that the contrast between South and North might have something to do with the fact "that in the North there is no fighting." But the only implication she draws from this fleeting subversive thought is that "a U.S. invasion might help equalize things, spreading hunger and squalor." [89]

What of the political system? "Obviously, in a short official stay in North Vietnam, I was not in a position to meet dissenters, if they existed." But wondering about the role of the Lao Dong (Communist) party, she asked one official about it and was told that it was of no importance; and when, to her surprise, she saw "that the question had given offense," she (who as a writer had always delighted in giving offense) dropped it altogether "to risk offending again." [90]

In any case, the North Vietnamese believed that "the license to criticize was just another capitalist luxury," rather like the large number of suitcases with which she was traveling ("I have never learned to travel light"). "This of course," writes McCarthy, famous precisely for her own unlimited use of the license to criticize, "is true. The fact that you can read about, say, police brutality or industrial pollution in the New York *Times* or even in a local paper is nothing to be especially proud of, unless something concrete results, any more than the fact that you can read both sides about Vietnam and watch it on television." To be sure, she concedes, "A free press is livelier than a government-controlled one, but access to information that does not lead to action may actually be unhealthy, like any persistent frustration, for a body politic." This is especially so where the war is concerned, because "in my opinion the Americans do not *have* a side in this war." [91]

Wilfully suppressing what her critical faculties might reveal ("as I got to know the North Vietnamese better, I grew ashamed to write little observations about them in my notebook"), she sought excuses and rationalizations for everything she either disliked or was offended by—not, like Sontag, by developing theories about Vietnamese culture, but usually by blaming the

Americans. "Until the Americans go home," there would be no freedom "from the self-imposed rationing system in the realm of ideas that limited [the North Vietnamese] diet to what was strictly necessary to the national interest, free to speculate, to question authority. . . . The Americans have blocked such possibilities for the young Vietnamese, and for the old, too."[92]

Unlike Sontag, she spoke to two American prisoners, but actually meeting them made her no less credulous than Sontag about the treatment they were getting. The two captured pilots she was taken to see were "in the living room of a Hanoi villa" (she was "not sure whether this was their actual place of confinement"), and the main impression they made on her was how unintelligent and uncultured they were: "I was taken aback . . . by a stiffness of phraseology and naive rote-thinking, childish." She was (as she had already made clear earlier) certain that they were neither "being fed lies nor, in my judgment, mysterious drugs"; in fact, "If these men had been robotized, I felt, it had been an insensible process starting in grade school and finished off by the Army," which had turned them into "somewhat pathetic cases of mental malnutrition." Indeed, "though one pilot told me he had read 'a lot' of Vietnamese history in jail, he seemed wholly unmodified by his experience, and the sole question he put me was 'Can you tell me how the Chicago Cubs are doing?' The second prisoner, an older man, had not changed his cultural spots either, except in one respect: he claimed to like Vietnamese candy."[93]

Nevertheless, the North Vietnamese captors of these deplorably uncultured war criminals to whom McCarthy spoke were as lacking in hate as the ones described by Sontag: "At the War Crimes Commission, Colonel Ha Van Lau, a delicate-featured, slender, refined officer from Hué, of mandarin ancestry (he reminded me of Prince Andrei in *War and Peace*), talked in an objective way about the problem of conscience for the U.S. pilots; some, he thought, were aware of what they were doing and some were naive or deceived . . . Shortly after their capture, or as soon as they are able, they are taken to see some bomb sites—the first step, it is hoped, in their reformation."[94]

Even more impressive than Colonel Ha Van Lau was the Prime Minister, Pham Van Dong, "a man of magnetic allure, thin, with deep-set brilliant eyes, crisp short electric gray hair, full rueful lips drawn tight over the teeth. The passion and direct- ness of his delivery matched something fiery, but also melan- choly, in those coaly eyes. An emotional, impressionable man, I thought, and at the same time highly intellectual." He tells her that in the book she has just written on South Vietnam she has "shown a deep feeling for the Vietnamese people. Feeling and understanding." She reciprocates by concluding from his own description of his policies that he presides over "a moral, ascetic government, concerned above all with the *quality* of Vietnamese life." [95]

Before she leaves, the Prime Minister again praises her book on South Vietnam and expresses the hope that she will now write a book about North Vietnam. She replies that it is too early to say; she may not have enough material for more than a few articles. "I feared he was disappointed." [96] He need not have been.

Unlike Susan Sontag and Mary McCarthy, Frances FitzGerald had no prior reputation as an anti-Communist when she took to writing about Vietnam; in fact, it was her articles about the war —which began appearing in various magazines in 1966 and which would form the basis of her 1972 book *Fire in the Lake*—that established her reputation in the first place. If the political and intellectual roots of McCarthy and Sontag were in the anti-Stalin- ist Left of the 1930s, and if their writings on Vietnam pointed toward the abandonment of that position by many of its former adherents, FitzGerald's roots were in the New Left of the 1960s, and her work pointed toward the softened version of its attitudes that would soon be known as the New Politics.

Still, FitzGerald's account of the Communists in the South— the National Liberation Front and the Vietcong—was no less idealized than the portraits of the North Vietnamese drawn by Sontag and McCarthy. Except in one curious respect: whereas both Sontag and McCarthy were impressed by the absence of hatred in the North Vietnamese Communists, FitzGerald be- lieved that the secret of Ho Chi Minh's success, as well as that of the NLF in the South, "was the systematic encouragement of hatred." For "Hatred was the key to the vast, secret torrents of energy that lay buried within the Vietnamese people, to a power that to those who possessed it seemed limitless and indestructible." In "calling upon the villagers to blame the 'feudalists' and the 'American imperialists and their lackeys' for their sufferings," the NLF was following a Communist party directive which ("quite correctly," in FitzGerald's opinion) "equated 'hatred of the enemy' with the masses' 'understanding of their own rights.' . . ."[97]

But if the gentleness and compassion of the North Vietnamese struck McCarthy and (despite her demurrers) Sontag as a great virtue, the NLF's systematic encouragement of hatred, being "a truly revolutionary act," was perhaps an even greater virtue to FitzGerald. "In calling upon the peasants to hate their enemies, the Front cadres were asking them not merely to change their ideas but to disgorge all of the pent-up feelings they had so long held back, to fight what was to them the extension of parental authority and stand up as equal members of the society." Following the example of the Vietminh and the Chinese Communists, "The revolutionary project of the NLF . . . was to use that released aggression as a creative force." Acknowledging (how could she not?) that the Vietcong practiced political assassination as "a basic ingredient" of its strategy, and "for the sake of its own security . . . had sometimes to execute men within its own ranks," she nevertheless denied that intimidation played a significant role in the spread of Vietcong control of the countryside: "Front soldiers were instructed not merely to avoid abusing the peasants. They were instructed to love them and to bring them into their own 'families.' . . ." Moreover, the Front "used political re-education rather than violence as its principal means of dealing with hostile people. . . . The lists of GVN [South Vietnamese government] officials to be assassinated or spies to be executed had to undergo long bureaucratic scrutiny before they could be put to use. . . . The NLF generally proscribed torture and preferred the bullet to any other means of dispensing death."[98]

Whenever it suited her purpose, FitzGerald quoted from

sources hostile to the Communists who, in trying to account for the success of the Vietcong, would sometimes point to the intelligent and disciplined way it combined terrorism and intimidation with gentler forms of persuasion. But the same or similar sources suddenly became suspect when they revealed that the Vietcong also used such techniques as "disembowelment with the villagers forced to be in attendance," [99] and putting the head of a recalcitrant peasant on a stake outside his village; [100] or when they conveyed the impression that "the NLF used foreign methods of organization in order to coerce a passive and generally apolitical peasantry"; or, still worse, when the NLF emerged from their work "as a sinister, disruptive force that has no local basis in legitimacy, and that quite possibly is the arm of a larger and more sinister power trying to impress similar methods of organization upon all nations throughout the world." [101]

To be sure, the role of the Communist People's Revolutionary Party (PRP) within the NLF "was much the same as that of the Communist parties in China and the Soviet Union. Its function was to provide political education and 'correct' political leadership at all levels of the bureaucracy." But this fact, like everything else that might seem "to support the claims of State Department propagandists," had to be seen in the proper Vietnamese context. "Americans, and particularly American liberals, find it difficult to understand how an elite, disciplined party could be an acceptable form of government for any people in the world. But the Vietnamese have always believed that some people know how to govern better than others. . . . Traditionally, those people the Vietnamese assumed to be best qualified were those who had studied government as a science and a system of morality. Whatever the virtues or vices of its policies, the PRP has laid strong claim to this tradition—its important modification being that it opened the opportunity for such study to the poorest members of the society." [102]

Even Marxism-Leninism itself had to be understood in the context of Vietnamese culture: "Upon his return to Vietnam in the 1940's, Ho Chi Minh set up his headquarters in a cave in the northern mountains above a swiftly rushing river. He renamed that mountain Marx and the river Lenin." Did this mean, as might reasonably be concluded, that Ho was imposing an alien ideology upon Vietnam? On the contrary: he was "making a symbolic connection between the ancient Vietnamese image that defined the country and the new history in which that country would live." In other words, "Through Marxism-Leninism he provided the Vietnamese with a new way to perceive their society and the means to knit it up into the skein of history. He showed them the way back to many of the traditional values and a way forward to the optimism of the West—to the belief in change as progress and the power of the small people. Through Marxism-Leninism he indicated the road to economic development, to a greater social mobility and a greater interaction between the masses of the people and their government." [103]

Though Susan Sontag, Mary McCarthy, and Frances Fitz-Gerald were all apologists for the Communist side in the Vietnam War, the fact that they were not Communists either in the sense of belonging to any Communist organization or in the sense of having a consistent record of support for the Soviet Union or China, contributed immeasurably to the weight of the pro-Communist element within the "antiwar" movement. The added fact that they were all very good writers meant that they were able to state the Communist case in a style acceptable to an audience that would normally be put off (just as they themselves were) by the crude propagandistic rhetoric of the hard-core and inveterate pro-Communist element.

Despite the touch of personal and literary class these writers gave to the pro-Communist case, however, and despite the unprecedented legitimacy they thereby helped it achieve, the number of open pro-Communists remained relatively rare even as late as the late sixties. At the same time, however, the number of anti-anti-Communists grew so large that they threatened to become the single most powerful faction in the American world of ideas.

In practice, and in its political effect, anti-anti-Communism was often hard to tell apart from pro-Communism. Indeed, the ridicule heaped by Frances FitzGerald on the anti-Communism of American foreign policy in the 1950s—or the statement made by two other pilgrims to Hanoi, Staughton Lynd and Tom Hayden, ". . . we refuse to be anti-Communist. We insist that the term has lost all specific content it once had. Instead it serves as the key category of abstract thought which Americans use to justify a foreign policy that is often no more sophisticated than rape" [104]—simply reinforced their support for the Communists in Vietnam.

But anti-anti-Communism did not in all or even most cases necessarily imply support for Communism in general or for the Communist side in Vietnam in particular. While some anti-anti-Communists subscribed (as the critic Diana Trilling in a polemic against them once put it) to "the belief that opposition to Communism constitutes a political, social, and cultural backwardness," [105] others like the Socialist Michael Harrington could say: "I am . . . an anti-Communist and an anti-anti-Communist." [106] Similarly the liberal Richard H. Rovere of *The New Yorker:* "I am against a good many things, Communism among them, but . . . I didn't particularly like to be described, as I sometimes was in the early 50's, as an anti-anti-Communist, though the term did have a certain accuracy as applied to me." [107]

Thus, too, Rovere's friend and sometime collaborator Arthur Schlesinger, Jr., who, while describing himself "as an unrepentant anti-Communist" and reaffirming "the obligation of the liberal to regard Communism with contempt [and] to reject its absolutisms," simultaneously asserted that "rational policy will give anti-Communism the priority it deserves, which has fallen now rather low. . . ." Since, said Schlesinger, Communism was no longer either a unified movement (witness the Sino-Soviet split) or a revolutionary one (in the developed countries "Communist parties are becoming bourgeoisified," while in the underdeveloped world "Communism has been a spectacular bust as a revolutionary creed" and "Nationalism is a far more powerful force"), the struggle to contain it no longer made sense. Indeed, containment "in some circumstances" might even now require encouraging and supporting "national Communism" as "the best barrier against an aggressive Communist state" in the same neighborhood. But however that might be, "Communism today is a boring, squalid creed, tired, fragmented and, save in very exceptional places and circumstances, wholly uninspiring. *La guerre est finie*." [108]

It followed that anti-Communism was obsolete as (in Rovere's words) "a foundation for a global policy." Or, in Dwight Macdonald's more colorful formulation: "As a universal menace, 'Communism,' *tout court,* has become a dead horse useful only for ritual floggings by our politicians." [109]

But calling anti-Communism obsolete was the kindest way the new anti-anti-Communists found to dispose of it. Thus, agreeing that "the *raison d'etre* for official anti-Communism as formulated in the 40's has largely disappeared," the sociologist (and Socialist) Lewis A. Coser went on to condemn it as "now in the main an ideological justification for an American global involvement on the side of those who try to hold back the tide of fundamental change in the underdeveloped areas of the world." [110] William Phillips, the editor of *Partisan Review* (who now apologized for having in the past occasionally swung "too far in the direction of 'obsessive anti-Communism' "), said that "to be an 'anti-Communist' today . . . one has to be pathologically single-minded, allergic to change, and in love with existing institutions." [111] His co-editor Philip Rahv added that "anti-Communism in the present-day meaning of the term . . . has no doubt helped to provide the ideological fuel needed by the policymakers in Washington (and the mass media at their service) for heating up the cold war whenever it suits their extremely narrow-minded, class-oriented conception of the national interest." [112] To the critic Harold Rosenberg, "The idea of setting up a world system either Communist or anti-Communist is a sick idea," and "Containment not only tries to stop *all* countries of whose ideology it disapproves, it also sabotages American freedom and the conflict of ideas." [113]

As Rovere pointed out, this attitude represented a great change "in the liberal and intellectual communities." Writing when Hubert Humphrey, who had been one of the founders of Americans for Democratic Action (ADA) in 1948, was Vice President under Lyndon Johnson, Rovere said: "Among Americans for Democratic Action there has been doctrinal controversy over Hubert Humphrey's enthusiasm for American policy in Vietnam. The ADA doves, who far outnumber the hawks, consider Humphrey a backslider. Humphrey insists that it is those in the antiwar majority who have lapsed into heresy: he hasn't left the church, but just about everyone else has. . . . This argument seems to me historically sound. The ADA . . . was established as a militantly anti-Communist organization. . . . Along with other liberal anti-Communists, they certainly did help to create a climate favorable to the war in Vietnam. Now they are appalled to discover where anti-Communism has led them, and they want out. But it is they more than Humphrey who have changed." [114]

This fact—that so many former anti-Communists were now joining the ranks of the anti-anti-Communists—did even more to lend respectability to the radical interpretation of the war than the conversion of a few former anti-Communists to the pro-Communist position. Here after all were people who had supported the policy of containment, including the war in Korea, about which Rovere himself had once written: "In Korea, the United States proved that its word was as good as its bond—and even better, since no bond had been given. History will cite Korea as the proving ground of collective security, up to this time no more than a plausible theory. It will cite it as a turning point in the world struggle against Communism." [115] Here were people who, like Schlesinger, had believed that in the past "the policy of containment" was "rational, wise, and brave," and who had even participated in Kennedy's decision to apply the same policy to Vietnam. Here, too, were people like Philip Rahv and William Phillips, the editors of a magazine, *Partisan Review,* whose anti-Stalinism had been its defining political characteristic for more than thirty years. Whatever the merits of the dismissal by all those people of Communism as either a relevant or a dangerous force and their correlative attack on or downgrading of anti-Communism—and I shall have something to say about those merits later on—when such as they took this position, the effect could only be to strengthen the influence of the radical view of the war according to which the Vietcong and Hanoi were right and good and the South Vietnamese and the United States were wrong and evil. And so it did.

"In liberal, academic, literary America," wrote Robert Pickus, who as a pacifist and the organizer of a moderate antiwar group called Negotiation Now knew what he was talking about, "political courage is required to maintain an *anti*-Communist stance. Here, anti-Communism is always 'blind.' If you believe Hanoi bears some responsibility for continuation of the killing in Vietnam, and are a careerist, or simply value non-hostile personal relations, you say nothing about it in the Math Department of the University of California, Berkeley." Even if (as Pickus himself was doing) "you are conducting a national campaign for a unilateral American ceasefire in Vietnam, you must nevertheless plan on losing significant money and support if you accurately depict the Vietcong's political leadership and their purposes."[116]

The third, and perhaps most powerful, of the three main currents running through the "antiwar" movement was anti-Americanism. By anti-Americanism I mean the idea that the United States was a force for evil in Vietnam. In this ethos, the diabolical role played by the Communists in the most extreme versions of the old anti-Communism was simply assigned to the United States. In the words of Noam Chomsky: "The Vietnam War is the most obscene example of a frightening phenomenon of contemporary history—the attempt by our country to impose its particular concept of order and stability throughout much of the world. By any objective standard, the United States has become the most aggressive power in the world, the greatest threat to peace, to national self-determination, and to international cooperation."[117]

As a background of anti-Communism combined with great literary ability made Susan Sontag and Mary McCarthy such effective apologists for Hanoi's view of the war, so it was Chomsky's reputation as a scholar in linguistics and the impression of scrupulous reasoning and meticulous scholarship he created in his heavily footnoted articles that gave the kind of credibility to his violent denunciations of American depravity in the waging of "a criminal war" that the cruder propagandists of the Students for a Democratic Society (SDS) and other such groups altogether lacked.

Like Mary McCarthy, Chomsky justified the one-sidedness of his analysis of the war by declaring that the United States had no side. "The simple fact is that there is no legitimate interest or principle to justify the use of American military force in Vietnam." Even "by accepting the presumption of legitimacy of debate" on Vietnam, "one has already lost one's humanity. . . . The war is simply an obscenity, a depraved act by weak and miserable men." Hence "We have to ask ourselves whether what is needed in the United States is dissent—or denazification." Unlike American policy in Vietnam this "question is a debatable one. Reasonable people may differ." But to Chomsky "it seems that what is needed is a kind of denazification."[118]

In this respect, however, Chomsky saw a significant difference between Nazi Germany and the United States. Whereas the Nazis tried to conceal the horrible things they did in the countries they invaded, one could read daily of American horrors in the American press itself: "I suppose this is the first time in history that a nation has so openly and publicly exhibited its own war crimes." But even this was turned by Chomsky to the moral disadvantage of the United States: as between showing "how well our free institutions function" and "how immune we have become to suffering," Chomsky thought it was "probably the latter" that accounted for the reporting of American atrocities by the American press. One was dealing with "moral degeneration on such a scale that talk about the 'normal channels' of political action and protest becomes meaningless and hypocritical."[119]

To Chomsky and the swelling number of those who accepted the anti-American perspective, the first crime the United States was committing in Vietnam was being there at all. "The unpleasant fact is that if one wishes to pursue the Munich analogy there is only one plausible contender for the role of Hitler," said Chomsky.[120] Daniel Ellsberg agreed: "The popular critique that we have 'interfered' in what is 'really a civil war,' " he wrote, "is as much a myth as the earlier official one of 'aggression from the North.' " This "simply screens a more painful reality: that the war is, after all, a foreign aggression. Our aggression." [121] According to Richard Falk, professor of international law at Princeton: "It seems clear that the basic premise of the Nuremberg judgment was that it was illegal to wage a war of aggression. From that perspective, there is little doubt that the fundamental role of the United States in Vietnam has been an illegal one." [122]

In the opinion of Hans J. Morgenthau (who in the course of the sixties moved away from his early criticisms of American policy as an imprudent extension of containment and began condemning the American role as both illegal and immoral), the United States was "fighting an entire people. And since everyone in the countryside of Vietnam is to a lesser or greater degree our potential enemy, it is perfectly logical to kill everyone in sight. . . . When we talk about the violation of the rules of war, we must keep in mind that the fundamental violation, from which all other specific violations follow, is the very waging of this kind of war." [123]

As to these "specific violations," the Committee of Concerned Asian Scholars asserted: "The fact is that U.S. war crimes are an accepted and regularly used method of waging war in Indochina." These crimes included—as Lewy summarizes the indictment—"the relocation of population and the creation of free-fire zones, the use of napalm and herbicides, and the treatment of prisoners," as well as atrocities committed by the military in the ordinary course of combat and "the indiscriminate killing of civilians through bombing and other tactics amounting ultimately to genocide." The United States, as the radicalized Roman Catholic priest Daniel Berrigan bluntly summed it all up, had "legitimated murder and expanded murder into genocide." [124]

Some of the books and articles from which I have been quoting were not published until late in Lyndon Johnson's Administration, and a few came out after he left office. But as we have already seen, their view of the war was in the air even before the escalations of 1965, and that view escalated in power and influence along with the American role itself. We have also seen that the Johnson Administration would not or could not take this attack from the Left seriously in 1965: these "noisy demonstrators" represented only "an infinitesimal fraction of the American people." A year later, upon being appointed to the White House staff, John P. Roche, a former president of ADA who, like Hubert Humphrey, had remained in the anti-Communist "church," told a reporter that the only opponents of the war were a few Jacobins on the Upper West Side of Manhattan.[125] And a year after that, in 1967, McGeorge Bundy (who had by this time left the Administration but was still closely tied to it) could say that while there were still "wild men in the wings" (by which he seems to have meant the opposition from the Right, the wild men on the Left scarcely meriting his attention), "on the main stage . . . the argument on Vietnam turns on tactics, not fundamentals."[126]

This patronizing attitude toward the radical opposition certainly bolstered Johnson's determination to fight the war on the political cheap, with "minimum disruption at home."[127] It was the political or ideological counterpart of his refusal to seek a declaration of war from Congress (which he could almost certainly have obtained up until 1967) and to mobilize the reserves (which the Pentagon Papers calls "the political sound barrier" that he would never break).[128] Thus, says Lewy, Johnson "rejected the view of some of his advisers that in order to hold the support of the country he would have to engage in some outright chauvinistic rabble-rousing and provide the American people with a vivid foe."[129] Instead he confined himself to using the "Treatment" in arguments over tactics "on the main stage," which meant that the moral question—the question of "fundamentals"—was left almost entirely to the radical opposition, whose arguments went almost entirely unanswered.

The reason was not that no answers could be found. As we shall see in due course, nothing is easier to refute than the *moral* case against the American intervention in Vietnam. Indeed, so preposterous was the diabolization of the American role in Vietnam—it was exceeded in naivete, foolishness, and immorality only by the beatification of the Communists—that Johnson and his people might well have been contemptuous of it simply on the merits. Why dignify such charges with a Presidential reply?

Surely it was self-evident that the United States was doing the right thing in trying to save South Vietnam from Communism.

But as the rise of the radical opposition itself demonstrated—and the pun here is intentional—this proposition was no longer self-evident. It was not even self-evident to many former anti-Communists to whom it had been so in relation to Korea (despite the fact that, as Rovere acknowledged, "while there are important differences between Korea in 1950 and Vietnam in 1967, there are more similarities than most liberals like to admit" and that "President Johnson has not thus far been less circumspect in his prosecution of this war than President Truman was in the other").[130]

Moreover, a new generation had appeared that knew everything about the evils, real as well as imagined, of American society and nothing about the evils of Communism or why the spread of Communism was both bad in itself and represented a danger to the United States. An effort to explain all this might well have failed, but it could hardly have led to more "disruption at home" than the refusal to press the moral argument did; and in any event, by abandoning the moral field to the radical opposition, the Administration allowed the war to lose its legitimacy in the eyes of an ever-widening public.

3.

For what Johnson and his people never understood until too late was that on the issue of Vietnam—and on a few other issues as well—the "wings" were becoming "the main stage." Or, to put it another way, New York (and its cultural colonies, the universities) was replacing Washington (and its numerical majority) as the source of political legitimacy. No matter that the radical opposition was and would remain a minority in the country at large, and even (although this was questionable by 1968) within the antiwar movement. The issue of Vietnam could not and would not be settled by numbers. To be fought successfully, the war had to have a convincing moral justification, and the failure to provide one doomed the entire enterprise. As Colonel Charles F. Kriete has said: "War requires for its successful pursuit the mobilization of a moral consensus on the legitimacy of both the objectives of violence and the means by which these objectives are pursued. . . . The maintenance of that consensus is one of the key objectives of national strategy, in both a political and a military sense, for when it fails, the war is lost." [131]

General Edward Landsdale puts the point more sharply: "This small clique, the Politburo [in Hanoi] brought ruin and tragedy to millions in Vietnam. Yet we never tried to arouse feelings among the Vietnamese or among Americans or among others in the world against this small clique of leaders—as we did against the Kaiser in World War I and again against Hitler in World War II. For some baffling reason, we accepted the self-portrait of Ho Chi Minh as a benevolent old 'uncle' who was fond of children—and of other Politburo leaders as speakers for a people they did not permit to have opinions. So we let their claims to leadership go unchallenged while their people suffered and died. . . ." [132]

Compounding the ironies here, the case Johnson and his people did work hard to make was much shakier than the moral case and much easier for critics of the war—moderate as well as radical—to beat down. This was the argument based on power politics. We were fighting in Vietnam not so much against the Vietcong or even against Hanoi but to contain China, just as we had fought to contain the Soviet Union in Europe and then Korea. In the words of an internal National Security Council memorandum of November 1964: "Communist China shares the same internal political necessity for ideological expansion today that the Soviet Union did during the time of the Comintern and the period just following the Second World War. . . . This will impel her . . . to achieve ideological successes abroad . . . our objective should be to 'contain' China for the longest possible period . . . and at the same time strengthen the political and economic structure of the bordering countries. . . . We should delay China's swallowing up Southeast Asia until (a) she develops better table manners and (b) the food is somewhat more indigestible." [133] Or, as Johnson himself put it in public: "In the forties and fifties we took our stand in Europe to protect the freedom of those threatened by aggression. Now the center of attention has shifted to another part of the world where aggression is on the march. Our stand must be as firm as ever." [134]

But even assuming that the Communists in Vietnam were surrogates of the Chinese (and the critics were right in denying this), the question arose as to whether their victory in Vietnam would have the dire consequences envisaged by the United States. Would such a victory lead to the toppling of all the other "dominoes" in Southeast Asia? This was not easy to prove; and even if it were to happen, in what way would American interests be seriously damaged? At a time when the Russians and the Chinese were competing for influence instead of cooperating, might not a more powerful China even have served American interests by acting to contain Soviet expansionism?

Such were the questions being raised by the doves in Congress and in the media, and answered most tellingly to Johnson's disadvantage and discomfiture by moderate critics of the war in the intellectual community like Theodore Draper, Arthur Schlesinger, Jr., and Robert W. Tucker. [135] Unlike the radicals, these critics did not call for immediate American withdrawal. The radicals, believing the United States to be waging a criminal war, wanted it to be punished by the humiliation of *surrender*. The word, and the italics, were Mary McCarthy's, who added: "The moral overtones are displeasing to the American public; surrender is a confession of failure. Yet we will be lucky, though we do not see it, if failure, finally, is the only crime we are made to confess to." [136]

This was not what the liberal or moderate doves were after. Some ("a firm minority" in Norman Mailer's knowledgeable estimate) did indeed want the United States to lose; or rather, it would be more precise to say, as Mailer did, that they "secretly desired Asia to go Communist." But since "they did not consider it expedient to grant this point," they "talked around it." [137] Talking around it meant advocating negotiations that would provide what Leslie H. Gelb and Richard K. Betts call "a face-saving way out" and that would spare the United States "withdrawal symptoms''[138] and the humiliation of surrender which to the radicals was a necessary element of a satisfactory end to the war.

"The others, the majority of the doves," said Mailer, "simply refused to face the possibility" that an American withdrawal would mean a Communist victory.[139] This refusal "to face the possibility" took the form of a belief that a compromise settlement could be negotiated if only the United States were willing. "The liberals," write Gelb and Betts, "called for a negotiated settlement, for cease-fires, for UN intervention, for Asian conferences, for dealing with the Vietcong, for truly free elections, and for a coalition government. . . . Liberal opponents of the war seemed to assume that Hanoi would negotiate on these terms if only Johnson would offer them."[140]

In response to this body of opinion, which he did take seriously, Johnson tried to prove that he was exploring every possible avenue to peace. He instituted bombing pauses and he made appeals to Hanoi. Once he even offered to extend the Great Society to North Vietnam (a gesture Schlesinger derided as "a form of imperialism unknown to Lenin: sentimental imperialism").[141] "We have put everything into the basket of peace except the surrender of South Vietnam," said Dean Rusk of the great "peace offensive" of 1965 (to which Hanoi replied, "Johnson puts everything in the basket of peace except peace"). And every "peace feeler" from Hanoi was explored (which, said John McNaughton of the Defense Department, was "like making smoke-signals in a high wind").[142] Throughout the entire Johnson Administration there were sixteen bombing pauses and a total of seventy-two peace initiatives.

Admittedly, as Gelb and Betts say, "only a few of the pauses were complete, and only a few of the initiatives had much significance." It is also true that Johnson had a tendency "to develop second thoughts and back off from an initiative" by increasing military operations after one had been launched.[143] This gave the critics an opening to argue that Johnson was not really interested in negotiations. But of course he was. Why else was he sending increasing numbers of American troops to Vietnam and dropping so many bombs on the North if not to persuade the Communists that they had no hope of taking over South Vietnam by force and that they would therefore have to settle for something short of that goal?

"President Johnson preferred a compromise settlement," write Gelb and Betts, "which by all odds he believed Hanoi would have to accept" once it realized that military victory was out of the question.[144] (Johnson: "My own feeling was that the only thing that might produce real peace talks would be a conclusion reached by the leaders in Hanoi that they could not win by military means.")[145] Gelb and Betts go on: "By traditional diplomatic standards of negotiations between sovereign states, the possible compromises would not have been fatuous. One was to guarantee that the Communists could remain in secure control of North Vietnam. The United States would not seek to overthrow this regime. The other compromise was to allow the Communists in South Vietnam to seek power in the same way Communist parties seek it in France and Italy."[146]

What Johnson did not want and would not accept was the "face-saving exit" some of his critics were looking for in negotiations: he was not willing to "compromise South Vietnam away to the Communists."[147] Yet nothing short of this would satisfy Hanoi. "Never once," wrote Johnson in his memoirs, "was there a clear sign that Ho Chi Minh had a genuine interest in bargaining for peace. Never, through any channel or from any serious contact, did we receive any message that differed significantly from the tough line that Hanoi repeated over and over again: Stop all the bombing, get out of Vietnam, and accept our terms for peace"—which, as Johnson rightly added, "prescribed the surrender of the South."[148]

Gelb and Betts confirm this assessment: Hanoi, they point out, was not interested in compromise for the simple reason that "the Vietnamese Communists, who were also the most dynamic of the Vietnamese nationalists, would not accept only part of a prize for which they had paid so heavily."[149]

Gelb and Betts proceed to make an interesting observation about the liberal or moderate opponents of the war, who "seemed to assume that Hanoi would negotiate . . . if only Johnson would offer" the right terms. "Reading through the lines of the liberal critique, however, it could be argued that they were saying that the United States should lose at the negotiating table, not on the battlefield—though they did not say this explicitly. Two leading war opponents, Richard Goodwin and Arthur Schlesinger, Jr., both put the arguments in that vein. In their books of this period they took as a given that the United States should not be driven from the battlefield but could negotiate a peace if the President only tried." [150]

The upshot is that there was no way for Johnson to satisfy the political demands of his liberal critics, and the only way he might have won the argument with them was by making the moral case for the war he persistently refused to make for fear of its domestic political costs.

Trying to fight the war on the political cheap, then, Johnson kept losing support among liberals as well as radicals. As President he had the power to go on fighting in spite of the opposition, and he did. But as the war escalated, it became more and more apparent that for the United States saving South Vietnam from Communism was probably beyond what Dean Acheson had called "the reasonable limits of its capabilities" in more than merely a political sense.

From 1965, when the decision to Americanize the war militarily was made, until the Tet offensive of 1968, the fortunes of war rose and fell. The "enclave" strategy (which gave priority to securing populated areas) was succeeded by the "big-unit" war and a strategy of attrition involving aggressive "search-and-destroy" tactics aimed at liberating areas already under Vietcong control; at the same time, bombers were used both to cut off infiltration from the North and to weaken the will of Hanoi. All this worked well enough to prevent what would have been certain victory for the Communists but not well enough either to clean the Vietcong out of the countryside, or to reduce infiltration from the North in any significant degree, or to weaken the will of Hanoi to persist in the struggle.

Did this mean that fighting in Vietnam was beyond the capabilities of the American military? General Westmoreland says no. He claimed then, and has claimed since, that a lack of political will was to blame for the American defeat.[151] "Cincinnatus" disagrees. "The Army chose not to adapt to the unique environment of Vietnam. It conducted big-unit operations against bands of guerrillas. It sought to achieve victory through attrition. It was uninterested in providing greater security for the people of the countryside and cities. It repeatedly relied on tactics already proven inadequate. It seemed not to understand the need for pacification and when it belatedly tried out that approach, it combined pacification with combat operations, thus negating both. It relied too heavily on technology and the lavish use of firepower. It refused to adopt more primitive tactics that could have dealt effectively with the sort of enemy it faced. It ignored calls for change that came from within. It continued to function as if it was pursuing enemy units of the Warsaw Pact nations across the plains of central Europe."[152]

Harsh as this judgment is, it is largely confirmed by writers more sympathetic to the American military like Edward N. Luttwak and Guenter Lewy. Thus Luttwak, making a similar observation about the failure of the army to adapt to local conditions, also speaks of the futility of the air war and of the gratuitous scale of the inflated naval role. Whatever the causes of "the absurd and tragic irrelevance" (in Luttwak's phrase) of so much of what the American military did in Vietnam, the point is that the kind of army the United States had, and the kind of bureaucratized and "civilianized" officer corps it had developed, were unfitted for the kind of war they were called upon to fight in Vietnam.[153]

Perhaps the best short statement of the point is by Henry Kissinger: "With rare and conspicuous exceptions like Douglas MacArthur, our modern generals have preferred to wear down the enemy through the weight of materiel rather than the bold stroke, through superior resources rather than superior maneuvers. In this they reflected the biases of a nonmilitary, technologically oriented society. But wars of attrition cannot be won against an enemy who refuses to fight except on his own terms. The Vietnam terrain, the nature of guerrilla warfare, the existence of sanctuaries, all combined to make it impossible for Westmoreland to wear down his adversary as he sought. Instead, the North Vietnamese hiding in the population and able to choose their moment for attack wore us down." [154]

No wonder there were GIs in Vietnam who chalked the legend UUUU on their helmets: "The unwilling, led by the unqualified, doing the unnecessary for the ungrateful." [155]

Debatable as these judgments of the American military performance may be, however, there can be no debate over what was called "the other war" in Vietnam—the war for the "hearts and minds" of the populace of the South. It was certainly beyond the "reasonable limits" of American capabilities. This was not because of the cynicism that expressed itself in another GI slogan —"Grab them by the balls, and their hearts and minds will automatically follow" [156]—but on the contrary because American ignorance constantly defeated American idealism.

It was an ignorance that could take comic as well as pathetic forms. For example: "The Americans often distributed their propaganda messages with pictures of voluptuous, scantily clad women. The Americans assumed the pictures would turn the thoughts of enemy troops toward home. But to most Vietnamese there's nothing captivating about overendowed women. 'Pinups just don't have the same appeal here,' says an American psywarrior, a little sadly." [157]

Or again, in order to fight the war of ideas more effectively, the Americans distributed 3,500 community-viewing television sets in rural areas. At first "the Vietcong shot up the sets," but after a while the guerrillas themselves "entered rural hamlets at night to watch their favorite programs and then slipped away when the evening's entertainment was over." [158]

So much for "propaganda of the word." But even "propaganda of the deed" often backfired because of American ignorance of Vietnamese ways. Such propaganda included everything from helping people rebuild villages (which had often been destroyed by the Americans themselves in pursuit of the elusive Vietcong) to public-health campaigns. One hardly knows whether to laugh or cry in reading about these campaigns. "Millions of posters, leaflets, and handbills were produced in a nationwide education program dealing with prevention, symptoms, and treatments of various diseases. . . . Other topics explained how to build a toilet (together with an exhortation—'USE TOILET ROOM WHEN YOU NEED'), how to prepare purified water, how to dispose of garbage ('This Is Your Home, Keep It Clean. Please Put Trash in Trash Cans'), and how to brush teeth. Banners exhorted the populace 'Not to Spit' (spreads tuberculosis), 'Wash Your Child With Soap,' 'Wash Vegetables Before Eating Them,' and 'Wash Your Hands Before and After Meals.' " [159]

Some of these earnest projects did in fact create good will, but when "In other cases, soap, candy, gum, coins, clothing, and similar items were handed out in the spirit of charity, . . . these acts sometimes caused friction, because those most in need were often overlooked." Even American friendliness toward children, bitterly acknowledged even by the Vietcong, "was resented by some because they felt that giving gifts created a habit of begging, degrading their parents and causing them to lose face." [160]

A former MACV Commander, General Fred C. Weyand, summed it all up in a postmortem on the Army's performance in Vietnam: "There are certain tasks the American military can accomplish on behalf of another nation. They can defeat enemy forces on the battlefield. They can blockade the enemy's coast. They can cut lines of supply and communication. They can carry the war to the enemy on land, sea, and air. . . . But there are also fundamental limitations on American military power . . . the Congress and the American people will not permit their military to take total control of another nation's political, economic, and social institutions in order to completely orchestrate the war. . . . The failure to communicate these capabilities and limitations resulted in the military being called upon to perform political, economic, and social tasks beyond its capability while at the same time it was limited in its authority to accomplish those military tasks of which it was capable." [161]

In short, it did indeed seem beyond the reasonable capabilities of the United States to win the war in Vietnam, even though it was equally clear that it *was* within the reasonable capabilities of the United States to deny victory to the Communists. Which is to say (as John McNaughton, McNamara's principal adviser on

Vietnam, put it) that by 1967, "an escalating military stalemate" had been reached.[162] It was in an effort to break this stalemate that the Communists launched the Tet offensive of 1968.

This offensive, beginning in January and ending in March, consisted of a coordinated surprise attack by the North Vietnamese and the Vietcong on nearly every city and every military base in South Vietnam. As American officials asserted then, and as almost everyone (even, to a considerable extent, Frances Fitz-Gerald[163]) now agrees, the offensive was a failure from the *military* point of view. Here, for example, is the assessment reached by Don Oberdorfer in his authoritative book on the subject: ". . . it is clear that the attack forces—and particularly the indigenous Vietcong, who did most of the fighting and dying—suffered a grievous military setback. Tens of thousands of the most dedicated and experienced fighters emerged from the jungles and forests of the countryside only to meet a deadly rain of fire and steel within the cities. The Vietcong lost the best of a generation of resistance fighters, and . . . because the people of the cities did not rise up against the foreigners and puppets at Tet . . . the Communist claim to a moral and political authority in South Vietnam suffered a serious blow. Under the stress of the Tet offensive, the South Vietnamese government faltered but did not fold. . . ."[164]

Oberdorfer's book did not appear until three years after Tet, but as Peter Braestrup's study of media coverage of the offensive *(Big Story)* makes irrefutably clear, the information on which he based his judgment was available at the time (and was indeed used to accurate effect by the Institute for Strategic Studies in London in its *Strategic Survey—1969*). Nevertheless, the almost universal impression created by press and television coverage of the offensive was of a great defeat for the Americans and the South Vietnamese.

On every point the situation was misrepresented by misleading stories and pictures and in some cases by outright falsehood. Thus the media continued to harp on the successes of Hanoi even after the assault on the cities had already been blunted; they spoke of rural areas having fallen under Communist control which were in fact being held by American and South Vietnamese forces; they said that the South Vietnamese troops in the provinces were refusing to fight when in fact they were refusing to cave in; they spoke of the "wily" North Vietnamese commander General Giap as a genius, although he had in fact made serious errors of military judgment (and would again in the Easter invasion of 1972 when "instead of concentrating all his forces for one overwhelming thrust, [he] attacked on three fronts simultaneously");[165] and they portrayed the siege of the marine base at Khe Sanh as comparable to the siege of Dien Bien Phu, when in fact the two had nothing in common, as was in the end demonstrated by the breaking of the siege with relatively light casualties.

When General Westmoreland or Lyndon Johnson or any of their surrogates tried to counter these impressions, they were ridiculed for "singing the same old song" of progress and optimism which had helped to create the "credibility gap" in the first place. The irony, however, was that in this respect American officialdom and the media had by now reversed roles. In the early days of the war, many journalists had challenged the optimistic official reports coming out of Saigon and Washington and had on the whole found their skepticism vindicated. This time it was the official reports that were generally accurate and the journalistic accounts that were unreliable. In the early days, moreover, the editors in New York had sometimes taken it upon themselves to censor or rewrite pessimistic stories they were getting from their correspondents on the scene; as the editors of *Time* told their chief correspondent in Southeast Asia, Charles Mohr, "he understood only a portion of 'the big picture.' "[166] With Tet the exact opposite occurred, and worse, since this time "when editors, pundits, and rewrite men 12,000 miles away went to work on 'the big picture,' "[167] they further falsified stories that were distorted to begin with.

This curious reversal of roles between the media and the government had already been foreshadowed by the stories of Harrison Salisbury in the New York *Times* in late 1966 and early 1967 about the effects of American bombing in the North. What Salisbury did in these stories written during a visit to North Vietnam was to create the impression that the United States, contrary to its stated policy of aiming only at military targets, was deliberately bombing nonmilitary ones. "Only after the articles had appeared," writes Lewy, "did a small number of persons learn that Salisbury, in effect, had given the authority of his byline to unverified Communist propaganda and that the New York *Times* had printed this information as though Salisbury had established it himself with his own on-the-scene reporting." Nor did either Salisbury or the *Times* ever "acknowledge that the dispatches dealing with the bombing of the city of Nam Dinh had borrowed extensively from a North Vietnamese propaganda pamphlet, *Report on U.S. War Crimes in Nam-Dinh City. . . .*"[168]

To this document—from which in his news reports he evidently adapted whole passages[169]—he gave such complete credence that Tom Wolfe could later write: "The North Vietnamese were blessed with a weapon that no military device known to America could ever get a lock on. As if by magic . . . in Hanoi . . . appears . . . Harrison Salisbury! Harrison Salisbury—writing in the New York *Times* about the atrocious American bombing of the hard-scrabble folks of North Vietnam in the Iron Triangle! If you had real sporting blood in you you had to hand it to the North Vietnamese. They were champions of this sort of thing . . . it seemed as if the North Vietnamese were playing Mr. Harrison Salisbury of the New York *Times* like an ocarina, as if they were blowing smoke up his pipe and the finger work was just right and the song was coming forth better than they could have played it themselves."[170]

But if Salisbury believed virtually everything he was told by his North Vietnamese hosts and virtually everything he read in their documents, he paid little or no attention to what could be found in American documents. Thus according to Salisbury, "No American communiqué has asserted that Nam Dinh contains some facility that the United States regards as a military objective." Yet on at least three occasions American communiqués *had* referred to the bombing of military targets in Nam Dinh, which far from being the harmless textile town Salisbury (relying entirely on his Communist guides) said it was, "happened to be a major transshipment point for supplies and soldiers moving South"[171] (as the Defense Department pointed out to no avail) and was therefore protected by anti-aircraft and surface-to-air missiles. The textile plants and residential buildings damaged in the American attacks had not been deliberately targeted and had been hit because they were located close to military facilities. Just as the Vietcong in the South mingled with women and children or even used them as soldiers so as to make it difficult for the Americans to know whether or not a particular village was a Vietcong stronghold or whether a particular civilian was a guerrilla in disguise with a hidden weapon, so in the North military facilities were often placed in residential areas and anti-aircraft batteries were even camouflaged as hospitals by the North Vietnamese. For unlike some of their supporters in the United States and Europe, the North Vietnamese knew very well that pilots were under the strictest orders to avoid nonmilitary targets.

That these orders were in effect when Salisbury was in the North we know from the fact that Secretary of the Air Force Harold Brown (who was later to serve as Jimmy Carter's Secretary of Defense) urged in an internal memo—more than a year *after* Salisbury's pieces were written—that these orders be changed "so as to permit bombing of military targets without the present scrupulous concern for collateral civilian damage and casualties." [172] The reason was not that Brown was eager to kill civilians and destroy residential housing but that the restrictions under which the pilots had to operate hampered their effectiveness. One pilot, who had trouble hitting a railroad yard in the Hanoi area because a nearby complex of buildings identified as a hospital was off limits to him, commented sardonically: "If it was in fact a hospital, it must have been a hospital for sick flak gunners, because every time we looked at it from a run on the railroad, it was a mass of sputtering, flashing gun barrels." What was worse, however, many pilots were being "shot down because the rules of engagement required approach angles and other tactics designed to reduce civilian casualties rather than to afford maximum protection to the attacking planes." [173] But Brown's request and others like it were all rejected, at a cost to American lives.

The Brown memo is in the Pentagon Papers, and is only one of hundreds of instances in which these documents, never intended for publication or for the eyes of anyone outside the government, confirm the accuracy and truthfulness of official statements and claims upon which doubt was cast at the time and continued to be expressed later on. Indeed, Leslie H. Gelb, who directed the Pentagon Papers project when he was in the Defense Department and who later became a New York *Times* correspondent, says: "The point that leaps out when internal estimates and high-level public statements are compared is that the two were not very far apart." What then, he asks, "was the credibility gap all about? In large part, it was not really a gap but a matter of emphasis." Acknowledging that there was also duplicity, he adds that there was "less than critics believed." [174] Yet it was to be precisely in connection with the Pentagon Papers that the reversal of roles between the government and the press—for which Harrison Salisbury's stories about the bombing of the North served as a dress rehearsal, and for which the Tet offensive became a kind of opening-night performance—would be established as a permanent change on "the main stage" of the Vietnam debate McGeorge Bundy had once talked about.

What came to be called the Pentagon Papers was a 7,000-page study, including thousands of classified documents, that a group of Pentagon analysts led by Gelb had been commissioned to undertake in 1967 by Secretary of Defense McNamara on the history of American involvement in Vietnam. In 1971 a copy was leaked to the New York *Times* by Daniel Ellsberg, who had worked on the project while serving under Gelb in the Defense Department and who not only turned against the war he had formerly supported with enthusiasm but became one of its most radical opponents. (At a conference on "War Crimes and the American Conscience" in 1970, Ellsberg "looked around a very large seminar table of participants—about forty distinguished people, among them Hannah Arendt and Telford Taylor," and it came to him that he was "the only person present who was a potential defendant in a war crimes trial"). [175]

Instead of publishing the entire study, however, the *Times* and its editors chose "to give its readers a more orderly, though also more concise, rendering of the history than the study itself."

This "rendering" consisted of long stories by various *Times* reporters together with a selection of "key texts" taken from the study. But as a well-known analyst of the media, Edward Jay Epstein, later demonstrated in a comparison of the full text of the study with the *Times* "renderings," "Substantial revisions in the history were made on major points." [176]

Two of these points we have already dealt with—the question of whether Johnson was lying when he said during the campaign of 1964 that he had no intention of bombing the North, and the question of whether the United States lied about the attacks in the Gulf of Tonkin. As to the first, according to the *Times,* the Pentagon Papers proved that Johnson was lying, but the full text of the study proves the opposite, placing the decision to begin bombing "in the early months of 1965." So too with the question of whether the government lied about the Gulf of Tonkin. "The conclusion of the Pentagon study that the Tonkin attacks were not deliberately provoked by the United States is not quoted in the *Times* account," Epstein writes. "On the contrary, the *Times*'s story strongly suggests that both Tonkin incidents might have been provoked by clandestine operations against North Vietnam by the United States. . . ." [177]

A final example of this reversal of roles—in which official American statements turned out to be more accurate and to deserve greater credibility than stories in the media—would occur in December 1972 when Nixon ordered the bombing of the Hanoi-Haiphong area by B-52s. Here again, as in the case of Salisbury's stories six years earlier, the "media tended to give more credence to the statements of the enemy than to the statements of the government of the United States." [178] Comparisons were drawn with the bombing of Hiroshima; charges of "carpet bombing" were made; and reports of huge numbers of civilian casualties were given great prominence. Yet the truth was that even though in terms of tons of bombs dropped the operation was indeed comparable to the heaviest bombings of World War II, civilian casualties were incredibly light, and the bombing was *not* indiscriminate (in fact, the "B-52 pilots were ordered under threat of court-martial not to deviate from their prescribed bombing runs even when SAMs were coming at them, and as a result many Americans died for the specific purpose of avoiding unnecessary civilian loss of life").[179]

Lewy: "The North Vietnamese themselves at the time claimed between 1300 and 1600 fatalities, and . . . such a number of victims . . . is surely not indicative of terror-bombing. Attacks explicitly aimed at the morale of the population took place against Germany and Japan during World War II and killed tens of thousands. According to an East German estimate, 35,000 died in the triple raid on Dresden in February 1945; the official casualty toll of the bombing of Tokyo with incendiaries on 9–10 March 1945, stands at 83,793 dead and 40,918 wounded. The Hanoi death toll, wrote the London *Economist*, 'is smaller than the number of civilians killed by the North Vietnamese in their artillery bombardment of An Loc in April or the toll of refugees ambushed when trying to escape from Quang Tri at the beginning of May. That is what makes the denunciation of Mr. Nixon as another Hitler sound so unreal.' "[180]

A few reporters would testify to this when they visited Hanoi several months later. Malcolm W. Browne of the *Times* wrote in March, for example, that "the damage caused by American bombing was grossly overstated by North Vietnamese propaganda." Then when the Defense Department had released aerial photographs of the results of the bombing, the *Times* after hesitating for several weeks finally ran a piece by Drew Middleton stating that the evidence did "not support charges made during the offensive that United States Air Force planes subjected Hanoi to the kind of carpet-bombing employed against German cities in World War II." But by then the earlier impression of "a crime against humanity," as Browne's colleague Anthony Lewis called the bombing, had taken hold, and "the *Times,* whose editorials had complained about wholesale devastation, did not acknowledge these findings in its editorial columns." The Washington *Post* was worse: "it tucked the information about what the aerial photographs revealed at the end of a news story about another subject . . . on page 24," and the editorial page, which had specifically charged carpet-bombing "across downtown Hanoi," never acknowledged the falsity of the charge. As for the other "prestige media" (*Time, Newsweek,* and the three major TV networks), they did not report on the new evidence at all.[181]

But to return to Tet, where this kind of thing really started, Braestrup believes that the distortions and misrepresentations were more a matter of the limited ability of the press corps to cover so complicated and strange a war as the one in Vietnam than a matter of ideology. No doubt ignorance and incompetence did play a part at Tet, and to that extent—given the crucial role of the media in influencing public opinion—the performance of the media might be considered yet another indication that the war was beyond the reasonable capabilities of the United States. But what seems a more likely explanation is that Tet provided the occasion for a growing disenchantment with the war to express itself.

When in 1965 the United States responded to a Vietcong attack on an American barracks at Pleiku by inaugurating the regular bombing of the North, McGeorge Bundy said, "Pleikus are streetcars."[182] That is, the contingency plans for a bombing campaign had been there, waiting for a chance to be implemented, Pleiku had come along, and those who had wanted to escalate the war grabbed it and hopped aboard. In that sense Tet was also a streetcar, but going in the opposite direction. For many, it marked the moment of conversion to the arguments of the anti-war movement.

Since 1975, certain veterans of that movement who in the past congratulated themselves on their role in driving Lyndon Johnson out of office and then in getting the United States out of Vietnam, have developed a curiously self-denigrating attitude and have taken to denying that they ever had any significant influence. Thus Professor Walter LaFeber of Cornell, brandishing the same public-opinion polls that Johnson himself used to take comfort from, asserts that "the effectiveness of the antiwar movement has been greatly overrated," and emphasizes "that the United States lost in Vietnam because it was defeated militarily. . . ." The reason for this belated attack of modesty seems to be LaFeber's anxiety lest the antiwar movement serve "as a scapegoat for . . . the national security managers whose policies failed in Vietnam."[183]

But such post-facto considerations aside, the mistake LaFeber makes is the same mistake Johnson and his people made when they assumed that because the arguments of the antiwar movement were accepted by only a minority, this meant that the American people supported the war. Certainly the American people did not want the United States to be defeated or humiliated, but neither were the American people ever enthusiastic about the war. The intensity was all on the side of the antiwar movement, whose moral arguments went unanswered because Johnson refused to answer them. Left to fend for themselves, the political and military arguments of the Administration and its supporters floated aimlessly in a moral vacuum, and so the war began to seem less and less legitimate in the eyes of more and more people in three strategically important sectors—the media, the Congress, and even within the inner circles of the Johnson Administration itself. These people grabbed the Tet "streetcar" not because (as they would claim) they no longer believed that the war could be won, but because they no longer believed that the American cause in Vietnam was just.

To be sure, most of them were not yet ready to denounce their country as immoral or criminal. Some would never be; others would reach this point only when they had Nixon to "kick around" again. In this, Nixon would ironically cooperate with them (as he so often inadvertently did with his political enemies). For if Johnson failed to make the moral case that might have neutralized or overcome the arguments of the antiwar movement, Nixon as President would (in Henry Kissinger's words) "reconcile the Republican Right to a withdrawal program and an inconclusive outcome. . . . By tranquilizing the Right, Nixon liberated the protest movement from its constraints; the center of gravity of American politics thus shifted decisively to the antiwar side even though the public had not changed its basic view."[184]

In the meantime, the groups in question seized on the argument that the war could not be won. And it is the very fact that a

military *victory* over the Communists should have been the occasion for this conclusion which proves that Tet was a pretext
for a prior decision to come as it were out of the closet. So
determined were these former supporters of the war to run in the
other direction that they persuaded themselves that Tet had been
a great defeat, just as the obverse self-delusion about body
counts and the like in the past had served to persuade many of
the same people that the war had been going well.

This was even more saliently the case with television than with
the newspapers. So much attention has been paid to what has
been called "the single most famous bit of reporting in South
Vietnam" [185]—Morley Safer's film of August 1965 on CBS showing marines using their cigarette lighters to set fire to the Vietnamese village of Cam Ne—that almost everyone thinks the
networks were as skeptical about the war in the early years as
some of the major newspapers, and as hostile to it as they themselves indubitably were in the later years. But careful studies
have shown that the Cam Ne program was a rare exception.
According to one such study, the network news programs "generally gave the impression that the Americans were in control,
on the offensive and holding the initiative, at least until Tet of
1968." [186]

A perfect measure of the change was that America's most influential newscaster, Walter Cronkite, who had earlier seen Vietnam as another expression of the "courageous decision that
Communism's advance must be stopped and that guerrilla warfare as a means to a political end must be finally discouraged,"
characterized Tet as a defeat and declared: "It is increasingly
clear to this reporter that the only rational way out . . . will be to
negotiate, not as victors, but as an honorable people . . ." [187]

Then, Edward Jay Epstein tells us, "In late 1968, Jack Fern, a
field producer for NBC, suggested to Robert J. Northshield a
three-part series showing that Tet had indeed been a decisive
military victory for America. . . . The idea was rejected because,
Northshield said later, Tet was already 'established in the public's mind as a defeat, and therefore it was an American
defeat.' " [188] From that point on, the networks for all practical

purposes joined the major newspapers and magazines as members of the antiwar movement.

The response in Congress to Tet demonstrates even more clearly that it was the arguments of the antiwar movement rather than the military facts of the case that turned the tide toward disengagement. "To any reasonably alert, well-read citizen," writes Peter Braestrup (and what he says would apply *a fortiori* to members of the Congress), "the attacks on the cities of Vietnam produced few new 'facts' about the U.S. commitment. By January 30, 1968, the costs—human and financial—of the war were already a matter of public record. The strain on the U.S. worldwide military and financial position was clear, as was the impact of the war's costs on domestic outlays. . . . The limited military benefits of step-by-step bombing of North Vietnam . . . had been aired in public, partly by McNamara himself. . . . The weaknesses—real and imagined—of the South Vietnamese regime and its army had been abundantly decried. . . . No *quick* end was in sight or even promised in 1967. . . . General Westmoreland himself had publicly foreseen no U.S. troop withdrawals before late 1969. Thus, for all their destruction and drama, the Tet attacks and their aftermath did not suddenly bring to light any basic new weaknesses or virtues in Administration Vietnam policy."[189] All the more remarkable, then, that so many congressmen should have seized on Tet in the way they did.

Much of the uproar both in the media and in the Congress has been attributed to the optimistic progress reports that had been streaming out of official circles in the period immediately preceding Tet. Not only did "the Tet attacks [come] without any prior White House warning of heavy fighting ahead"; they also "followed by less than 10 weeks the end of an Administration 'progress' propaganda campaign designed to show that the enemy was 'losing.' " But Braestrup is undoubtedly right in his belief that Tet would have triggered "a vigorous outcry in Washington . . . even without the credibility gap over Vietnam policy that the White House and Defense Secretary McNamara had been helping to widen since 1962." For "like a delayed time fuse," wrote John Finney of the New York *Times* Washington Bureau at the time, "the current Communist offensive in Vietnam seems to be setting off within the Senate a critical political reaction against the *validity* as well as the *credibility* of the Administration's policy. . . ." [190] (His italics.)

This reaction included not only calls from doves for negotiation, neutralization, bombing halts, and a "full-scale reexamination of the purposes and objectives of our policy in Vietnam" (Fulbright), but also calls from hawks for escalation. Yet it is a measure of how mistaken Johnson had been to worry more about pressure from the Right than from the Left that "as time went on, Congressional hawks seemed to object less and less to the sentiments of the doves; most hawks remained silent." [191] Like the majority of Americans, the hawks were unable to work up any enthusiasm for a war whose purpose had been defined in terms so bloodless that they could not justify or redeem the blood being shed for its sake; and so they were by now reduced, again like the majority of Americans, to the negative demand that the United States not be defeated or humiliated.

But the most telling demonstration of how Tet served as a "streetcar" was the reaction within the White House itself. An outside advisory group, the so-called Wise Men—which included former high officials like Dean Acheson, George Ball, and Mc-George Bundy, as well as retired military men like General Matthew Ridgway and General Maxwell Taylor—was summoned to the White House by Johnson for briefings on Tet. "At the end of our discussion," wrote Johnson in his memoirs, "it appeared to me that six advisers favored some form of disengagement, one was in between, and four were opposed." Johnson was shaken: "I knew this group had not been reading the detailed reports on Vietnam each day, as I and my principal advisers had, but . . . I had always regarded the majority of them as very steady and balanced. If they had been so deeply influenced by the reports of the Tet offensive, what must the average citizen in the country be thinking?" Johnson "remained convinced that the blow to morale was more of our own doing than anything the enemy had accomplished with its army," and he would have been even more convinced if he had known how his own special counsel, Harry McPherson, who unlike the Wise Men *had* "been reading the detailed reports on Vietnam each day," was responding to Tet. [192]

As McPherson later told an interviewer: "I would go in two or three mornings a week and study the cable book and talk to Rostow and ask him what had happened the day before, and would get from him what almost seemed hallucinatory from the point of view of what I had seen on network television the night before." McPherson recognized how extraordinary it was that "people like me—people who had some responsibility for expressing the Presidential point of view—could be so affected by the media as everyone else was, while downstairs, within 50 yards of my desk, was that enormous panoply of intelligence-gathering devices—tickers, radios, messages coming in from the field." His own explanation was that "like everyone else who had been deeply involved in explaining the policies of the war and trying to understand them and render some judgment, I was fed up with . . . the optimism that seemed to flow without stopping from Saigon." [193]

Yet in a message from Saigon to which McPherson would have had access, General Westmoreland himself had warned "that the enemy has already made a crucial decision . . . to undertake . . . a maximum effort," and the Chairman of the Joint Chiefs of Staff, General Earle G. Wheeler, had said publicly only about two weeks before Tet "that there may be a Communist thrust similar to the desperate effort of the Germans in the Battle of the Bulge in World War II." [194]

It is true that most other official statements of that period were of "the light at the end of the tunnel" variety that McPherson was by now "fed up with." Yet it is also true that the warnings of Westmoreland and Wheeler had turned out to be accurate, and so had their predictions that the offensive would be defeated. Indeed, in the pre-Tet period "the optimism that seemed to flow without stopping" came not so much from Saigon as from Washington, where in an effort to shore up support for the war Johnson had ordered an emphasis on the progress we were making. He never went public with Westmoreland's warning about the coming offensive; and when the general delivered a speech in Washington declaring "that whereas in 1965 the enemy was winning, today he is certainly losing," [195] he did not (presumably on Johnson's instructions) say anything about the heavy fighting ahead.

Others might have been misled by all this, but there was no reason why McPherson should have been. As an intimate of the President—who had acknowledged privately that he "foresaw the North Vietnamese using 'kamikaze' tactics in the weeks ahead, committing their troops in a wave of suicide attacks" and that "we face dark days ahead" [196]—McPherson should have expected the offensive; and with access to "that enormous panoply of intelligence-gathering devices," he should have known that the media reports of a disaster were wrong. That he accepted the false version over the true one could only mean that he had chosen to do so—in all probability because he had lost faith, not in the possibility of winning, but in the justice of the war. Like more and more people who had once supported the effort, McPherson needed "a call to blood, sweat, and tears," but all Johnson gave him (and to make matters more poignant, in words McPherson himself might well have written) was what Braestrup, referring to a Johnson press conference held only six weeks before Tet, describes as "an assurance that the nation's costly investment in Vietnam was beginning to show a profit." [197]

It was not enough—not for McPherson, not for the Wise Men, not for the American people, and not even in the end for Lyndon Johnson himself. *We are defeating ourselves,* Johnson thought as he left the meeting with the Wise Men, and of course he was right. His belief that disagreement with his policies "passed the bounds of reasonable debate and fair dissension" and that "this dissension prolonged the war, prevented a peaceful settlement on reasonable terms, encouraged our enemies, disheartened our friends, and weakened us as a nation" [198] has found substantial support from no less surprising a source than the director of the Pentagon Papers study, Leslie H. Gelb, and no less authoritative a source than the North Vietnamese.

"What was important," writes Gelb, "was not so much what was going on in Vietnam but what was happening in America. . . . The war could be lost only if the American public turned sour on it. American public opinion was the essential domino. U.S. leaders knew it. Hanoi's leaders knew it." [199] One may doubt from the way Johnson and his people talked about the war that "U.S. leaders knew it" or at any rate understood it. But there can be no question that Hanoi's leaders did. Indeed, in the years to come, when Henry Kissinger would engage in secret negotiations with the North Vietnamese, he would frequently be subjected to gloating lectures on the strength of antiwar sentiment in the United States and would on several occasions tell his opposite number that this was not a fit subject for discussion. For example:

> KISSINGER: We'll take care of our public opinion and you of yours.
> XUAN THUY: Since your public opinion speaks on the situation, therefore we must give an interpretation.
> KISSINGER: I won't listen to it at these meetings.[200]

Thus did the North Vietnamese go on fighting in the reasonably secure belief that even if they lost on the battlefield, American public opinion—like French public opinion before it—would force the United States to withdraw on terms that would eventually ensure the Communist conquest of the South.

In saying that "we were defeating ourselves," Johnson was not only right about the country as a whole. He was also right in a personal sense: He had defeated himself in trying to fight the war on the political cheap. Since Harry Truman his party had been the more resolute of the two major parties in acting to contain the expansion of Communism. Though the Republicans tended to be more rhetorically fervent in their anti-Communism, they also tended (as witness Eisenhower and Dulles) to be more cautious in practice. It was the Democrats who had taken the country into Korea and the Republicans who had taken it out; it was the Democrats who had taken the country into Vietnam, after a Republican Administration had refused to intervene, and soon it would be up to another Republican Administration to take it out.

But the Democratic party of 1968 was not the Democratic party of 1948. In 1948 those elements in the party who had opposed containment—who believed that the Soviet Union had no aggressive or expansionist intent and who favored a conciliatory policy rather than one of resistance—broke with Truman and backed the third-party candidacy of Henry Wallace. As we have already seen, so poorly did they do in the Presidential election of that year—winning only about a million votes instead of the 10 million they had expected—that they lost all power and influence in the arena of electoral politics. Thanks to Vietnam, however, they had been able for the first time since 1948 to make themselves heard politically; and thanks to the emergence of Eugene McCarthy, they had the first candidate behind whom to rally since Henry Wallace.*

The difference was that whereas Henry Wallace had failed miserably in his challenge to Truman, Eugene McCarthy—to the utter astonishment of everyone in those far-off days when a sitting President was considered beyond challenge from within his own party—did extraordinarily well against Johnson in the New Hampshire primary. This was a "demonstration," more convincing than any on the campuses or the streets, that the antiwar movement had become more potent than the public-opinion polls suggested, and it made a candidate out of Robert Kennedy (who had previously accepted the conventional wisdom concerning the invincibility of a sitting President).

Kennedy had been inching very cautiously toward an antiwar position, and as the brother of the man who had committed the United States to military intervention in Vietnam, he was able to rally the swelling tribe of disaffected Democrats much better than McCarthy, who put many of them off because his constituency was largely made up (to his own barely concealed dismay) of unreconstructed Wallace Progressives and their actual or spiritual children. (McCarthy was not of this political breed and was therefore not the natural leader of the movement. The natural leader was George McGovern, a supporter of Henry Wallace in 1948 who could reasonably be called an unreconstructed Wallace

---

* I have always thought the impish Zeitgeist was playing a joke on the United States in throwing up a McCarthy (Eugene) and a Wallace (George), each of whom represented the opposite political force from his namesake predecessor (Joe and Henry) twenty years earlier. As we have seen in the case of the "credibility gap" and of the ADA, such reversals were not confined to names alone.

Progressive himself; and as a measure of the immense distance the Democratic party would finally move because of Vietnam, he was to become its nominee for President in 1972.)

With his party so badly split, Johnson decided not to run. Thus the antiwar forces had grown strong enough to force Johnson to abdicate, and if Robert Kennedy had not been assassinated they might even have taken over the Democratic party as early as 1968. As it was, Johnson's Vice President, Hubert Humphrey, won the nomination. But given his inability either to dissociate himself from Johnson's Vietnam policy or to defend it whole-heartedly, he never managed to unite the party, and in the end he lost in a very close race to the Republican nominee, Richard Nixon.

In 1952, Adlai Stevenson, the hand-picked heir and successor to Harry Truman, had been defeated by the Republican candidate, Dwight Eisenhower, because (among other things) Eisenhower had promised to end the Korean War. Now, in 1968, Hubert Humphrey, Lyndon Johnson's hand-picked heir and successor, was beaten by his Republican opponent Richard Nixon because (more, probably, than anything else) Nixon promised to end the Vietnam War.

Here there was no reversal of roles: history was straight-forwardly repeating itself. But in the more immediate historical context, the one framed by 1962 rather than 1952, a great transformation had come over the United States. The ceiling on American military involvement in Vietnam had been reached, and after Tet there would be no talk of increasing the number of troops. From now on the only questions would concern the speed and the manner of the American withdrawal from Vietnam. The argument over whether the United States had any business or right to be in Vietnam was over. The American role had lost its legitimacy, and the only questions that remained were whether the United States would also lose the war, and if so how badly it would be damaged by this first experience of defeat in its entire history.

FOUR:

WHY WE WITHDREW

SURPRISING as it may seem in retrospect, many people in the antiwar movement expected Richard Nixon to order an immediate American withdrawal from Vietnam.

It was not that these people were ignorant of Nixon's record as a hard-line anti-Communist. On the contrary, it was one of the reasons for the hatred—no milder word will do—he inspired in them. This hatred was much deeper and more pervasive than the hostility provoked by Lyndon Johnson, even taking into account the by-now routine denunciations of him as a murderer comparable to Adolf Hitler ("Hey, Hey, LBJ, How Many Kids Did You Kill Today?" was a familiar chant at antiwar rallies by 1968). Johnson had come in for such opprobrium only since 1965, whereas Nixon had been regarded as an arch villain since he had first attracted national attention through his prominent role in the investigations that led to the conviction of Alger Hiss. To most liberals, not to mention radicals, Nixon was no better than Joe

McCarthy (than whom they could think of no one worse); and like Joe McCarthy, he was detested even by anti-Communists on the Left who believed that Hiss had indeed been a Soviet agent.

In the years that followed the Hiss case, Nixon—as a senator from California, then as Eisenhower's Vice President—remained true to the militant anti-Communist position on which his political career had been founded. As we have already seen, it was Nixon who in the 1952 Presidential campaign had attacked Adlai Stevenson as a graduate of Dean Acheson's "Cowardly College of Communist Containment," which allegedly had been responsible for the loss of Eastern Europe and China to Communism. As we have also seen, in 1954 Nixon had been one of the chief advocates within the Eisenhower Administration of American military intervention to save Dien Bien Phu; in fact, unlike his fellow advocates who wanted to use only air and naval forces, Nixon wanted to send in American combat troops. In the early sixties, as a private citizen (having been defeated both by John Kennedy when he ran for President in 1960 and by Pat Brown when he ran for governor of California in 1962), he denounced what he would call in his memoirs "Kennedy's naive willingness to accept a 'neutralist' coalition regime [in Laos] that was known to be a convenient cover for the Communist Pathet Lao guerrillas."[1]

As for Vietnam, Nixon had criticized the reluctance of both Kennedy and Johnson "to support the measures needed to defeat the Communists." These measures, he believed, should include not only the bombing of North Vietnam but "ground raids into Laos to cut off the pipeline of Vietcong arms and supplies known as the Ho Chi Minh trail." When visiting Saigon in 1964, he had a conversation with Henry Cabot Lodge, who had been his running mate in 1960 and was now ambassador to South Vietnam, and was amazed when "Lodge argued against pursuing the Vietcong forces into Laos or Cambodia." What amazed him even more was Lodge's view that the way to fight the Vietcong was not by shooting at them but by distributing food to the hungry peasants from whom Lodge told him they drew their strength. "I could hardly believe that I was hearing this from one as versed as Cabot Lodge in the tactics and techniques of international Communism."[2]

All of this was consistent with Nixon's entire public record, and all of it was familiar—if not in detail, then in general—to those people in the antiwar movement who expected that the first thing Nixon would do upon becoming President was announce an immediate American withdrawal from Vietnam. Why, then, did they entertain such implausible expectations? Why did they think that the man they themselves regarded as the great anti-Communist villain of the age would scuttle a bloody effort to resist the expansion of Communism? Why did they believe that a man who had always attacked his opponents for being weak and irresolute in the fight against Communism—and specifically and emphatically in the case of Vietnam—would simply give up the fight altogether?

For one thing, because during the campaign Nixon had held out the tantalizing prospect that he might. He would later deny that he had ever spoken of having a "secret plan" to end the war, but whether he used the term or not, he certainly created the impression that he had such a plan, even (in David Halberstam's words) "touching his breast pocket as if the plan were right there in the jacket—implying that to say what was in it might jeopardize secrecy."[3] Rumors had also been circulating to the effect that Nixon had told Republican doves like Congressman Pete McCloskey that he would end the war in six months if he were elected. Given the near universal conviction among the doves after Tet that the war was unwinnable, what else could such a timetable mean but an immediate American withdrawal?

Curiously, these rumors acquired greater plausibility from the very hatred of Nixon so common in the circles that believed them. Since in such circles Nixon was given credit for nothing, not even for being sincere in his anti-Communism, they saw no anomaly in the prospect of a cynical betrayal of everything he had always stood for. "Would you buy a used car from this man?" read the legend across a photograph of Nixon looking exactly like the "Tricky Dick" of liberal demonology, only more sinister. In the case of Vietnam it was a question that gave hope to the antiwar movement.

But there were also more sophisticated versions of the theory that Nixon would go for an immediate withdrawal. One was based on the historical precedent of Eisenhower's withdrawal from Korea. Might not Nixon, who had benefited politically from the growing public disillusion with "Johnson's war" in Vietnam, just as Eisenhower had in the case of Truman's policy in Korea, follow Eisenhower's example and consolidate his gains by calling a halt to an even more unpopular war than Korea had been? "There were some undeniably compelling political arguments to recommend this particular course," wrote Nixon in later years. "As one of my friends in Congress put it, 'You didn't get us into this war, so even if you end it with a bad peace, by doing it quickly you can put the blame on Kennedy and Johnson and the Democrats. Just go on TV and remind people that it was Kennedy who sent the 16,000 Americans in there, and that it was Johnson who escalated it to 540,000. Then announce that you're bringing them all home, and you'll be a hero.' "[4]

And indeed, Nixon himself had brought up the Eisenhower precedent when he reportedly told a group of Southern delegates at the Republican National Convention that, in dealing with Korea, Eisenhower had shown the way to bring a war to a successful conclusion. "I'll tell you how Korea was ended. We got in there and had this messy war on our hands, Eisenhower let the word go out—let the word go out diplomatically—to the Chinese and the North Koreans that we would not tolerate this continued war of attrition. And within a matter of months they negotiated. . . . Well, as far as the negotiation [in Vietnam] is concerned that should be our position."[5]

The other theory that gave hope to the antiwar movement was also based on a historical precedent—de Gaulle's withdrawal from the Algerian war in 1961. As de Gaulle had been a hard-liner on Algeria, Nixon was a hard-liner on Vietnam; therefore —so the theory went—he could get away politically with liquidating the American role more easily than a Democrat, even a hawkish Democrat like Humphrey.

On the basis of such reasoning (and forgetting that it had taken de Gaulle five years to get out of Algeria) many opponents of the war had refused to support Humphrey in the 1968 campaign. Few if any had actually supported Nixon; but as they well understood, they were contributing to his election by cries of "Dump the Hump" or softer expressions of anti-Humphrey sentiment, up to and including the refusal to vote. They were thus afforded the satisfaction of punishing Humphrey for what they saw as his unprincipled failure to join all the other liberal apostates from the anti-Communist "church," without at the same time having to feel guilty about helping the detested Richard Nixon become President of the United States.

It was in fact a measure of the depth of their opposition to the war that to get America out of it they were even willing to pay the price of seeing Richard Nixon in the White House. Thus when it became clear that Nixon had no intention of ordering an immediate withdrawal, their rage against him knew no bounds. He had betrayed them in breaking what they had taken to be a promise that he would betray himself.

To complicate the dynamics of this sorry drama even further, Nixon *did* intend to liquidate the American combat role in Vietnam. But not immediately or all at once. He even intended if possible to make peace. But not at the expense of turning South Vietnam over to the Communists. No one doubted that an *immediate* American withdrawal from Vietnam would mean just that, but those who expected it from Nixon thought that he would use his notorious cunning to disguise his acquiescence in a Communist victory—that he would, in other words, take the cosmetic or face-saving exit that Johnson had rejected before him. When they discovered that they were wrong, they accused Nixon of lying about getting out even when he began steadily reducing the number of American troops in Vietnam.

To be sure, the more radical members of the antiwar movement wanted the United States to be punished by the experience of humiliation if not by an international war-crimes tribunal, and not even the face-saving exit would satisfy them. The more moderate members of the movement would have been willing to settle happily for an end to the American combat role. But by now this was the only significant substantive difference between the radicals and moderates. In the past, moderates had objected to the war largely on political grounds, concentrating their fire on such arguments as the domino theory, the need to contain China, and the importance of maintaining American credibility. Now more and more of them were joining the radicals in denouncing the war as "immoral" and reconciling themselves to the prospect of a Communist victory.

Surely, they said, the people of South Vietnam would be better off without an American Army that—in a phrase that had become notorious during Tet—was forced "to destroy the country in order to save it." Surely with the war over, the people of South Vietnam would be better off for that fact alone, spared finally from the killing and the bombing (by our planes, supposed to be protecting them) and the refugee camps to which so many of them had already been driven. As for the putative horrors of Communist domination, would the people of South Vietnam be any worse off under the rule of Communism than they now were under the rule of General Thieu?

In the early years, liberal critics had attacked the repression and corruption of Diem and his immediate successors as obstacles to a successful struggle against the Vietcong; now (in an echo of the old Dulles idea that the "taint of colonialism" had weakened the case for American intervention at the time of Dien Bien Phu) the repressive and nondemocratic features of the South Vietnamese government were used to demonstrate not so much the futility of the struggle as its moral emptiness. Surely we were not fighting for freedom or democracy in South Vietnam; what then *were* we fighting for? Was political life under Thieu in the South—with his rigged elections and his jails featuring those underground "tiger cages" fit only for wild animals— better than life under Communism in the North?

Nor was there any real reason to believe that a Communist victory would result in the "bloodbath" predicted by supporters of the war; as the sociologist Nathan Glazer, whose anti-Communist credentials were old and solid, would later write, to speak of a bloodbath was "hypocritical when hundreds of thousands of South Vietnamese civilians [had] already died largely as a consequence of American military action." One could, Glazer said, double or triple the estimated number of landlords who had been "slaughtered when the North Vietnamese state was set up" and still one would come "nowhere near the number of civilians killed in the war."[6]

Richard Nixon did not believe that the people of South Vietnam would be no worse off under Communism than they were under Thieu. "I was aware that many Americans considered Thieu a petty and corrupt dictator unworthy of our support," he would write in his memoirs. "I was not personally attached to Thieu, but . . . the South Vietnamese needed a strong and stable government to carry on the fight against the efforts of the Vietcong terrorists, who were supported by the North Vietnamese army in their efforts to impose a Communist dictatorship on the 17 million people of South Vietnam."[7]

Nor did Nixon have any doubt as to what such a dictatorship would mean to those 17 million South Vietnamese, "many of whom had worked for us and supported us": it would abandon them "to Communist atrocities and domination. When the Communists had taken over North Vietnam in 1954, 50,000 people had been murdered, and hundreds of thousands more died in labor camps. In 1968, during their brief control of Hué, they had shot or clubbed to death or buried alive more than 3,000 civilians whose only crime was to have supported the Saigon government."[8] There would, then, be a bloodbath, followed by the institution of what Nixon's new National Security Adviser (and future Secretary of State), Henry Kissinger, called "the icy totalitarianism of North Vietnam."[9]

But what was even more important to Nixon as President of the United States than the effect on South Vietnam of a Communist victory was its probable effect on the United States. "If we suddenly reneged on our earlier pledges of support, because they had become difficult or costly to carry out, or because they had become unpopular at home, we would not be worthy of the trust of other nations and we certainly would not receive it." He would act on "what my conscience, my experience, and my analysis told me was true about the need to keep our commitment.

To abandon South Vietnam to the Communists now would cost us inestimably in our search for a stable, structured, and lasting peace."[10]

In his ultimate objective, then, Nixon differed not in the slightest from Kennedy and Johnson; like them, he was determined to save South Vietnam from Communism. And like them too, he wanted to do it at the lowest possible cost. Kennedy had tried to do it with minimum involvement in the military operation in Vietnam; Johnson had tried to do it with minimum political disruption at home. Both had succeeded in the sense that South Vietnam had still not fallen to the Communists, but both had also failed to limit the cost. Johnson had been forced (as Kennedy would have been if he had lived) to pay a far higher price in military involvement than he had wished, and his effort to limit political disruption at home had resulted in more disruption than he had envisaged in his worst nightmares. Now it was Nixon's turn.

With an immediate withdrawal ruled out, the question of what he called "the option to the Right" arose—that is, escalation. At its most extreme this would involve either bombing the elaborate system of irrigation dikes in North Vietnam or using tactical nuclear weapons. Nixon ruled out both of these "knockout blows" on the ground that they "would have killed hundreds of thousands of civilians."[11]

But what about a lesser form of escalation? This would involve tying down North Vietnamese troops along the DMZ (Demilitarized Zone) by holding out the threat of an invasion; mining Haiphong Harbor "to cripple the enemy's supply lines"; and authorizing "free pursuit of the Communist forces into Laos and Cambodia," where they had sanctuaries from which they drew supplies and launched "hit-and-run attacks against our forces in South Vietnam."[12] All these moves would be reinforced by canceling the bombing halt that Johnson had declared in connection with his announcement not to run for re-election and that had been extended when—to everyone's surprise—the North Vietnamese agreed to begin negotiations in Paris.

Nixon, however, ruled out even this lesser form of "the escalation option" from the beginning. There were three main reasons. First, it would have meant six months of intensified fighting and "there was no way that I could hold the country together for that period of time in view of the numbers of casualties we would be sustaining." Second, "resorting to the escalation option would also delay or even destroy any chance we might have to develop a new relationship with the Soviet Union and Communist China." [13] But the third reason was perhaps the most important, and it came out in a conversation Nixon had in October 1969 with Sir Robert Thompson, the British expert on guerrilla warfare. (Among Thompson's other distinctions was the following comment he had made during the recently concluded Presidential campaign: "There are now some contenders for the American Presidency who quite blithely advocate that the present government of South Vietnam should accept a coalition government with the NLF, when, as far as I am aware, they have not yet announced their own readiness to appoint Mr. Stokely Carmichael as Secretary of Defense or Mr. H. Rap Brown as head of the F.B.I." [14] I do not know whether Nixon was aware of this memorable statement, but he would certainly have appreciated it, as would Kissinger, who was destined to make a similar point in his memoirs: "In the United States, a homogeneous society, the appointment of any member of the opposition party to a Cabinet is considered as newsworthy as it is extremely rare. The idea that a civil war can be ended by joining the people who have been killing each other in one government is an absurdity. Generally, a coalition government is a gimmick or an excuse, not a solution. It works best where it is least needed.") [15]

When, in their meeting of October 1969, Nixon asked Thompson "whether he thought it was important for us to see it through in Vietnam," Thompson replied, "Absolutely. In my opinion the future of Western civilization is at stake in the way you handle yourselves in Vietnam." Nixon also asked Thompson what he thought of the idea of escalation. Thompson was against it "because it would risk a major American and worldwide furor and still not address the central problem of whether the South Vietnamese were sufficiently confident and prepared to defend themselves against a renewed Communist offensive some time in the future."[16]

Nixon had already come to the same conclusion himself. Indeed, it was for this reason above all that he had decided on the strategy he would follow. His way of trying to save South Vietnam from Communism at minimum cost to the United States would be to turn the job over to the South Vietnamese themselves.

This idea was not, of course, invented by Nixon. Nor had it ever really been the intention of the United States to "Americanize" the war in Vietnam to the extent that had been done. "In the final analysis," Kennedy had said in September 1963, "it is their war. They are the ones who have to win or lose it." The following year, running against Goldwater, Johnson had made his by-now notorious promise that he would not send "American boys" to do the fighting that "Asian boys" had to do for themselves, and even as late as 1968, Johnson had said: "We and our allies can only help to provide a shield behind which the people of South Vietnam can survive and can grow and develop. On their efforts—on their determination and resourcefulness—the outcome will ultimately depend."[17]

Yet the truth was that since 1966 the war *had* been fought, in Lewy's words, "essentially as an American war, with the South Vietnamese increasingly watching from the sidelines." The main factor behind this development (which can perhaps be seen as the military correlate to the political considerations behind the coup against Diem) was the "frustration experienced by the members of the American advisory program, which eventually led the military to conclude that by doing the job themselves they would save much irritation and seemingly wasted effort."[18]

It was only in response to Tet that serious plans began to be made to "de-Americanize" the war. A ceiling of 550,000 was placed on American troops, and a new emphasis was put on increasing the size and the quality of the South Vietnamese army. While still in office, Johnson said that he looked forward to a time when the American share of the responsibility for the security of South Vietnam would be greatly diminished,[19] but not until

Nixon became President did the process of disengagement actually get underway.

This process of "de-Americanization"—or "Vietnamization," as it came to be called instead at the insistence of Nixon's Secretary of Defense, Melvin Laird—began in June 1969 with the announcement that 25,000 American troops would soon be withdrawn and that additional withdrawals would follow at a rate to be determined by developments at the Paris peace talks, the level of enemy activity, and the progress of the South Vietnamese army. But as Nixon also stressed in a speech on November 3 of that year, which finally dashed all hope that he intended to withdraw immediately, the United States would (as he paraphrased the statement in his memoirs) "continue fighting until the Communists agreed to negotiate a fair and honorable peace or until the South Vietnamese were able to defend themselves on their own—whichever came first." [20] Kissinger would put it more succinctly: "We were clearly on the way out of Vietnam by negotiation if possible, by unilateral withdrawal if necessary." [21]

2.

The negotiations to which Nixon and Kissinger were referring were not the ones that had begun in Paris in the last months of the Johnson Administration. The Paris talks, from the moment they started to the moment they ended, were nothing more than a battlefield of political warfare. No serious discussions were ever held there, and no movement toward a political settlement was ever made. (Kissinger would later say that the Paris talks broke all records in the history of negotiations for the number of sessions held without any progress of any kind to their credit.) The real negotiations were the secret talks, also held in Paris, between Kissinger and the North Vietnamese, represented by Le Duc Tho and Xuan Thuy, that began in August 1969.

The story of these negotiations, which is told at great length and in fascinating detail in *White House Years,* the first volume of Kissinger's memoirs, is also summed up in a brief passage in the same book: "Hanoi . . . continued to insist that the United States establish a new government under conditions in which the non-Communist side would be made impotent by the withdrawal of the American forces and demoralized by the removal of its leadership. If the United States had the effrontery to withdraw without bringing about such a political upheaval, the war would go on and our prisoners would remain. Over the years we moved from position to position, from mutual to unilateral withdrawal, from residual forces to complete departure. But Hanoi never budged. We could have neither peace nor our prisoners until we achieved what Hanoi apparently no longer trusted itself to accomplish: the overthrow of our ally."[22]

This was, from the very beginning, the issue that blocked a negotiated settlement: Hanoi's demand that on its way out of Vietnam, the United States pause to overthrow Thieu, and the refusal of the United States to agree. "We were not," explains Kissinger, "prepared to do for the Communists what they could not do for themselves. This seemed to us an act of dishonor that would mortgage America's international position for a long time to come. Our refusal to overthrow an allied government remained the single and crucial issue that deadlocked all negotiation until October 8, 1972, when Hanoi withdrew the demand."[23]

Nor was it only because it would have been damaging politically to the United States that Kissinger opposed the overthrow of Thieu. Kissinger was no more "personally attached to Thieu" than was Nixon (and Thieu later came to loathe Kissinger, whom he blamed for selling out South Vietnam in the Paris Peace accords of 1972). Nevertheless, throughout *White House Years* Kissinger defends Thieu against his American critics who kept demanding that he institute liberal reforms in the midst of a bloody war and with more than 300,000 enemy troops and guerrillas in his country, and who would not even give him credit for the reforms he had actually put through under these impossible conditions: "There is no question that in response to our pressures the Saigon government made extraordinary efforts to broaden its base and to agree to a political contest with the Communists. A significant land reform program was instituted; an electoral commission on which the Communists would be represented was put forward. Saigon's politics were more pluralistic and turbulent than its American critics cared to admit—and vastly better in human terms than the icy totalitarianism of North Vietnam, which was in fact the alternative at stake. . . . Attacking Thieu too often was not an advocacy of concrete reform but an alibi for our abdication."[24]

The hope for a negotiated end to the war was, thus, dim; and it was dimmed still further by the steady withdrawal of American troops, which all but destroyed the North Vietnamese incentive to offer concessions. To make matters worse and more bitter, Nixon and Kissinger were constantly being accused of responsibility for the failure of negotiations even after the American concessions that would allegedly move things forward had been made and then rejected by Hanoi. For example, the New York Times "began calling for a cutback of search-and-destroy missions in April 1969. Its own news columns on July 25 reported that such a reduction was about to take place. Within two weeks, the Times was calling for a standstill cease-fire. Even this proved insufficient. Nixon offered it on October 7, 1970; Hanoi promptly rejected it. The Times continued its criticism."[25] In this manner, says Kissinger, we expended most of our energy in effect negotiating with ourselves.

The critics, then, could not "be satisfied for long, *even by the adoption of their proposals*," and they sometimes even blamed the United States for failing to accept proposals that Hanoi had not only not offered but had already ruled out. Thus Roger Hilsman, who had been Assistant Secretary of State for Far Eastern Affairs under Kennedy, once published an article charging that Nixon was "rebuffing a Communist offer of a more-or-less immediate Vietnam peace on terms that many Americans might find perfectly acceptable."[26] The offer as spelled out by Hilsman included four points, every one of which Hanoi had earlier explicitly rejected in the secret negotiations.

With a negotiated settlement unlikely, and with the United States determined to withdraw, the only remaining hope was necessarily invested in Vietnamization. Everything possible had to be done to ensure that the South Vietnamese would be able to hold the Communists off after the Americans had left. Moreover, everything possible had to be done to protect the retreating American troops, who might become more vulnerable to attack as their numbers dwindled. These were the two considerations that led Nixon to expand American operations into Cambodia, first by bombing (which began secretly in March 1969) and then by authorizing a joint American–South Vietnamese invasion, or "incursion," a year later (April 1970).

These Cambodian operations triggered perhaps the most passionate protests against the war mounted up to that point. They would also later give rise to a controversy over the issue of whether in going into Cambodia Nixon had created the conditions for the eventual takeover of that country by the Communist Khmer Rouge, who proceeded to turn Cambodia into what has accurately been called the Auschwitz of Asia. (I will have something to say about this issue later.) At the time, however, the main reason for the protests was the belief that in going into Cambodia, Nixon had proved that he had no real intention of withdrawing from Vietnam.

For months he had talked of American withdrawals and of Vietnamization; yet here he was expanding the war into another country instead. Having disappointed the hope that he would order an immediate withdrawal from Vietnam upon becoming President, he was now betraying the promise of a gradual withdrawal as well. It was "a shocking escalation" (St. Louis *Post-Dispatch*), "a deeper entrapment" *(Wall Street Journal)*, "a virtual renunciation of the President's promise of disengagement from Southeast Asia" (New York *Times*).[27]

In vain did Nixon explain "that this was not an invasion of Cambodia" but an attack on sanctuaries in a strip of territory "completely occupied and controlled by North Vietnamese forces." In vain did he promise that "we would withdraw once they had been driven out and once their military supplies were destroyed." In vain did he say that the purpose of this incursion was "to protect our men who are in Vietnam and to guarantee the continued success of our withdrawal and Vietnamization programs." In vain did he assert that the point "was not to expand the war into Cambodia, but to end the war in Vietnam."[28] The press refused to believe him, and in Congress it was the same: "The President," said Senator Edmund Muskie, "has decided to seek a military method of ending this war rather than a negotiated method." Said Senator Walter Mondale: "This is not only a tragic escalation, which will broaden the war and increase American casualties, but is outright admission of the failure of Vietnamization."[29]

The truth was almost exactly the opposite. "After 1969," writes Kissinger, "the war in Vietnam had turned into a race between our withdrawals, the improvement of the South Vietnamese army, and the ability of Hanoi to interrupt the process by launching offensives. As the American combat role dwindled, anything that weakened Hanoi's combat capability was crucial for us."[30] In attacking the sanctuaries in Cambodia from which the North Vietnamese had been drawing supplies and launching attacks with complete impunity for years (and with, as the London *Economist* said, "barely a chirp of protest from the rest of the world" over this violation of Cambodian neutrality which the Cambodians themselves were too weak to prevent), Nixon was trying to make it more difficult for the Communists to launch offensives against South Vietnam.[31]

Whether or not the incursion into Cambodia was a success in that sense—whether it helped Vietnamization along or hindered it—remains debatable. The Communists were certainly hampered in that area in the next two years, but since in the end Vietnamization did fail, one can say that the Cambodian operations were ultimately of no avail. But what is no longer debatable is that the purpose of both the bombing and the invasion of Cambodia was neither to escalate the war nor "to seek a military method . . . rather than a negotiated method" of ending it. It is beyond dispute now, and should have been clear then, that the Cambodian operations were a tactic in an overall strategy of American withdrawal.

From Nixon's point of view, moreover, they represented exactly the opposite of what Muskie thought they did. Nixon always doubted that the North Vietnamese would accept a compromise settlement unless they felt that they had no choice; therefore, all his "brutal" military moves (the Cambodian operations, the subsequent incursion into Laos, the Christmas 1972 bombing of North Vietnam) were aimed not at an American victory but at persuading the North Vietnamese that a military victory was out of reach for *them*. If, even so, they remained unwilling to negotiate an end to the war, then they would at least be weakened by the time the unilateral American withdrawal was completed and they were left to fight the South Vietnamese alone. By that time, presumably, the South Vietnamese forces would conversely have been strengthened and would be able to hold off the Communists with the help of American arms.

Did Nixon also contemplate an open-ended commitment to use American air power in that case? He sometimes suggested that he did. But on the other hand, in a memo to Kissinger in May 1972, during the so-called Easter offensive the North Vietnamese had just launched, he spoke of the need to "win—not just a temporary respite from this battle, but if possible, tip the balance in favor of the South Vietnamese for battles to come when we no longer will be able to help them with major air strikes."[32] Kissinger was tormented by the question Le Duc Tho once asked him during the secret negotiations: "Before, there were over a million U.S. and puppet troops, and you failed. How can you succeed when you let the puppet troops do the fighting?"[33] This question apparently did not torment Nixon. He believed in Vietnamization, and he went into Cambodia to give it a better chance.

In addition to the strategic rationale, there was also the matter of American casualties. "In 1969," writes Lewy, "the province with the largest American casualty toll was Tay Ninh . . . ; the heavy fighting there, involving some 50,000 North Vietnamese regulars who shuttled back and forth across the Cambodian border, provides the background for the secret bombing of Communist sanctuaries in Cambodia . . . as well as for the April 1970 incursion into that country."[34] On this matter the figures refute Mondale's prediction that the incursion into Cambodia would lead to an increase in American casualties. During the attack on the sanctuaries itself, of course, there was an increase, but there-after the number dropped steadily, thanks both to continued withdrawals and to the diminished capacity of the North Viet-namese to attack from behind the safe haven of the Cambodian border.

The incursion into Laos the following year had the same stra-tegic purpose as the Cambodian operations, but the results were much less encouraging to believers in the viability of Vietnami-zation. This time the objective was to disrupt the elaborate sys-tem of roads known as the Ho Chi Minh Trail that the North Vietnamese had built in supposedly neutral Laos and through which they had for years been sending both troops and supplies into South Vietnam. The incursion into Cambodia had been a joint American–South Vietnamese undertaking, but in the inter-vening period Congress had forbidden American participation on the ground in any operation outside Vietnam. This meant that except for air support the South Vietnamese would be on their own; therefore it also meant that Vietnamization would get its first major test in Laos.

Nixon said then, and reaffirms in his memoirs, that "the net result was a military success. . . . American and South Vietnam-ese casualties were reduced, and Vietnamization continued at a steady pace."[35] Kissinger is more candid. "The South Vietnam-ese divisions were simply not yet good enough for such a com-plex operation as the one in Laos." While claiming that it slowed Hanoi down and—in combination with the Cambodian operation —"enabled us just barely to blunt the North Vietnamese offen-sive in 1972," Kissinger recognizes that the Laos operation se-verely damaged the credibility of Vietnamization. "The South Vietnamese had fought better than before," but they had failed in their main objective.[36] Worse still, as they were withdrawing, some of their men were photographed clinging in panic to the skids of the evacuation helicopters. Even Nixon acknowledges that this "undercut confidence in the success of Vietnamization and the prospect of ending the war."[37]

Did it also undercut his own confidence? Not if we take the account in his memoirs at face value. But if we assume that the performance of the South Vietnamese in Laos did shake his belief that South Vietnam would be able to defend itself on its own after the Americans left—and there are suggestions that it did—we can understand why a negotiated settlement should now have presented itself to him as the only way out.

As we have already seen, Nixon had said that the United States would "continue fighting until the Communists agreed to negotiate a fair and honorable peace or until the South Vietnamese were able to defend themselves on their own—whichever came first." [38] He had—so Kissinger repeatedly tells us—always been skeptical about the willingness of the Communists to compromise, which is to say that he had expected Vietnamization to "come first." Now that this seemed unlikely, the main hope of saving South Vietnam from Communism would be invested in a negotiated settlement that would bring an end not only to the American war in Vietnam but to the war between North Vietnam and South Vietnam as well.

Nixon understood, however, that so long as the North Vietnamese believed they could win on the battlefield they would refuse to accept such a negotiated settlement. Consequently, when the expected North Vietnamese offensive was finally launched in the spring of 1972—"It was more than just an offensive," says Nixon accurately. "It was a full-scale invasion"—Nixon "felt that if we could mount a devastating attack on their home territory while pinning down their Army in the South, we would be in a very good position for the next round of negotiations." [39] Kissinger emphatically agreed. "If we defeated the offensive, we would get a settlement out of it. The North Vietnamese had thrown everything into their effort; if it failed, they would have no choice except to negotiate." [40]

Nixon (very likely whistling in the dark) "viewed the North Vietnamese invasion as a sign [that] they clearly felt that Vietnamization was working" (for "if it were not, they would have waited and let it fail"). [41] Kissinger saw in Hanoi's insistence "that we overthrow the South Vietnamese government" a mark of "Hanoi's uncertainty whether it could accomplish the objective by itself even after our withdrawal." Nevertheless, both

Nixon and Kissinger rejected the view held by many in the Administration "that the conclusive test of Vietnamization was at hand."[42]

A memorandum submitted to Kissinger by his own staff said: "We all recognize that the key is not what we do but what the South Vietnamese do." But neither Kissinger nor Nixon "recognized any such thing."[43] Determined to defeat the offensive, Nixon ordered a resumption of bombing of the North (including Hanoi) and then the mining of all North Vietnamese ports. At the same time, he and Kissinger put diplomatic pressure on the Soviets (who were eager for a summit meeting at which the SALT I treaty would be signed and the Basic Principles of Détente proclaimed) and the Chinese (with whom relations had by now been opened) to use their influence with Hanoi.

In the end, after these measures had been put into effect, the North Vietnamese invasion stalled; and despite all predictions to the contrary, the Soviets did not call off the summit meeting (the supposed risk of which had struck the Boston *Globe* as "even more immoral than our involvement in the war itself").[44]

What, asks Lewy, did the failure of the 1972 invasion signify for the status of Vietnamization? After analyzing the uneven performance of the South Vietnamese, he concludes by endorsing the judgment of Sir Robert Thompson that while "it is untrue to say that the battles were won solely by American air power, it would be true to say that they could not have been won without it." In other words, Lewy writes, "the 1972 offensive did not really constitute a conclusive test of Vietnamization."[45]

It did, however, bear out the expectation of Nixon and Kissinger that only after a military showdown would Hanoi be willing to accept a settlement that did not involve American collusion in the overthrow of the Saigon government. Since a Vietnamese equivalent of the Pentagon Papers is unlikely to materialize, we may never know what exactly impelled Hanoi in October 1972 to accept American proposals it had rejected over and over again for three long years. According to Lewy, "Even though the 1972 offensive had failed to bring about a South Vietnamese collapse, the Communists now controlled much additional territory and they considered themselves to be in a stronger position for accepting the American peace proposals secretly handed their representatives in Paris in October 1971."[46] According to an investigative report by Tad Szulc, the Soviets put pressure on Hanoi after receiving assurances from Nixon and Kissinger at the May summit meeting that the United States was prepared to make certain concessions of its own. But Szulc also says that the North Vietnamese, "whose military fortunes were declining after their spring-summer successes," were eager to reach a settlement before the Presidential election. They feared that Nixon—who on the eve of a summit meeting had dared to risk a confrontation with the Soviet Union in mining the North Vietnamese harbors—might harden his position after being re-elected (which the polls showed unmistakably would happen). Having stalled for three years, they now set a deadline of October 31 and fought to meet it "almost as maniacally as they fought the war."[47] The quotation is attributed by Szulc to Kissinger, and it accords entirely with Kissinger's own subsequently published account in *White House Years*.

Kissinger, too, was in a hurry. Unlike the North Vietnamese, he understood that even though Nixon was certain to be re-elected by a large margin, the antiwar forces in Congress would also be strengthened by the election, which would in turn weaken his bargaining position. Nixon did not see it that way; just as Hanoi feared, he preferred, says Kissinger, "to bring matters to a head by drastic escalation immediately after the election."[48] Nevertheless he went along with Kissinger's recommendation that an agreement be concluded by October 31.

When, however, Thieu balked at the agreement secretly arrived at by Kissinger and Le Duc Tho, Hanoi went public as a way of forcing the United States to stand by the terms already negotiated even if this meant doing so without Thieu's concurrence. This would, of course, have been a triumph for the North Vietnamese, whose major concession had been to drop their insistence that the Saigon government be overthrown and who were delighted to see Thieu emerge as the major obstacle to a peaceful settlement. It was only at this point that the United

States also went public through the medium of a press conference held by Kissinger at which he made the famous announcement that "we believe that peace is at hand." The purpose of this announcement was simultaneously to reassure Hanoi that the United States intended to stick by the agreement and to put pressure on Thieu to accept it.

In any case, there was no truth in the charge later made that the announcement was an election-eve ploy. If there was a ploy involved here, it was Hanoi's, not Nixon's. "Nixon was quite positive that an agreement was unnecessary for the election; its benefit would be too marginal to warrant any risks," Kissinger says plausibly.[49] Nixon is equally emphatic and just as plausible: "The opinion polls confirmed my own intuition that, in terms of voter support, my handling of the war was generally viewed as a positive issue for me and a negative one for McGovern, who was perceived as weak and favoring surrender. Therefore, any settlement that was hastily completed in time for the election would look cynical and suspicious. The hawks would charge, however unfairly, that I had given away too much in order to meet a self-serving deadline, and the doves would claim, however erroneously, that I could have obtained the same terms in 1969."[50]

In the event, both charges would be made anyway. Indeed, Thieu had already said that he regarded the agreement as a sellout even though the North Vietnamese had made several major concessions. The most important were these: They had accepted the continuance of the Thieu government in power; they had agreed to a continuation of economic and military aid to that government; they had agreed to internationally supervised elections to determine the political future of the South; and they had for all practical purposes dropped their insistence on a coalition government. The main thing they got in return was American acquiescence in the continued presence of North Vietnamese troops in the South (although, incredibly, they still denied that there were any North Vietnamese troops in the South).

Thieu objected to many points of detail and insisted on strengthening the safeguards against a coalition government. But for him the main problem was the North Vietnamese troops.

Frequently bursting into tears—of rage rather than sorrow, Kissinger thought—Thieu "said that the United States had obviously 'connived' with the Soviets and China to sell out South Vietnam. He would not be a party to it."[51]

Kissinger replied that in the past Thieu himself had agreed to the continued presence of North Vietnamese troops in the South as part of every joint American–South Vietnamese proposal for a cease-fire in place since October 1970. He also pointed out that Hanoi had now accepted an American demand that infiltration of additional Northern troops into the South be halted—which, if observed, would mean the eventual disappearance by attrition of those already there.

Further to reassure Thieu, the United States then stepped up the supply of military equipment to replace battle losses. Most important of all, Thieu was promised that the United States would come to the aid of South Vietnam if the North should violate the agreement (and Nixon put this promise in writing—not once but twice).

Nevertheless, Thieu refused to sign, and the October 31 deadline passed. When negotiations resumed after the election, the North Vietnamese not only turned down most of the points Thieu had raised, but withdrew several concessions they had made earlier and in general raised new difficulties of a substantive as well as a technical nature. Kissinger thought they had become greedy, having taken heart from Thieu's intransigence and the growing indications that the new Congress (which, as he had anticipated, was even more antiwar than its predecessor) would force Nixon to bend.

On December 13, negotiations broke down once again. Five days later, on December 18, Nixon (in "the most difficult decision I made during the entire war")[52] ordered what came to be known as the Christmas bombing of North Vietnam. It lasted until December 30, and almost immediately upon its termination on New Year's Day, negotiations resumed and were then brought to a successful conclusion in little over a week.

Again, in the absence of a North Vietnamese equivalent of the Pentagon Papers, it is impossible to prove that it was the Christmas bombing that forced Hanoi back into serious negotiations. Lewy thinks it may have contributed, but he also argues that the North Vietnamese finally signed the cease-fire because its terms —"the unanimity principle adopted for the inspection machinery, which virtually guaranteed that supervision of adherence to the agreements would be ineffective, and the legitimation of the presence of NVA forces in the South"—were favorable to them.[53] But if so, why should they have backtracked before the bombing when the same terms were available?

Szulc is more skeptical than Lewy about the effect the bombing had on the course of negotiations, his argument being that "agreement with Hanoi was probably possible in December 1972 without the final paroxysms of the Christmas bombings" and that the differences between the October 1972 and January 1973 texts do not "justify the death and destruction wrought by American planes—not to mention American losses."[54] Kissinger addresses this charge directly in his memoirs: "Were the changes significant enough to justify the anguish and bitterness of those last months of the war? Probably not for us; almost surely for Saigon, about whose survival the war had, after all, been fought."[55]

Does this then mean that the real purpose of the bombing, as Szulc further charges, was "to induce Thieu to sign the Paris agreement, the price being the 'brutalizing' of the North"?[56] Not necessarily. As Ambassador Martin F. Herz of Georgetown University points out in his book on the Christmas bombing: "No one can say with any assurance what, if anything, the North Vietnamese were prepared to sign in December."[57] Nor is there any evidence for the charge that the main purpose of the bombing was to induce Thieu rather than Hanoi to accept the agreement. If anything, in fact, the evidence points in the opposite direction.

Thus on December 19, when the bombing was already in progress, Nixon sent Thieu a letter telling him that if the North Vietnamese "agreed to resume negotiations, it was imperative that he join us in offering reasonable terms Hanoi would be willing to accept." This, he said, was the "absolutely final offer on my part for us to work together in seeking a settlement along the lines I have approved or to go our separate ways."[58] This letter had been drafted by Kissinger because "We did not want Thieu to believe that the attacks on the North heralded a new period of open-ended warfare; nor did we want him to be misled by the critical outcry against us." Nixon then ("contrary to his habit of signing my drafts without change") toughened the language because "I don't want him to take any heart from the fact that we are hitting Hanoi. . . ."[59] None of this is absolutely incompatible with the theory that the bombing was meant to reassure Thieu, but it strongly suggests that this theory is mistaken.

As against Szulc, Herz believes that the bombing probably did have the intended effect on the North Vietnamese: "Certainly they seemed eager to come to terms after the bombing, an eagerness they had conspicuously failed to display before. . . . As an invitation to resume serious negotiations, the bombing was not a subtle move; it was not a militarily effective move; it was certainly not a popular move; but it appears to have been a diplomatically effective one."[60] Sir Robert Thompson is much more emphatic: "In my view, on December 30, 1972, after eleven days of those B-52 attacks on the Hanoi area, *you had won the war. It was over!* . . . They would have taken any terms. And that is why, of course, you actually got a peace agreement in January, which you had not been able to get in October."[61]

One thing about the bombing *is* certain, however: practically all the comment it elicited in the United States was wrong. We have already seen that the casualties and civilian damage were amazingly light (about 1,500 killed, according to Hanoi's own figures, as against the 35,000 in Dresden and 84,000 in Tokyo during the World War II raids with which it was compared, and fewer than the North Vietnamese themselves had just killed by their artillery bombardment of An Loc).[62] Yet Senator George McGovern in an interview on NBC called it "the most murderous aerial bombardment in the history of the world," "the most immoral action that this nation has ever committed in its national history," and "a policy of mass-murder that's being carried on in the name of the American people."[63] Senator Harold Hughes concurred: "It is unbelievable savagery that we have unleashed on this holy season; the only thing I can compare it with is the savagery at Hiroshima and Nagasaki."[64] Anthony Lewis of the New York *Times* added his note to this temperate chorus, characterizing the bombing not only as "a crime against humanity" but "the most terrible destruction in the history of man."[65] An editorial in the Washington *Post* agreed: the bombing, it declared, was "the most savage and senseless act of war ever visited, over a scant ten days, by one sovereign people upon another."[66]

In addition to being wrong about the destruction the bombing was causing and about the moral weight that could legitimately be assigned to it in comparison with such horrors as Auschwitz and Hiroshima even by those who considered it unjustified, the critics (although that seems too tame a word to describe the people who used such language as I have just quoted) were wrong in their predictions. McGovern said that the bombing had "destroyed any immediate hopes for peace."[67] Senator Mike Mansfield declared: "I think that bombing will just put steel in their backbones and prolong the war."[68] Senator Jacob Javits said: "The North Vietnamese have not been bombed into a settlement, and there is nothing to indicate that our renewed air strikes are going to have that effect now."[69] Yet whether or not the bombing caused the North Vietnamese to resume negotiations, it certainly did *not* have the effect these three senators, and most of the editorialists and columnists, so confidently asserted it would.

A similar but much more serious question that has been raised concerning the agreement that was finally signed (by Thieu as well as Hanoi) in Paris on January 23 was whether the same terms, or roughly the same terms, might not have been negotiated in 1969. The answer to this question is obviously no, since it was not until October 1972 that Hanoi made an agreement possible by dropping its theretofore unyielding insistence that the Saigon government be overthrown. Even Szulc acknowledges this: "In all fairness to Kissinger, it must be recognized that a settlement, as distinct from an American cave-in which Nixon would not have tolerated, became possible only in October [1972], when Hanoi and the Vietcong dropped their demand that Thieu be ousted as a sine qua non of peace." But he then goes on to write:

"It must have been predictable . . . from the time the first bombing halt was negotiated in 1968 that the North Vietnamese would never leave the South. Other than the effort at Vietnamization, therefore, there is no satisfactory reason for Kissinger to have refused to recognize reality for three years." But this "effort at Vietnamization" was the only alternative to what Szulc himself describes as "an American cave-in which Nixon would not have tolerated." [70]

The fact is that having by 1968 already fought for over five years to prevent the Communists from taking over South Vietnam by force, the United States was not prepared to let them take it over at the negotiating table. Indeed, the United States was unwilling to do this even under cover of diplomatic arrangements—like a coalition government by some other name—that would have disguised or retarded the process sufficiently to ensure "a decent interval" between the American withdrawal and the Communist victory and thus save the American face.

Yet it is precisely "a decent interval" that Nixon and Kissinger have been charged with contriving through the Paris agreement of 1973. Thieu's accusation of a sellout was seconded by the commander of the Australian army advisory team in Vietnam who called the agreement "a shameless bug-out." [71] Sir Robert Thompson put it more delicately but no less devastatingly in asserting that the Paris agreement restored Hanoi's "chance of winning the war in Indochina and practically eliminated the risk of losing it." [72] The reason, Thompson explained on another occasion, was that the "cease-fire agreement restored complete security to the rear bases in North Vietnam, in Laos, in Cambodia, and in the parts of South Vietnam that it held. It subjected the South Vietnamese rear base again to being absolutely open to military attack." [73]

Nor were the South Vietnamese and their more hawkish supporters the only ones to interpret the Paris agreement in this way. Even among opponents of the war the theory of the "decent interval" was found credible. "During 1968," wrote Daniel Ellsberg before the Paris agreement, "Henry Kissinger frequently said in private talks that the appropriate goal of the U.S. policy was a 'decent interval'—two to three years—between the withdrawal of U.S. troops and a Communist takeover in Vietnam.''[74] Several years later, after the collapse of Saigon, Earl C. Ravenal, another radical exponent of the antiwar position, went so far as to defend Thieu's bitter reaction: "After all, the United States had extricated itself from Vietnam by bargaining for its prisoners, coercing the enemy in a convincing but locally irrelevant way, fabricating an overhead deal with its ally's mortal adversary, signing a cosmetic and imperfect agreement on behalf of the local contestants, and forcing it down its ally's throat.''[75]

Needless to say, this is not how Kissinger and Nixon see the Paris agreement. They both certainly admit to having forced the agreement down Thieu's throat (even after Nixon told Kissinger that "we must have Thieu as a willing partner in making any agreement. It cannot be a shotgun marriage").[76] But they both believed then, and continued to believe, that the agreement was a good one.

Kissinger states the case forcefully: "All of us who negotiated the agreement of October 12 were convinced that we had vindicated the anguish of a decade not by a 'decent interval' but by a decent settlement. We thought with reason that Saigon, generously armed and supported by the United States, would be able to deal with moderate violations of the agreements; that the United States would stand by to enforce the agreement and punish major violations; that Hanoi might be tempted also by economic aid into choosing reconstruction of the North if conquest of the South was kept out of reach; that we could use our relations with Moscow and Peking, in addition, to encourage Hanoi's restraint; and that with our aid the South Vietnamese government would grow in security and prosperity over the time bought by the agreement, and compete effectively in a political struggle in which without question it had the loyalty of most of the population. Perhaps the Vietnamese parties could even work out a peaceful modus vivendi.''[77]

Although this passage was written three years later, and following the fall of the South, it is impossible to doubt after a reading of the memoirs of the two men that it accurately states what Kissinger and Nixon believed they had accomplished at the time. Far from admitting defeat and cunningly contriving a "decent interval" for themselves, they thought they had scored a great victory over the Communists. "We have done it," Kissinger and his aide Winston Lord said to each other in Paris on October 12 when it became clear to them that Hanoi had accepted the American terms. Kissinger's deputy, Alexander M. Haig, Jr., who had served in Vietnam (and would later become Ronald Reagan's Secretary of State), was also present, and even though he was anxious about Thieu's response, he "declared with emotion that we had saved the honor of the military men who had served, died, and suffered there." [78]

Then came Kissinger's report to Nixon upon his return to Washington. Playing on the theme that the three major goals of Nixon's foreign policy were to achieve an opening with China, détente with the Soviet Union, and an honorable end to the war in Vietnam, and assuming that the first two had already been accomplished, Kissinger began his report to the President (so writes Nixon) with "the broadest smile I had ever seen. 'Well, Mr. President,' he said, 'it looks like we've got three out of three!' " [79]

After Kissinger completed his description of the negotiating session and the provisions of the agreement (which were not even as good from both the American and South Vietnamese points of view as the agreement finally signed in January), Nixon's response was that "these provisions alone amounted to a complete capitulation by the enemy: they were accepting a settlement on our terms." [80] The following week, en route to Saigon to brief Thieu, Kissinger and all his staff (with one exception) "thought that Thieu would be overjoyed by the agreement," and Kissinger characterized it in his meeting with Thieu as "a major collapse of the Communist position." [81]

When Thieu remained noncommittal, Kissinger cabled Nixon that "we were up against a paradoxical situation in which North Vietnam, which had in effect lost the war, was acting as if it had won; while South Vietnam, which had effectively won the war, was acting as if it had lost." Nixon agreed, and when Thieu subsequently rejected the entire plan as what he would later publicly call "an agreement to surrender," Nixon also agreed with Kissinger's statement that Thieu's "demands verge on insanity." [82] He instructed Kissinger to "advise President Thieu in the strongest terms that for the four years I have been in office and, indeed, for the period before that when I was out of office, no American public figure has stood up more staunchly for the proposition that there can be no Communist government imposed on the people of South Vietnam." [83]

Finally, in a diary entry dated December 30, 1972, the day he announced the resumption of negotiations, Nixon wrote: "The real question is whether the announcement today will be interpreted in the public mind as having been the result of a policy that worked. Of course, it will not be so interpreted by our opponents in the media and the Congress. . . . Henry always looks at it in terms of the merits, and on the merits we know that what this is is a very stunning capitulation by the enemy to our terms." [84]

Only the eyes of an unmitigated animus could see in all this a deliberate deception aimed at avoiding humiliation by buying a "decent interval" between an American surrender and its ultimately inevitable consequence in the fall of the South to Communism. If Nixon and Kissinger were practicing deception here, it was self-deception, not the deception of others, whether of Thieu or Hanoi or the American people or the rest of the world. Their euphoria over Hanoi's willingness to accept terms they had been offering for years was not, however, a product of this self-deception. On the contrary, they were entitled to feel triumphant at having brought Hanoi to that point by (as they understandably saw it) resolve, steady nerves, and above all the courage to take very tough military measures and to see them through in the face of commensurately brutal attacks on their political judgment and moral character.

Nor was self-deception present in their expectations of what the likely aftermath of the agreement would be. They hoped that the cease-fire would hold; they thought it just possibly might; but they had no illusions as to the odds that it would. "I sympathized with Thieu's position,'' writes Nixon. "Almost the entire North Vietnamese Army—an estimated 120,000 troops that had poured across the DMZ during the spring invasion—were still in South Vietnam, and he [Thieu] was naturally skeptical of any plan that would lead to an American withdrawal without requiring a corresponding North Vietnamese withdrawal. I shared his view that the Communists' motives were entirely cynical. I knew, as he did, that they would observe the agreement only so long and so far as South Vietnam's strength and *America's readiness to retaliate forced them to do so.*'' [85]

This was in October. Then, on December 7 (that is, while the negotiations over the changes demanded by Saigon in the October draft were proceeding in Paris but before the Christmas bombing began), Kissinger cabled Nixon: "It is now obvious as the result of our additional exploration of Hanoi's intentions that they have not in any way abandoned their objectives or ambitions with respect to South Vietnam. What they have done is decide to modify their strategy by moving from conventional and main force warfare to a political and insurgency strategy within the framework of the draft agreement." Two conclusions followed from this analysis: "Thus, we can anticipate no lasting peace in the wake of a consummated agreement, but merely a shift in Hanoi's modus operandi. *We will probably have little chance of maintaining the agreement without evident hair-trigger U.S. readiness, which may in fact be challenged at any time, to enforce its provisions.*'' [86]

The words I have italicized in both of the above statements were the key to the entire agreement. Nixon knew that it was the key at least as well as Kissinger did, which is why he promised Thieu in the clearest terms that the United States would react with force in the event of a serious violation by North Vietnam of the agreement. On November 14, Nixon had written in a letter to Thieu: "You have my absolute assurance that if Hanoi fails to abide by the terms of this agreement it is my intention to take swift and severe retaliatory action.'' [87] And then on January 5, he reiterated the same promise: "Should you decide, as I trust you will, to go with us, you have my assurance of continued assistance in the post-settlement period and that we will respond with full force should the settlement be violated by North Vietnam."[88]

Thieu was not convinced. Nixon says that he "seemed almost desperate. He argued that the cease-fire would not last more than three months: then, when the last American had gone, the Communists would resume their guerrilla warfare. But this time they would fight with knives and bayonets, being careful not to do anything sufficient to justify American retaliation. In this way my guarantees to enforce the agreement would never be put to the test, and the Communists would have a free hand against him and his government."[89]

In recording this argument in his memoirs, Nixon makes no comment on it, but Kissinger (whose account of Thieu's objectives is briefer but substantially the same as Nixon's) says that it turned out to be "totally correct." A little later on, however, he also says that "we believed that Saigon was strong enough to deal with guerrilla war and low-level violations." As for "massive violations," those would be deterred, in accordance with the theory of Vietnamization, by "the implicit threat of our retaliation." And as a further deterrent, "We would use our new relationships with Moscow and Peking to foster restraint" in Hanoi.[90]

3.

No one contemplating these words in the light of what subsequently happened can reasonably believe that Kissinger and Nixon were deceiving anyone but themselves. What subsequently happened was this. No sooner was "America's Vietnam war" over, in Kissinger's poignantly telling phrase,[91] than the North Vietnamese began violating the cease-fire provisions. The South Vietnamese, with American cooperation, were also guilty of violations (which, characteristically, were the ones stressed by Szulc in his 1974 article). But the difference between the two sets of violations was that those committed by the South Vietnamese were measures of self-defense, whereas those committed by the North Vietnamese were aimed at conquest.

The most important of the violations on either side was the continued infiltration of North Vietnamese troops. The United States protested and threatened. Nixon: ". . . we have informed the North Vietnamese of our concern about this infiltration . . . and I would only suggest that based on my actions over the past four years, that the North Vietnamese should not lightly disregard such expressions of concern. . . ."[92] But this implicit threat of renewed bombing was soon rendered meaningless by Congress, first in voting to cut off funds for all U.S. military action in and over Indochina, and then by enacting the War Powers Resolution, which added the final nail to the coffin of Nixon's promises to Thieu to enforce the Paris agreement. "I knew," writes Nixon, "that since Congress had removed the possibility of military action I had only words with which to threaten. The Communists knew it too."[93]

Indeed they did. Years earlier, General Nguyen Van Vinh, chairman of the reunification department of the North Vietnamese Communist party (Lao Dong), had written: "Whether or not the war will resume after the conclusion of agreements depends on the comparative balance of forces. If we are capable of dominating the adversary [without war], the war will not break out again, and conversely."[94] Since the prospects of domination by political means combined with guerrilla operations were looking dim—to that extent Vietnamization really *was* working—and with "the comparative balance of forces" radically altered by the removal of the American threat, the North Vietnamese began planning a large-scale invasion of the South.

At this point, one of the two illusions by which Nixon and Kissinger had deceived themselves was exploded. If they had really expected the Soviet Union to restrain Hanoi for the sake of the "new relationship" they had so recently forged in signing the Basic Principles of Détente at the Moscow Summit of 1972, they now discovered, as Lewy drily puts it, that "this was not to be."[95]

As the infiltration of North Vietnamese soldiers proceeded (45,000 in the first year after the Paris agreement was signed, bringing their strength from 140,000 in January 1973 to 185,000 in

March 1974), the Soviets poured increasing quantities of heavy weapons into Hanoi—tanks, artillery pieces, and the latest air-defense systems armed with surface-to-air missiles.

The Soviets also supplied adequate quantities of ammunition for all these weapons—a crucial point because the American weapons that had been shipped to the South Vietnamese were soon rendered useless by a progressive reduction of economic aid which led to severe shortages of ammunition (as well as of spare parts and fuel). "By the fall of 1974," Lewy says, "available funds were no longer sufficient to allow the one-for-one replacement of lost aircraft, tanks, or artillery pieces permitted by the Paris agreement. . . ."[96]

North Vietnam's Chief of Staff, General Van Tien Dong, would later explain what this meant: "The reduction of U.S. aid made it impossible for the puppet troops to carry out their combat plans and build up their forces. . . . Nguyen Van Thieu was then forced to fight a poor man's war. Enemy firepower had decreased by nearly 60 percent because of bomb and ammunition shortages. Its mobility was also reduced by half due to lack of aircraft, vehicles, and fuel."[97] (In Cambodia, too, the government forces fighting the Khmer Rouge Communists, who were soon to murder nearly half the population of their own country, finally had to surrender because they literally ran out of ammunition after a cutoff of American aid.) Thanks to the Soviets—and the Chinese, who also disappointed Nixon's expectation that they would try to foster restraint—the North Vietnamese suffered no such problem of shortages.

By this time, in encouraging the Egyptians to attack Israel in 1973, the Soviets had already violated the provisions in the Basic Principles of Détente calling for the United States and the Soviet Union to exercise a restraining influence on third parties lest they themselves be drawn directly into the conflict. Conceivably, therefore, Nixon and Kissinger were no longer counting on Soviet help to make the Paris agreement work. Nor could they still have been counting on the United States; as Nixon says, congressional action had turned his promise to retaliate into empty words. Here then the second of the two illusions behind the Paris agreement was blasted—and it was to be even more cruelly blasted when Congress (in an act neither Nixon nor Kissinger nor anyone else would have anticipated in 1973) in effect cut Saigon off without a bullet in the very midst of a full-scale invasion by the North Vietnamese army. Gerald Ford was now the President, Nixon having resigned as a result of Watergate, but Kissinger was still Secretary of State. Both he and the new President pleaded and cajoled, but to no avail. Thieu then in a last desperate act released the text of the two letters Nixon had sent him promising that the United States would enforce the Paris agreement. The response in Congress and in the media was to disavow a moral obligation that had been contracted by a disgraced President, and to justify itself by citing Nixon's failure to secure congressional ratification of this commitment as yet another sign of the contempt for the Constitution that had brought about his downfall.

Believers in the "decent interval" interpretation of the Paris agreement might well counter the analysis I have been offering here by asking how men as astute as Richard Nixon and Henry Kissinger could ever really have persuaded themselves that they would be in a position to order the bombers back into Vietnam after the American withdrawal was complete (and the American prisoners of war had all been released). Kissinger's answer is simple: If not "for the collapse of executive authority as a result of Watergate, I believe we would have succeeded."[98]

He explains: "The argument was later advanced that it was not within the President's power to give such assurances without explicit authorization by the Congress. This idea not only did not occur to us; it would have struck us as inconceivable that the United States should fight for years and lose 45,000 men [sic] in an honorable cause, and then stand by while the peace treaty, the achievement of their sacrifice, was flagrantly violated. . . . In Vietnam this meant the agreement would have been a blatant subterfuge for surrender. We could have done that earlier and with much less pain. Honor, decency, credibility, and international law all combined to make it seem beyond controversy that we should promise to observe the treaty and see it enforced.

What else could be the meaning of a solemn compact ending a war, ratified by an international conference?'' [99]

Even McGeorge Bundy, who accuses Kissinger and Nixon of "contempt for the clear opinion of the Congress, and ultimately contempt for democracy itself," acknowledges that "there is every reason to believe that the assurances were offered in full good faith." [100] But Bundy disagrees that Watergate was responsible for what Congress ultimately did (or rather failed to do) in 1975. Accusations against Nixon and Kissinger of contempt for democracy in their dealings with Thieu come with a special ill grace from a repentant hawk like Bundy, against whom the same charge has been made. Yet in refusing to put the blame on Watergate, I think he is right. As Kissinger and Nixon both give every indication of having known, antiwar sentiment was growing so strong that, Watergate or no, it was bound to place severe limits on any future action any President might wish to take in Indochina. Indeed, it had already set the very limits of flexibility and time within which Kissinger (as he complains over and over again) had to negotiate with the North Vietnamese. How then could he and Nixon have believed that they would be in a stronger position in the future?

There were three reasons. First of all, says Kissinger, "We thought we would be in a better moral and political position to assist Saigon to maintain its freedom in the name of a peace program in which the American people could take pride than in the context of open-ended warfare tearing our country apart." [101]

In case this prediction should turn out to be wrong, they had something else to fall back on: Nixon's strength of will and his ability to resist the fiercest pressures when once he had decided on a controversial course. In a memo to Kissinger on the implementation of his order to bomb the North and mine Haiphong harbor in response to the Easter offensive of 1972, Nixon had said: "We have the power to destroy his war-making capacity. The only question is whether we have the *will* to use that power. What distinguishes me from Johnson is that I have the *will* in spades." [102]

That Nixon was not merely bragging had by the signing of the

Paris agreement been abundantly confirmed, as even McGeorge Bundy acknowledges: "This image of the fierce and single-handed Richard Nixon is what Mr. Kissinger almost surely has in mind when he uses the sonorous phrase 'executive authority.' And this Nixon did indeed have a record; he had dared to mine Haiphong on the eve of his cherished Moscow summit, and he had dared to bomb Hanoi on the eve of Christmas and the brink of peace. Reinforced by his achievement of peace, as by his assured four years of office, what might he not do if provoked?" [103]

But the most important reason of all for the confidence of Nixon and Kissinger in their future ability to enforce the Paris agreement was their conviction that the alternative would seem unthinkable to the American people. The alternative was the "pitiful, helpless giant" Nixon had warned the United States would become if it were defeated in Vietnam. Like his immediate predecessors, Nixon saw in Vietnam a significance beyond itself, but his version of the domino theory was global rather than narrowly geographical: "If, when the chips are down, the world's most powerful nation, the United States of America, acts like a pitiful, helpless giant, the forces of totalitarianism and anarchy will threaten free nations and free institutions throughout the world." [104] Given this wider context of significance, it was essential that the United States not be defeated in the struggle against the forces of totalitarianism in Vietnam. But given also the need for the United States to withdraw from Vietnam, it was essential that a strategy of withdrawal be designed that would not lead to or merely act as a cover for an ultimate defeat. "A decent interval," in other words, might serve partisan political purposes, but so far as the interests of the nation, and of "free nations and free institutions throughout the world," were concerned, it would only postpone the day of reckoning.

A great deal therefore depended on the success of the strategy of withdrawal from Vietnam which Nixon and Kissinger began putting into effect the minute they assumed office. To be sure, this strategy had already been envisaged by Johnson and his people, and just before Tet, Westmoreland had even predicted that American troop withdrawals would begin in 1969. But it was Nixon and Kissinger who were charged with the responsibility of carrying out the de-Americanization, or Vietnamization, of the war at such a pace and in such a way as to give Saigon a fair chance of surviving future Communist assaults. And this is what they believed they had done.

There was another sense in which more was riding on the success of Vietnamization than the fate of Vietnam alone. In addition to showing the way to an American withdrawal from Vietnam that would not result in a clear and unobstructed path for the "forces of totalitarianism and anarchy," Vietnamization was to Nixon and Kissinger the paradigm and first testing-ground of a strategy of American retreat from the version of containment defined by the Truman Doctrine.

The Truman Doctrine had committed the United States (at least in principle) to intervention anywhere and everywhere in the world against the spread of Communism; it had enjoyed a bipartisan national consensus up to and through the early years of American intervention in Vietnam; and it had in the later years of that intervention lost so much support that no President could now remain obedient to its imperatives. This is why even Richard Nixon—who had once upon a time denounced the Truman version of containment as "cowardly" and might have been expected upon becoming President himself to enunciate a more aggressive doctrine aimed not at holding the line against the spread of Communism but rather of liberating or "rolling back" the boundaries of the Communist world—was forced to move in the opposite direction. About six months after becoming President, Nixon enunciated a new doctrine—the Nixon Doctrine—that was intended to supplant the Truman Doctrine.

Here is how he describes it in his memoirs: "In the past our policy had been to furnish the arms, men, and matériel to help other nations defend themselves against aggression. That was what we had done in Korea, and that was how we had started out in Vietnam. But from now on, I said, we would furnish only the matériel and the military and economic assistance to those nations willing to accept the responsibility of supplying the manpower to defend themselves." This was not, Nixon hastens to add, "a formula for getting America *out* of Asia, but one that provided the only sound basis for America's staying *in* and continuing to play a responsible role in helping the non-Communist nations and neutrals as well as our Asian allies to defend their independence." [105]

Nixon said nothing here about the use of American air power either in Vietnam or anywhere else, but there is no question that he looked forward to a time when even that degree of direct American military involvement would become unnecessary in Vietnam itself and *a fortiori* in other places to which we had not committed ourselves so deeply. The point of the Nixon Doctrine was to salvage as much of containment as possible by depending on local forces to deter or hold the line against Communist expansion.

In Vietnam, and some other cases, the local forces would be the threatened countries themselves; in other areas, the local forces might be a regional surrogate (like Iran under the Shah which with the help of American arms would act as the "policeman" of the Persian Gulf). With the deepening of the Sino-Soviet split and the forging of a de facto Sino-American alliance, even Communist China was expected to become such a regional surrogate. Having gone into Vietnam to contain Chinese expansionism at a time when China was still regarded as a Soviet proxy, the United States in getting out of Vietnam would attempt to use China as an American proxy in containing Soviet expansionism there. At the same time, the United States, through the system of incentives for good behavior built into détente, would attempt to restrain the Soviet Union itself and secure its cooperation in restraining Hanoi and all its other troublesome third-world clients.

If the Soviets were to explode one of the two illusions on which this brilliantly coherent strategy was based almost immediately after the Basic Principles of Détente were signed, the American people would explode the second almost immediately after the Paris agreement on Vietnam was signed. Not only did the American people refuse to allow the use of air power to enforce the agreement; they even refused to send the "máteriel and the military and economic assistance" without which South Vietnam could not possibly defend itself. The Nixon Doctrine thus failed its first and most important test. (A few years later, under Jimmy Carter, whatever was still left of it would follow the Truman Doctrine into the fabled trash can of history when the United States would first help to weaken, and would then do nothing to bolster, its surrogate in the Persian Gulf when the Shah's turn came to be threatened and finally overthrown.)

If, then, Kennedy tried to apply containment in Vietnam on the military cheap, and Johnson tried to make it work on the political cheap, Nixon tried to salvage it on the strategic cheap. All three failed. That these were failures of leadership is certain. Kennedy failed in prudential wisdom; Johnson failed in political judgment; Nixon failed in strategic realism.

These were all the more failures of leadership in that the actions taken by all three Presidents were taken without any pressure from below. The decision to enter the war was made by Kennedy and his advisers; the decision to escalate the war was made by Johnson and his advisers; and the decision to withdraw gradually rather than all at once was made by Nixon and his advisers. None of these major decisions owed much, if anything at all, to popular pressure. The people went along, but they were never enthusiastic about the war, feeling for the most part incompetent to judge and willing on the whole to give their leaders the benefit of the doubt. For America the war in Vietnam was not a people's war, it was a war of the elites, conceived and executed by "the best and the brightest" who later—and with exactly the same dogmatic assurance—opposed and denounced what they alone had wrought.

But this cannot be said of the decision to cut off the South Vietnamese and leave them weakened in the face of a major North Vietnamese buildup and vulnerable to a massive North Vietnamese invasion. Those decisions were made not by a small elite but by a majority of the members of the Congress of the United States. At least a measure of responsibility for them therefore also belongs to the people whose representatives they were and whose wishes they believed themselves to be carrying out.

Imprudent though it might have been to try to save South Vietnam from Communism, it was also an attempt born of noble ideals and impulses. The same cannot be said of what the United States did in abandoning South Vietnam to Communism in 1975. Perhaps nothing would have helped by then. Except for a few military men, almost everyone thinks that South Vietnam was defeated by its own internal weaknesses as most dramatically manifested in the ignominious collapse of its army in the face of the North Vietnamese invasion. "Our" Vietnamese had always seemed less motivated, less willing to fight, than the Communists, and now after years and years of military training and billions and billions of dollars of military aid, after elections and rural pacification and land-reform programs, the South Vietnamese army was unable to stand and defend the country in the last life-and-death battle it would be called upon to fight. Nevertheless, we will never know whether the outcome might have been different if the South Vietnamese had not been forced to fight "a poor man's war" and if their morale had not been so disastrously affected by the sense of abandonment and the defeatism this naturally aroused.

At one time it had been said that the success of the Vietcong against Diem and then Thieu proved that the people of South Vietnam did not support the non-Communist government in Saigon and that they in fact would welcome the Communists as liberators and national heroes. Yet far from rising up to join the Vietcong in the Tet offensive of 1968, the people of South Vietnam fought; and by the time the offensive was over, the Vietcong cadres had been decimated. From that point on, North Vietnamese troops did 80 percent of the fighting in the South, and the war could no longer be represented as an internal insurgency or a "people's war." Indeed, the Communists had lost the "people's war," and the war they finally won was a straightforward conventional war fought by regular uniformed troops equipped with tanks and planes and missiles, not an insurgency fought by primitively armed guerrillas in black pajamas. To have lost such a conventional war to a stronger invading army no more proves that South Vietnam was an unviable or illegitimate state than the fall of France in 1940 to the Nazis proved that France was unviable or illegitimate.

Moreover, despite the unpopularity of Thieu, and despite widespread corruption, and despite the allegedly superior claim of the Northerners to the nationalist feelings of all Vietnamese, the people of South Vietnam had no wish to live under Communism or the domination of the North. As Robert Shaplen of *The New Yorker,* no friend of the Thieu regime, had said earlier, the South Vietnamese "may not love the government more but they seem to be loving the Communists less." [106]

We know that the people of South Vietnam had no wish to live under Communism from the fact that a million of them had left the North and come to the South at the time of the 1954 partition of the country; we know it from the fact that during the last sixty days of the war hundreds of thousands of them voted with their feet by fleeing from their Communist "liberators"; and we know it from the fact that after the Communist victory, hundreds of thousands more risked their lives in leaky boats rather than remain in a Communist Vietnam. "Under French colonial domination, throughout the long war years, even during the catastrophic famine of 1945 when two million starved to death," writes Doan Van Toai, a former NLF sympathizer now in exile himself, "Vietnamese simply did not willingly leave their homeland—the land of their ancestors' graves." [107] That such a people should leave their homeland in such numbers and at such risk tells us all we need to know about their hearts and minds.

In abandoning these people at the end, the United States demonstrated that saving South Vietnam from Communism was not only beyond its reasonable military, political, and intellectual capabilities but that it was ultimately beyond its moral capabilities as well.

FIVE:

WHOSE IMMORALITY?

LOOKING back on this entire story, one can, if one wishes, make the consoling point that everyone on all sides of the argument turned out to be wrong about the political character and implications of the Vietnam War.

Those supporters of American intervention who thought the problem was to contain Chinese expansionism were wrong: shortly after the Americans left, Communist Vietnam was at war with Communist China, thereby vindicating those opponents of American intervention who had always stressed the ancient enmity between the two countries.

But this was only a partial vindication. Those who said that Hanoi was not a Chinese proxy also tended to think that the Vietcong was not a North Vietnamese proxy, and about this *they* were wrong. To be sure, the National Liberation Front, true to its character as a front, included elements that were not Communist, as well as Communists and sympathizers who thought they were fighting "for democracy, freedom and peace" and who believed that the fall of Saigon would lead to "a domestic policy of national reconciliation, without risk of reprisal, and a foreign policy of nonalignment." But Doan Van Toai—whose words I have just quoted, who was arrested and jailed many times for leading student demonstrations against the Thieu regime and against American involvement, and who never joined the Vietcong only because the NLF felt he could be more useful as an intelligence agent—was deceived about this, as were what he calls "the most prestigious intellectuals in the West." Shortly after the North Vietnamese army conquered the South, the Provisional Revolutionary Government (PRG, into which the NLF had been transmuted) was disbanded; and far from being appointed to positions of power in the new Vietnam, many of its members were arrested. "Today," wrote Doan Van Toai in 1981, "among 17 members of the Politburo and 134 members of the Vietnamese Communist party, not a single one is from the N.L.F." (though there were a few "who had been North Vietnam Communist party representatives with the N.L.F.").[1] Although not all members of the NLF knew it then, they had indeed been acting as proxies for Hanoi, and those who persisted in thinking otherwise were eliminated in the end as unreliable. In the view of General Fred C. Weyand, this might even have been one of the purposes of the Tet offensive of 1968: "Applying the test of *cui bono* (for whose benefit) it can be seen that the real losers of Tet-68 were the South Vietnamese Communists (the Vietcong or PRG) who surfaced, led the attacks, and were destroyed in the process. . . . Just as the Russians eliminated their Polish competitors [with] the Warsaw uprising, the North Vietnamese eliminated their Southern competitors with Tet-68. They thereby insured that the eventual outcome of the war would be a South Vietnam dominated and controlled, not by *South* Vietnamese Communists, but by the *North* Vietnamese."[2] Be that speculation as it may, the fact remains that the war in Vietnam was a case of external aggression, and those who said that it was merely a civil war were wrong.

On the issue of the Soviet role in Vietnam, everyone was

wrong as well. In its earliest stages, the insurgency in South Vietnam was seen as a "war of national liberation" of the kind Nikita Khrushchev explicitly predicted would lead to the triumph of Communism in the third world (then known as the undeveloped world). As such, it represented to supporters of American intervention a case of attempted Soviet expansionism at a third remove (that is, through Peking to Hanoi and through Hanoi to the Vietcong). But the Sino-Soviet split made nonsense of the idea that the Russians could be using the Chinese to further their own imperialistic aims. One of the greatest of all the ironies of the Vietnam War, however, is that it ended by vindicating the original idea that a Communist victory would be tantamount to an expansion of Soviet power. Having won the war with the help of Soviet arms, and then having conquered Laos and Cambodia, Hanoi went on to ally itself with the Soviet Union against "the Chinese menace," at which point (in the words of a high official of the Singapore government, S. Rajaratnam) the Vietnamese found themselves "fighting for a Soviet Indochina."[3] Yet by the time the people who had predicted some such result of an American defeat in Vietnam were thus vindicated, all but a very few had long since changed their minds and gone over to the other side.

But what of the notorious domino theory? Here, too, everyone was wrong. Those who said that the fall of Vietnam to Communism would be followed by the fall of Laos and Cambodia were right, but they were wrong in thinking that the dominoes would topple all throughout Southeast Asia "at least down to Singapore but almost as certainly to Djakarta," in Johnson's words.[4] This does not, however, mean that the domino theory has been "discredited," as is so often glibly claimed. For believers in the domino theory turned out to be right in thinking that an American defeat in Vietnam would give encouragement to other Communist insurrections or "wars of national liberation" backed by the Soviet Union. Thus, no sooner had Vietnam fallen than Soviet proxies in the form of Cuban troops appeared in Angola to help the Communist faction there overwhelm its pro-Western rivals in a civil war. With local variations, the same pattern was repeated over the next few years in Ethiopia, Mozambique, South Yemen, and Afghanistan, all of which were taken over by Communist parties subservient to or allied with the Soviet Union with the help of Soviet proxies or massive infusions of Soviet arms. Still, if the domino theory was in one sense vindicated by Vietnam, it was not in the sense most of its proponents foresaw.

From a strictly *political* point of view, then, no one (to borrow a phrase from George McGovern's campaign for the Presidency in 1972) was "right from the start." The fall of Vietnam to Communism led to some of the consequences that had been predicted, but not to others.

Nor was anyone "right from the start" about the consequences for the United States of a defeat in Vietnam. On the one hand, those who predicted the upsurge of a new isolationism were right. The new isolationism became powerful enough to capture the Democratic party—the party that had given the nation the Truman Doctrine, the Korean War, and the Vietnam War—and thus managed to establish itself in the very center of American political life for the first time since 1941.

Admittedly, when George McGovern, as the Democratic candidate for the Presidency in 1972, campaigned under the all but explicitly isolationist slogan "Come Home, America," he was defeated by Nixon in one of the great landslides in American electoral history. Nevertheless, the new isolationism remained strong enough to produce results in the form of a weakening of "the imperial Presidency"—that is, the main institutional capability the United States possesses for conducting an overt policy of intervention to contain the spread of Communism—and then of the CIA, the main institutional capability the nation possesses for conducting a covert policy of containment. It is true that these assaults on the powers of the Presidency and the CIA were triggered by the abuses exposed in connection with the Watergate scandal. But it would be naive to suppose that they did not reflect a new impulse within the political culture of the United States to pull back from the responsibilities of containment by making any future act of anti-Communist interventionism much more difficult (if not indeed impossible) to undertake.

That this was the animating purpose behind the twin assaults on "the imperial Presidency" and the CIA came out very clearly when in 1975 Congress cut off a nascent effort by Ford and Kissinger to help the pro-Western guerrillas in Angola in their struggle against the Soviet-backed faction there (which finally triumphed after Cuban troops, acting as Soviet proxies, intervened in force). With the election of Jimmy Carter in 1976, the retreat from containment was given full Presidential sanction. In his first major foreign-policy address, Carter—not content with even the severe reduction in the scope of containment already accomplished by the Nixon Doctrine—congratulated the nation on having overcome its "inordinate fear of Communism" and went on to assert that "historical trends have weakened the foundation" of the two principles that had guided American foreign policy in the past: "a belief that Soviet expansion was almost inevitable and that it must be contained."[5]

On this issue, then, Lyndon Johnson and some of his chief advisers like Dean Rusk and Walt Rostow, who worried about a resurgence of isolationism, were right.

On the other hand, Johnson was wrong in predicting that this resurgence would be accompanied by "a divisive debate about 'who lost Vietnam' "[6] and a concomitant resurgence of McCarthyism. This fear that American intervention in Vietnam would give rise to a new McCarthyism was expressed as early as 1962 by Hans J. Morgenthau and as late as the closing stages of the war by Henry Kissinger. Yet nothing of the sort ever developed—at least not on the Right. After the war was over, military men like Westmoreland defended themselves by saying that they had lost because the politicians had denied them the means by which to win, but hardly anyone seemed to listen. In the Army itself, no "stab-in-the-back" syndrome ever developed after Vietnam;[7] instead there was a great deal of soul-searching, self-criticism, and strategic analysis. Nor did a stab-in-the-back theory take hold in the country at large: one need only compare the obscurity and even disgrace into which Westmoreland fell to the adulation that greeted MacArthur when he made similar complaints about the limitations imposed on him in Korea by the politicians.

As to insinuations of disloyalty and even treason, if they were promiscuously thrown around in the wake of Korea, the situation after Vietnam was in this respect characterized by extreme prudishness. Not only were critics of the war spared accusations of disloyalty; they were celebrated as prophets to whom the country should have listened and heroes who had shown the courage to "tell the truth to power."

Even opponents of the war who had openly sided with the Vietcong and Hanoi—who had marched with Vietcong flags, who had parroted the propaganda of the Communists in speeches and articles and books, who had visited Hanoi and had come back with reports of how well American prisoners-of-war were being treated, and who had denounced their own country as an aggressor and a perpetrator of crimes against humanity—were spared the wrath of public opinion, not to mention prosecution, for acts that at any other time and in any other country would certainly have been regarded as treason. More than spared: Tom Hayden, who had done most of these things, was received at the White House by President Jimmy Carter; Ramsey Clark, who had done most of these things, was sent on a diplomatic mission by the same President Carter; Jane Fonda, who had done most of these things, was rewarded with greater and greater popularity, higher and higher fees, and more and better prizes.

Indeed, in another of those reversals of role to which the war kept giving rise, the only substantial signs of McCarthyism in the Vietnam era appeared on the Left. Thus the investigations of the CIA by several congressional committees in the seventies were a mirror image of the congressional investigations of Communists in the fifties. Like the committees of the McCarthy period, those investigating the CIA featured daily leaks of sensational revelations to a cooperative press, which then helped spread the idea that the Communist once supposedly under every American bed had been replaced by a CIA agent.

Thus too attributions of guilt by association—another feature of McCarthyism—became as standard in the writings of the Left as they had been in such right-wing publications of the fifties as *Red Channels*. For example, when Jeane Kirkpatrick was appointed ambassador to the United Nations by Ronald Reagan in

1981, an article in the *Nation*[8] (subsequently quoted in many other magazines of the Left) connected her with the CIA through her husband, Evron Kirkpatrick, whose brother had allegedly been a high official of the agency. But the official in question (Lyman Kirkpatrick) was not Evron Kirkpatrick's brother or any relation at all. Here, then, was a classic McCarthyite smear: the assumption of guilt by association with even the evidence of association turning out to be false.

If, moreover, McCarthyism means character assassination based on accusations for which there is no solid foundation, the charges of war crimes against both the military and the civilian leadership of the country can also be seen as a symptom of its resurgence on the Left. According to Nixon, Ronald Reagan told him at the time that "CBS under World War II circumstances would have been perhaps charged with treason" for the way it was handling the Christmas bombing,[9] but Reagan never said any such thing in public, and if he had, he would have been ignored or shouted down. So much for McCarthyism of the Right. On the Left, however, accusations of the most serious kind were freely made and widely circulated with impunity, often by means of self-appointed kangaroo courts whose deliberations were respectfully treated by people who had in the past professed outrage at the violation of due process by congressional investigators. Indeed, what Lewy calls "a veritable industry publicizing alleged war crimes"[10] emerged both in the United States and abroad (in the form of the International War Crimes Tribunal organized by Bertrand Russell).

This activity was by no means confined to fringe groups on the Left. In 1970, ten congressmen sponsored a conference in Washington on "War and National Responsibility" in which other congressmen and senators participated along with such nonradical luminaries as Hannah Arendt, Benjamin V. Cohen, Hans J. Morgenthau, Louis Pollak, and Telford Taylor. Though some of the forty participants did not agree that the United States was committing war crimes in Vietnam, few disagreed strongly, and all were only too willing to lend their presence to a conference in which the dominant view was that of Richard A. Falk (professor of international law at Princeton): "The evidence is so abundant and so unambiguous that war crimes *are* being committed in Vietnam by the United States Government that there is no longer any excuse for silence or acquiescence on the part of American citizens." [11] Said the editors of the volume that emerged from the conference (whose title, *War Crimes and the American Conscience,* dispensed with the cautious euphemism of the conference's title): "It would have been inconceivable only a few years ago that a serious and searching discussion of war crimes—including American war crimes—could be conducted under congressional auspices at the Capitol of the United States." [12] Again, so much for McCarthyism of the Right.

To say that a book like *War Crimes and the American Conscience* was a species of McCarthyism is to say that the charges it made were irresponsible and that the way it made those charges showed contempt for the rules of evidence and for the procedures by which accusations can fairly be judged. Of course such conferences and tribunals were not courts of law and were bound by no rules other than those they themselves decided upon; in that sense they had a "right" to do what they did. Nevertheless, in exercising that right, they freely defamed and slandered individuals and groups on the basis of false or faulty or tainted evidence, and witnesses of dubious credibility, in proceedings presided over by biased judges.

The Russell tribunal, for example, was convened, as Russell himself put it, "in order to expose . . . barbarous crimes . . . reported daily from Vietnam." [13] This assumption of guilt before trial was further strengthened by the membership of the tribunal, which was made up entirely of such outspoken supporters of North Vietnam as Jean-Paul Sartre, Stokely Carmichael, Dave Dellinger, and Isaac Deutscher. Not surprisingly, the proceedings largely "relied on evidence supplied by VC/NVA sources or collected in North Vietnam by persons closely aligned politically with the Communist camp." [14] So biased was the entire enterprise that even a radical antiwar activist like Staughton Lynd declined to participate, and even to Richard Falk it seemed "a juridical farce" (which did not prevent him from saying shortly thereafter that it had done a good job of turning up evidence of American war crimes and had "developed persuasively some of the legal implications it seems reasonable to draw from that war").[15]

In the United States itself, similar enterprises were launched. One such was the Vietnam Veterans Against the War (VVAW), whose activities included holding hearings all over the country. At one of these hearings, in Detroit in 1971, more than a hundred veterans were reported to have testified to "war crimes which they either committed or witnessed." Senator Mark Hatfield inserted the transcript of the proceedings into the Congressional Record and demanded an investigation of the charges by the Naval Investigative Service (since mostly marines had been involved). This investigation yielded the following: a refusal by many of the witnesses to be interviewed (despite assurances that they would not be questioned about atrocities they themselves might have committed); inability on the part of one witness to provide details of the atrocities he had described at the Detroit hearings; and "sworn statements of several veterans, corroborated by witnesses"[16] that they had not even attended the hearings at which they allegedly had testified.

But if from a procedural point of view, these (and many others that could be cited) are examples of left-wing McCarthyism, the substantive allegations of criminality "established" by such procedures go beyond McCarthyism in the strict sense. For what the war-crimes industry did was to charge people who had committed certain acts with violating laws that these acts did not in fact violate. (It would be as though a member of the Communist party had been accused of committing a crime in joining the party even though membership in the Communist party was never against the law in the United States.)

For example, one of the crimes with which the United States was most frequently charged was connected with the practice of clearing areas of civilians and then declaring them "free-fire zones" (or "specified strike zones")—that is, areas that could be bombarded by planes and artillery at will. The refugees thus "generated" were placed in camps, and anyone who remained behind was considered Vietcong. Once the area was cleared, evacuees were free to return to their homes, and efforts were made by the authorities to help them do so.

According to an ecumenical committee of American theologians (including among others a black Protestant, Martin Luther King, Jr.; a white Protestant, Harvey Cox; a Roman Catholic, Robert F. Drinan; and a Jew, Abraham Joshua Heschel), this practice was a crime—a "violation of Article 49 of the Civilians Convention of 1949, an article framed to avert repetition of the forcible relocations that took place in World War II." [17] Yet as was so often the case with such confidently asserted accusations by public figures with no special knowledge either of military matters or of international law, this indictment was based on a faulty or ignorant interpretation of the law.

For one thing, the article of the Geneva Convention invoked here applies only to armed international conflict; yet these theologians and those who agreed with them regarded Vietnam as a civil war and therefore had no intellectual right to subject it to laws applicable only to wars between different nations. But assuming that the Vietnam War was an international conflict—as both the United States and South Vietnam claimed it was—and applying Article 49 of the Geneva Convention Relative to the Protection of Civilian Persons in Time of War, we find that this article unambiguously permits the evacuation of civilians from a combat zone and can even be read to *require* "total or partial evacuation of a given area if the security of the population or imperative military reasons so demand." [18]

Other international codes subsequently added their weight to this requirement, as when in 1956 the International Committee of the Red Cross proposed that belligerents "protect the civilian population subject to their authority from the dangers to which they would be exposed in an attack—in particular by removing them from the vicinity of military objectives and from the threatened areas." [19] So too the Secretary General of the United Nations in 1970 (while the war was still going on) proposed that the General Assembly "call on all authorities involved in armed conflicts of all types to do their utmost to insure that civilians are removed from, or kept out of, areas where conditions would be likely to place them in jeopardy or expose them to the hazards of warfare."[20]

The lavish use of firepower by the United States in Vietnam undoubtedly caused destruction of property and civilian casualties. But did it constitute a war crime? Professor Falk had no doubt that it did. The American way of fighting the war, he charged, involved "the massive use of cruel tactics directed indiscriminately against the civilian population in flagrant violation of the minimum rules of war."[21] The same group of theologians who were so certain that the United States was guilty of violating Article 49 of the Geneva Convention were equally certain that American actions in Vietnam also violated "the minimal standards of constraint established by the Hague Convention of 1907 and the Geneva Conventions of 1929 and 1949." In short, "our nation must be judged guilty of having broken almost every established agreement for standards of human decency in time of war."[22]

The tactics condemned here were developed in order to fight an enemy, the Vietcong, whose own tactics involved "clutching the people to their breast" by converting rural hamlets into fortified strongholds that were camouflaged to look like peaceful villages; by disguising themselves as civilians; and by using villagers of all ages and both sexes—little children, women, old men—to plant mines and booby traps and engage in other military activities. As it happens, all *these* practices are clearly forbidden by the laws of war which seek to ensure that innocent civilians are not taken for combatants. Consequently, resistance fighters are required to carry arms openly and have "a fixed distinctive sign recognizable at a distance," and "the presence of a protected person may not be used to render certain points or areas immune from military operations."[23] Professor Falk, so tender of international law when American actions were under consideration, argued that the Vietcong was justified in disregarding these rules on the ground that adherence to the Geneva Convention would have made it impossible for the guerrillas to fight effectively. They had "no alternative other than terror," and they could not wear uniforms or take the care required by international law of wounded or captured enemies. On the other

hand, "the cumulative effect of counterguerrilla warfare is necessarily barbaric and inhumane to such an extent as to taint the
entire effort with a genocidal quality."[24] Or, in the succinct formulation of Gabriel Kolko, a leading revisionist historian of the
cold war: "The war crime in Vietnam is the war itself."[25]

Again, this idea was not confined to the radical fringe of the
antiwar movement. One of the leading "moderate" critics of
the war, Hans J. Morgenthau, made much the same point about
the nature of the American military effort: "We are not fighting
an army. We are not even fighting a group of partisans in the
woods, as the Germans did in Yugoslavia. We are fighting an
entire people. And since everyone in the countryside of Vietnam
is to a lesser or greater degree our potential enemy, it is perfectly
logical to kill everyone in sight."[26]

By these criteria, there was no point in arguing over whether
this or that American battlefield tactic violated this or that provision of the laws of war: the very act of fighting against the
Vietcong was intrinsically or by definition criminal and therefore
gave rise by a "perfectly logical" progression to subsidiary criminal acts. What difference could it then make to Falk or Morgenthau that the laws of war *permit* attacks upon a village or town
that is occupied by a military force or has been fortified, or upon
civilian homes used to store war materials, or even hospitals if
(in the language of the Geneva Convention) "they are used to
commit, outside their humanitarian duties, acts harmful to the
enemy"[27] and due warning has been given to cease such use?
Could it make any difference that the American commander who
destroyed an entire village in response to a single sniper's bullet
was within his legal rights so long as he was honestly exercising
his best judgment as to the size of the enemy force, even though
(as the Nuremberg tribunal declared) "the conclusion reached
may have been faulty"?[28]

None of this would make any difference to Falk, or to Kolko,
or to Morgenthau, or to another "moderate" member of the antiwar movement, Jonathan Schell, whose reports in *The New
Yorker* were so influential in establishing the impression of indiscriminate use of American firepower against civilians in South
Vietnam (they even influenced Robert McNamara when he was

still Secretary of Defense).[29] At the conference on war crimes convened by the ten congressmen, Schell said there were only two alternatives for the United States: "The first is simply to leave and to permit the Vietcong or the North Vietnamese or some combination of them to take over at their leisure." This he found "regrettable," but the second alternative was much worse: it was "to continue what we are now doing—to commit more massacres and to destroy other provinces as we have destroyed Quang Ngai. This course of action—that is to say, our present course of action—leads to the total destruction of the society in South Vietnam."[30]

In other words, whether or not the American effort to save South Vietnam from Communism was intrinsically criminal, it could not be pursued without leading to genocide. Just as we were being forced to destroy the country physically in order to save it, so we were wiping out its entire population for the same purpose.

Of all the crimes with which the United States was charged, genocide was the most serious. Genocide means murdering, or trying to murder, an entire people, and it was in order to reinforce the charge that the United States was doing precisely this in Vietnam that the statistics of bombs dropped and ordnance used were so regularly compared to the tonnages used in World War II (as though such statistics had anything to do with the genocidal program the Germans carried out against the Jews by means of gas chambers); and this is also why the talk of indiscriminate attacks on civilians was so steady and so loud.

Yet at the very time charges of genocide were being made, it was known that the population of South Vietnam was *increasing*. Indeed, no less fervent an antiwar activist than Daniel Ellsberg, speaking in 1970, cautioned against use of the term "genocide" by the movement "even if it is strictly warranted," because "the population of South Vietnam has almost surely increased each year in the last five."[31] So had the population of North Vietnam, despite charges that American bombing was taking a heavy toll of civilian casualties. According to the *United Nations Demographic Yearbook 1974,* the population of South Vietnam went from 16.12 million in 1965 to 19.95 million in 1973, and that of

North Vietnam from 18.71 million in 1965 to 22.70 million in 1973; the annual rates of growth were roughly double that of the United States. "This fact," comments Lewy, "makes the charge of genocide a bit grotesque."[32]

But what about indiscriminate and excessive firepower resulting in an unusually high number of civilian casualties? Here, too, the charge can be characterized as "a bit grotesque." According to Lewy's calculations—which are generous in their definition of civilian and extremely cautious in their reliance on official "body counts"—"the Vietnam War during the years of active American involvement was no more destructive of civilian life, both North and South, than other armed conflicts of this century and a good bit less so than some, such as the Korean War."[33] Whereas as many as 70 percent of those killed in Korea were civilians, in Vietnam the proportion was at most 45 percent, which was approximately the level of civilian casualties in World War II. And of course a substantial percentage of these civilians were killed not by the Americans or the South Vietnamese but by the Vietcong and the North Vietnamese, especially after 1969, when there was a steady decline in American bombing and shelling and combat increasingly occurred farther away from areas in which the rural population lived.[34]

The fact that American battlefield tactics were not in themselves criminal does not mean that the laws of war were never violated in Vietnam. The most notorious such violation was the massacre of anywhere from 200 to 400 inhabitants—most of them old men, women, and children—of the hamlet of My Lai in the village of Son My in March 1968. These executions were justified by no military necessity and were carried out against nonresisting and unarmed persons, and they therefore constituted acts of murder not only under international law but under the specific directives of the American command in Vietnam. Moreover, they were committed in the wake of other violations of these directives, including the failure to issue a warning prior to an attack on a village or hamlet and the concomitant failure to make "maximum effort . . . to minimize noncombatant casualties during tactical operations."[35] For over a year this atrocity was concealed; then an American soldier, who was not connected with the division of which the offending company was a part and who had heard about the massacre, brought it to the attention of the authorities.

Was the My Lai massacre characteristic of the way all "search-and-destroy" missions were carried out? Some said that it was. For example, the psychiatrist Robert Jay Lifton, a well-known antiwar activist, declared: "My Lai epitomizes the Vietnam war . . . because every returning soldier can tell of similar incidents, if on a somewhat smaller scale. . . ."[36] Three other psychiatrists agreed: *"The most important fact about the My Lai massacre is that it was only a minor step beyond the standard, official, routine U.S. policy in Vietnam."*[37] And Hans J. Morgenthau was "firmly convinced that what happened in My Lai and elsewhere were not accidents, or deviations . . . , but the inevitable outgrowth of the kind of war we are waging."[38]

Yet no evidence existed at the time—and none has materialized since—to substantiate the charge that My Lai was typical. Nor is it likely, given the number of antiwar journalists reporting on Vietnam, that if other such atrocities had occurred, they could have been kept secret. Telford Taylor, who had been a prosecutor at Nuremberg and was now a strong opponent of the war, disputed the judgment of Lifton and others on this point: "It has been said that 'the massacre at Son My was not unique,' but I am unaware of any evidence of other incidents of comparable magnitude, and the reported reaction of some of the soldiers at Son My strongly indicates that they regarded it as out of the ordinary."[39]

So, too, Daniel Ellsberg, who believed the war was criminal and even saw himself (having been a government official) as a potential defendant in a war-crimes trial: "My Lai was beyond the bounds of permissible behavior, and that is recognizable by virtually every soldier in Vietnam. They know it was wrong: No shots had been fired at the soldiers, no enemy troops were in the village, nobody was armed. The men who were at My Lai knew there were aspects out of the ordinary. That is why they tried to hide the event, talked about it to no one, discussed it very little even among themselves."[40]

The other question raised by My Lai was the question of responsibility. The officer in charge, Lt. William Calley, who was tried and convicted and punished for the crime, not surprisingly found defenders in political circles that considered such actions justified by the circumstances in which they had been committed. But in what may seem paradoxical at first sight, perhaps his most fervent defenders came out of the ranks of the antiwar movement because they feared that by assigning guilt to Calley or other individuals, the truly guilty parties would be absolved. Said the team of three psychiatrists led by Edward M. Opton, Jr.: *"The major responsibility and guilt for the massacre lie with the elected officials who make U.S. policy in Vietnam and with the high military officials who have misled both elected officials and the general public as to what they have been doing under the name of those policy directives."* In addition to elected officials and high military officials, *"America's citizens share in the responsibility for My Lai. . . . We as a people do bear much of the* responsibility for My Lai. The guilt is in large part collective."[41] Lifton too believed that the guilt was collective, that the American people shared in a "moral or criminal culpability . . . in relationship to the Vietnam War . . . since all of us are part of America and we, one way or another, live in the American realm and contribute to national and military efforts. . . ."[42]

This revival of the doctrine of collective guilt by a movement generally called "liberal" was one of the more bizarre cultural phenomena of the Vietnam period. For nothing could be more repugnant to the moral and legal tradition of liberalism than the idea that an individual can be held responsible for an act he himself did not commit. But the underlying reasoning—that "My Lai epitomizes the Vietnam war" because "the war crime in Vietnam is the war itself"—is a reminder that the discussion of My Lai and other atrocities was disingenuous. The point was not to expose instances of wrongdoing, or to institute training and command procedures that would more effectively deter violations of the law and punish them more severely when they occurred; the point was to discredit the entire American effort to save South Vietnam from Communism.

This is why convincing refutations of the charge that the United States was committing war crimes could be so easily shrugged off by many who had either voiced the charges themselves or nodded in agreement when they were voiced by others. For example, when Lewy's *America in Vietnam* came out in 1978, the response from those former members of the antiwar movement who even bothered to notice was to dismiss his meticulous examination of the issue of war crimes as "legalistic," and then to shift the ground immediately to the question of morality. Leaving it "for the lawyers to decide" how well Lewy had made his case "that American military operations were conducted in substantial conformity with the laws of war," Terry Nardin and Jerome Slater, two academic reviewers with a clear antiwar point of view, went on to assert that "no legal expertise is needed, however, to see the fallacy of Lewy's further conclusion that because the American way of war was not illegal, it was not immoral. It is simply a *non sequitur* that whatever is not prohibited by the laws of war is therefore morally acceptable."[43]

The political theorist Michael Walzer concurred: "In fact, Lewy argues only the legal case, as if morality were a realm to which scholarly qualification doesn't extend. . . . The task Lewy sets for himself turns out to be surprisingly simple, for the laws of war are so vaguely stated and so radically incomplete that a brief for the defense is readily put together. Lewy's brief is 'legalistic' in the common sense of that word, but I would hesitate to say it is wrong. . . . The result, however, is likely to leave the reader more uncomfortable with the law than easy with the war."[44] Finally, Theodore Draper: "It is a continuing shame . . . that the shamefulness of this war should be incidentally mentioned in a book designed to cover up the shame by taking refuge in narrow and dubious legalisms."[45]

Having conceded in the face of Lewy's analysis that "the charge made by some radicals at home that we were fighting a genocidal war in Vietnam was both ignorant and silly," these critics can then blithely assert that "though he scores easy victories against what we might call the gesticulations of the Left—the rhetorical exaggerations and the anti-American or self-hating extravagances of the peace movement—he leaves its core position untouched."[46] Namely, that the war was "a study in military immorality" (Walzer), that "the manner in which it was fought constituted a dramatic collapse of both reason and morality" (Nardin and Slater), that it was marked by "immoral conduct" (Draper).

What Draper and the others then do is fall back on a rehearsal of the familiar catalogue of horrors to which the war in Vietnam gave rise. Quoting from Lewy himself—not that they needed him for this purpose—they describe once again how the designation of a given area as a "free-fire zone" led to the "generating" of refugees, the vast majority of whom were old people, women, and children; how numbers of these were killed because they insisted on returning to their homes after being sent to squalid refugee camps. They speak of how "the fatuous policy of 'body counts' encouraged the indiscriminate lumping of combatants and noncombatants," of how "American military doctrine called for methods that were insensitive to political and human costs"; they emphasize—again taking terms and examples out of Lewy's own book—American "atrocities" and "massacres" and the lenience with which the perpetrators of these crimes were treated by the military courts. They cite the astronomical statistics of bomb tonnages dropped both on South and on North Vietnam, and they speak of how South Vietnam was turned by these bombs and by napalm and defoliants and herbicides into "a barren wasteland."[47]

In dwelling on the horrors of the war in Vietnam, these critics provide ample confirmation of Lewy's argument "that the suffering inflicted upon large segments of South Vietnam's rural population during long years of a high technology warfare . . . undermined the efforts of the Saigon regime to win the allegiance of the people . . . and contributed to the spread of a feeling of resignation, war-weariness, and an unwillingness to go on fighting against the resolute opponent from the North."[48]

What then accounted for the use of such "counterproductive" tactics? Reading the critics, one gets the impression that it was all a matter either of the innate immorality of the military or— what often comes to the same thing in their analyses—the product of the workings of an inflexible bureaucracy. Yet there was a reason that so much firepower was employed in Vietnam. "The American way of war," as it came to be called in the polemics of the period, was based on the motto "Expend Shells Not Men."[49] Was it immoral of American commanders to follow this rule? The antiwar movement thought so, and Lewy's critics still do. "The American way of war was largely responsible for the very high civilian death toll," says Walzer.[50] To rely, as the Americans did, "on massive firepower is not merely a disproportionate response to enemy fire; it is a response that shifts the burden of war from the soldier, who would otherwise have to assume the risks of entering the village to root out enemy soldiers, to the civilian population," write Nardin and Slater (who cite Walzer's book, *Just and Unjust Wars,* as their moral authority).[51] The implication is that it was immoral for American commanders to be more concerned with the lives of their own men than with the lives of Vietnamese who might have been part of the elusive enemy force.

Leaving aside the fact that the civilian death toll in Vietnam was *not* "very high" as compared with Korea and World War II (to repeat: the proportion of civilian deaths was much lower in Vietnam than in Korea and roughly the same as it was in World War II), there is something bizarre in charging an American officer with immorality for adopting methods whose purpose was to minimize American casualties. By normal standards, the men in the field surely had a better case when they made the opposite complaint about the rules of engagement (ROE) which restricted their use of firepower in order to minimize civilian casualties. According to Roger Hilsman, "The military fretted under the limitations, citing incidents in which they took casualties that might have been avoided with more thorough preparatory bombing."[52] These limitations included cumbersome clearance procedures for calling in artillery fire or air strikes—procedures which, in the judgment of Senator Barry Goldwater (who thought they and not the air strikes were shameful) "had as much to do with our casualties as the enemy themselves."[53] No wonder, then, that the rules of engagement were often violated in practice by commanders in the field who—in a tradition that was in the past held to be a special moral glory of the American military—were determined to do everything in their power to protect the men for whose lives they were responsible.

Because of this, stupid though the American way of war no doubt was in the political context of Vietnam—where it served to arouse the hostility of the very people whose "hearts and minds" were being courted and whose support was a necessary ingredient of victory—it could not reasonably be considered immoral. Nor could it even be considered extraordinarily brutal. Writing in 1970, not, obviously, to defend the United States, but out of the expectation that things might yet get worse both in Vietnam and elsewhere, Daniel Ellsberg warned his fellow activists in the antiwar movement that "an escalation of rhetoric can blind us to the fact that Vietnam is . . . no more brutal than other wars in the past—and it is absurdly unhistorical to insist that it is. . . ."[54]

Even granting to writers like the sociologist Peter L. Berger that "the war was marked by a distinctive brutality . . . flowing in large measure from its character as a war of counterinsurgency,"[55] Ellsberg's point was so obviously true that it poses a difficult intellectual problem. One can easily enough understand how the young of the 1960s—who were in general notoriously deficient in historical knowledge or understanding, and who therefore tended to look upon all the ills around them, including relatively minor ones, as unique in their evil dimension—would genuinely imagine that never in all of human experience had there been anything to compare in cruelty and carnage with the war in Vietnam. But how did it happen that so many of their elders and teachers, who did have historical perspective and had even lived through two earlier and bloodier wars, should have taken so "absurdly unhistorical" a view of Vietnam? The answer is, quite simply, that they opposed—or had turned against—the American effort to save South Vietnam from Communism. Being against the end, they could not tolerate the very means whose earlier employment in Korea and in World War II they had not only accepted but applauded.

In World War II, as Lewy says, "despite the fact that the

Allies . . . engaged in terror-bombing of the enemy's civilian population and generally paid only minimal attention to the prevention of civilian casualties—even during the liberation of Italy and France—hardly anyone on the Allied side objected to these tactics." The reason was that "the war against Nazism and fascism was regarded as a moral crusade in which the Allies could do no wrong. . . ."[56]

So, too, with the Korean War, in which practically all the major population centers were leveled, dams and irrigation systems were bombed, napalm was used, and enormous numbers of civilians were killed. Yet there was no morbidly fascinated dwelling on those horrors in the press, and very little moral outrage expressed. For the Korean War was seen as an extension of World War II not merely in the strategic sense of representing a new phase in the resistance to aggression through the principle of collective security, but also in being part of a moral crusade against Communism. As such it was a continuation of the struggle against totalitarianism, whose first battles had been fought and won in the Second World War.

The fact that this aspect of the Korean War was rarely emphasized in the offical pronouncements, which tended to dwell upon the strategic element, does not mean that it was considered less important. It means rather that it was taken so entirely for granted as to need little if any explicit stress. The consensus of the period was that Communism represented an evil comparable to and as great as Nazism. This was the feeling in the country at large, and it was even the prevalent view within the intellectual community where Communism was regarded—not least by many who had earlier embraced it—as the other great embodiment of totalitarianism, the twentieth century's distinctive improvement upon the despotisms and tyrannies of the past. In one of the most influential books of the Korean War period, *The Origins of Totalitarianism,* Hannah Arendt brought Nazism and Communism together under the same rubric as systems of total control (in contrast to the traditional despotisms which exercised lesser degrees of domination over the individuals living under them). Indeed, Arendt went even further, arguing that Hitler, for all his anti-Communist passion, had looked admiringly to Lenin and

Stalin for lessons in the practical implementation of his own brand of totalitarianism.

To go to war in order to contain the spread of Communism was therefore on the same moral plane as going to war against Nazism had been, "and those who fought such a war could do no wrong" either. "There was hideous bloodletting in Korea," wrote Richard H. Rovere in 1967, "and few liberals protested it";[57] he himself, as we have seen, celebrated the Korean War as "a turning point in the world struggle against Communism."[58] Having then believed that "we had an obligation" to go to the aid of the government in South Vietnam when it was threatened by a combination of internal and external Communist aggression, by 1967 he had come to feel that the American role was indefensible. "People who used to say there are things worse than war now say there are things worse than Communism and that the war in Vietnam is one of them."[59] Rovere himself was clearly one of those people, and their number was now legion. It was because they no longer thought that Communism was so great an evil that they saw the American war against it as a greater evil than it truly was, either by comparison with other wars, or more emphatically, in relation to the political system whose extension to South Vietnam the war was being fought to prevent.

2.

Here then we arrive at the center of the moral issue posed by the American intervention into Vietnam.

The United States sent half a million men to fight in Vietnam. More than 50,000 of them lost their lives, and many thousands more were wounded. Billions of dollars were poured into the effort, damaging the once unparalleled American economy to such an extent that the country's competitive position was grievously impaired. The domestic disruptions to which the war gave rise did perhaps even greater damage to a society previously so self-confident that it was often accused of entertaining illusions of its own omnipotence. Millions of young people growing to maturity during the war developed attitudes of such hostility toward their own country and the civilization embodied by its institutions that their willingness to defend it against external enemies in the future was left hanging in doubt.

Why did the United States undertake these burdens and make these sacrifices in blood and treasure and domestic tranquillity? What was in it for the United States? It was a question that plagued the antiwar movement from beginning to end because the answer was so hard to find. If the United States was simply acting the part of an imperialist aggressor in Vietnam, as many in the antiwar movement professed to believe, it was imperialism of a most peculiar kind. There were no raw materials to exploit in Vietnam, and there was no overriding strategic interest involved. To Franklin Roosevelt in 1941 Indochina had been important because it was close to the source of rubber and tin, but this was no longer an important consideration. Toward the end of the war, it was discovered that there was oil off the coast of Vietnam and antiwar radicals happily seized on this news as at last providing an explanation for the American presence there. But neither Kennedy nor Johnson knew about the oil, and even if they had, they would hardly have gone to war for its sake in those pre-OPEC days when oil from the Persian Gulf could be had at two dollars a barrel.

In the absence of an economic interpretation, a psychological version of the theory of imperialism was developed to answer the maddening question: *Why are we in Vietnam?* This theory held that the United States was in Vietnam because it had an urge to dominate—"to impose its national obsessions on the rest of the world," in the words of a piece in the *New York Review of Books,*[60] one of the leading centers of antiwar agitation within the intellectual community. But if so, the psychic profits were as illusory as the economic ones, for the war was doing even deeper damage to the national self-confidence than to the national economy.

Yet another variant of the psychological interpretation, proposed by the economist Robert L. Heilbroner, was that "the fear of losing our place in the sun, of finding ourselves at bay, . . . motivates a great deal of the anti-Communism on which so much of American foreign policy seems to be founded." This was especially so in such underdeveloped countries as Vietnam, where "the rise of Communism would signal the end of capitalism as the dominant world order, and would force the acknowledgment that America no longer constituted the model on which the future of world civilization would be mainly based." [61]

All these theories were developed out of a desperate need to find or invent selfish or self-interested motives for the American presence in Vietnam, the better to discredit it morally. In a different context, proponents of one or another of these theories— Senator Fulbright, for example—were not above trying to discredit the American presence politically by insisting that *no* national interest was being served by the war. This latter contention at least had the virtue of being closer to the truth than the former. For the truth was that the United States went into Vietnam for the sake not of its own direct interests in the ordinary sense but for the sake of an ideal. The intervention was a product of the Wilsonian side of the American character—the side that went to war in 1917 to "make the world safe for democracy" and that found its contemporary incarnations in the liberal internationalism of the 1940s and the liberal anti-Communism of the 1950s. One can characterize this impulse as naive; one can describe it, as Heilbroner does (and as can be done with any virtuous act), in terms that give it a subtly self-interested flavor. But there is no rationally defensible way in which it can be called immoral.

Why, then, were we in Vietnam? To say it once again: because we were trying to save the Southern half of that country from the evils of Communism. But was the war we fought to accomplish this purpose morally worse than Communism itself? Peter L. Berger, who at the time was involved with Clergy and Laymen Concerned About Vietnam (CALCAV), wrote in 1967: "All sorts of dire results might well follow a reduction or a withdrawal of the American engagement in Vietnam. Morally speaking, however, it is safe to assume that none of these could be worse than what is taking place right now." Unlike most of his fellow members of CALCAV, Berger would later repent of this statement. Writing in 1980, he would say of it: "Well, it was *not* safe to assume. . . . I was wrong and so were all those who thought as I did." For "contrary to what most members (including myself) of the antiwar movement expected, the peoples of Indochina have, since 1975, been subjected to suffering far worse than anything that was inflicted upon them by the United States and its allies.''[62]

To be sure, the "bloodbath" that had been feared by supporters of the war did not occur—not in the precise form that had been anticipated. In contrast to what they did upon taking power in Hanoi in 1954 (when they murdered some 50,000 landlords), or what they did during their brief occupation of Hué during the Tet offensive of 1968 (when they massacred 3,000 civilians), the Communists did not stage mass executions in the newly conquered South. According to Nguyen Cong Hoan, who had been an NLF agent and then became a member of the National Assembly of the newly united Communist Vietnam before disillusionment drove him to escape in March 1977, there were more executions in the provinces than in the cities and the total number might well have reached into the tens of thousands. But as another fervent opponent of the war, the New York *Times* columnist Tom Wicker was forced to acknowledge, "what Vietnam has given us instead of a bloodbath [is] a vast tide of human misery in Southeast Asia—hundreds of thousands of homeless persons in United Nations camps, perhaps as many more dead in flight, tens of thousands of the most pitiable forcibly repatriated to Cambodia, no one knows how many adrift on the high seas or wandering the roads."[63]

Among the refugees Wicker was talking about here were those who came to be known as "the boat people" because they "literally threw themselves upon the South China Sea in small coastal craft. . . ."[64] Many thousands of these people were ethnic Chinese who were being driven out and forced to pay everything they had for leaky boats; tens of thousands more were Vietnamese fleeing voluntarily from what Nguyen Cong Hoan describes as "the most inhuman and oppressive regime they have ever known."[65] The same judgment is made by Truong Nhu Tang, the former Minister of Justice in the PRG who fled in November 1979 in a boat loaded with forty refugees: "Never has any previous regime brought such masses of people to such desperation. Not the military dictators, not the colonialists, not even the ancient Chinese overlords."[66]

So desperate were they to leave that they were willing to take the poor chance of survival in flight rather than remain. Says Nguyen Cong Hoan: ". . . Our people have a traditional attachment to their country. No Vietnamese would willingly leave home, homeland, and ancestors' graves. During the most oppressive French colonial rule and Japanese domination, no one escaped by boat at great risk to their lives. Yet you see that my countrymen by the thousands and from all walks of life, including a number of disillusioned Vietcongs, continue to escape from Vietnam; six out of ten never make it, and for those who are fortunate to make it, they are not allowed to land."[67] Adds one of the disillusioned who did make it, Doan Van Toai: "Among the boat people who survived, including those who were raped by pirates and those who suffered in the refugee camps, nobody regrets his escape from the present regime."[68]

Though they invented a new form of the Communist bloodbath, the North Vietnamese (for, to repeat, before long there were no Southerners in authority in the South, not even former members of the NLF and the PRG) were less creative in dealing with political opposition, whether real or imagined. The "re-education camps" they had always used for this purpose in the North were now extended to the South, but the result was not so much an indigenous system of Vietnamese concentration camps as an imitation of the Soviet Gulag. (*The Vietnamese Gulag*, indeed, was the name Doan Van Toai gave to the book he published about the camps in 1979.) The French journalist Jean Lacouture, who had supported the Communists during the war to the point (as he now admitted) of turning himself into a "vehicle and intermediary for a lying and criminal propaganda, [an] ingenuous spokesman for tyranny in the name of liberty,"[69] now tried to salvage his integrity by telling the truth about a re-education camp he was permitted to visit by a regime that had good reason to think him friendly. "It was," he wrote, "a prefabricated hell."[70]

Doan Van Toai, who had been in the jails over which so much

moral outrage had been expended in the days of Thieu, describes
the conditions he himself encountered when he was arrested by
the Communists: "I was thrown into a three-foot-by-six-foot cell
with my left hand chained to my right foot and my right hand
chained to my left foot. My food was rice mixed with sand. . . .
After two months in solitary confinement, I was transferred to a
collective cell, a room 15 feet wide and 25 feet long, where at
different times anywhere from 40 to 100 prisoners were crushed
together. Here we had to take turns lying down to sleep, and
most of the younger, stronger prisoners slept sitting up. In the
sweltering heat, we also took turns snatching a few breaths of
fresh air in front of the narrow opening that was the cell's only
window. Every day I watched my friends die at my feet."[71]

Toai adds: "One South Vietnamese Communist, Nguyen Van
Tang, who was detained 15 years by the French, eight years by
Diem, six years by Thieu, and who is still in jail today, this time
in a Communist prison, told me: . . . 'My dream now is not to be
released; it is not to see my family. My dream is that I could be
back in a French prison 30 years ago.' "[72]

No one knows how many people were sent to the Vietnamese
Gulag. Five years after the fall of Saigon, estimates ranged from
150,000 to a million. Prime Minister Pham Van Dong, who so
impressed Mary McCarthy with his nobility in 1968, told a
French magazine ten years later that he had "*released* more than
one million prisoners from the camps,"[73] although according to
the figures of his own government he had arrested only 50,000 in
the first place.

These prisoners naturally included officials of the former government of South Vietnam, but many opponents of the Thieu
regime could also be found among them, some of whom were by
1981 known to have died in the camps. One such was Thic Thien
Minh, "the strategist of all the Buddhist peace movements in
Saigon, . . . who was sentenced to 10 years in jail by the Thieu
regime, then released after an outpouring of protest from Vietnamese and antiwar protesters around the world," and who died
after six months of detention by the Communists in 1979. Another was Tran Van Tuyen, a leader of the opposition to Thieu in

the Saigon Assembly. A third was the philosopher Ho Huu Tuong, "perhaps the leading intellectual in South Vietnam," who died in a Communist prison in 1980. All these—along with other opponents of Thieu possibly still alive, like Bui Tuong Huan, former president of Hué University; Father Tran Huu Thanh, a dissident Catholic priest; and Tran Ngoc Chau, whose own brother had been a North Vietnamese agent—were arrested (and of course held without trial) "in order," says Toai, "to preempt any possible opposition to the Communists."[74]

Before the Communist takeover, there had been a considerable degree of political freedom in South Vietnam which manifested itself in the existence of many different parties. After the North Vietnamese conquest, all these parties were dissolved; as for the NLF, "they buried it," in the bitter words of Truong Nhu Tang, "without even a ceremony," and "at the simple farewell dinner we held to formally disband the NLF in late 1976 neither the party nor the government sent a representative." The people of Vietnam, who "want only the freedom to go where they wish, educate their children in the schools they choose and have a voice in their government," are instead "treated like ants in a colony. There is only the opportunity to follow orders strictly, never the opportunity to express disagreement. Even within the [Communist] party, the principle of democracy has been destroyed in favor of the most rigid hierarchy. Stalinism, discredited throughout most of the Communist world, flourishes under the aged and fanatic Vietnamese leadership."[75]

Reading these words, one recalls Susan Sontag, Mary McCarthy, and Frances FitzGerald expending their intellectual energies on the promulgation of theories of Vietnamese culture calculated to deny that the people of Vietnam cared about freedom in the simple concrete terms set forth by Tang. One recalls Sontag saying that "incorporation" into a society like that of North Vietnam would "greatly improve the lives of most people in the world." One also recalls that both Sontag and McCarthy were troubled by the portraits of Stalin they saw all over the North; they were there, Sontag thought, because the Vietnamese could not bear to waste anything. Perhaps that is also how she would explain why portraits of Soviet leaders began appearing in public buildings, schools, and administrative offices throughout South Vietnam after 1975, and why the following poem by To Huu, president of the Communist Party Committee of Culture and a possible successor to Pham Van Dong,[76] was given a prominent place in an anthology of contemporary Vietnamese poetry published in Hanoi in the seventies:

> *Oh, Stalin! Oh, Stalin!*
> *The love I bear my father, my mother, my wife, myself*
> *It's nothing beside the love I bear you.*
> *Oh, Stalin! Oh, Stalin!*
> *What remains of the earth and of the sky!*
> *Now that you are dead.*[77]

Written on the occasion of Stalin's death, this poem no doubt earned its place in an anthology twenty years later by virtue of its relevance to the spirit of the new Communist Vietnam. For if the Vietnamese Communist party is Stalinist, so is the society over which it rules. "Immediately after the fall of Saigon, the Government closed all bookshops and theaters. All books published under the former regimes were confiscated or burned. Cultural literature was not exempt, including translations of Jean-Paul Sartre, Albert Camus and Dale Carnegie [!]. . . . The new regime replaced such books with literature designed to indoctrinate children and adults with the idea that the 'Soviet Union is a paradise of the socialist world.' "[78]

As with books, so with newspapers. Under the old regime, under constant attack throughout the world for its repressiveness, there had been *twenty-seven* daily newspapers, three television stations, and more than twenty radio stations. "When the Communists took over," writes the political analyst Carl Gershman, "these were all closed down, and replaced by two official dailies, one television channel, and two radio stations—all disseminating the same government propaganda."[79]

All the other freedoms that existed, either in full or large measure, under the Thieu regime were also eliminated by the Communists. Freedom of movement began to be regulated by a system of internal passports, and freedom of association was abolished to the point where even a large family gathering, such as a wedding or a funeral, required a government permit and was attended by a security officer.

Freedom of religion, too, was sharply curtailed. The Buddhists, who were so effective an element in the opposition to Diem, soon learned that there were worse regimes than his. A Human Rights Appeal drafted by the Unified Buddhist Church and smuggled out by the Venerable Thich Manh Giac when he escaped by boat, charged that the government, "pursuing the policy of shattering the religious communities in our country, . . . has arrested hundreds of monks, confiscated hundreds of pagodas and converted them to government administration buildings, removed and smashed Buddha and Bodhisattva statues, prohibited celebration of the Buddha's birthday as a national holiday, . . . and forbidden monks to travel and preach by ordering restrictions in the name of 'national security.' "[80]

Unlike demonstrations by Buddhists in 1963, this appeal fell on deaf ears; whereas a raid on a Buddhist temple led directly to the overthrow of Diem, a similar raid by the Communist police in April 1977 went unnoticed; and whereas the self-immolation of a single Buddhist monk in 1963 attracted the horrified attention of the whole world, the self-immolation of twelve Buddhist nuns and priests on November 2, 1975, in protest against Communist repression, received scarcely any notice either in the United States or anywhere else.

When all this is combined with the terrible economic hardships that descended upon Vietnam after 1975—hardships that were simultaneously caused by the new regime and used by it to justify resettling millions of people in the so-called New Economic Zones, remote jungle areas where they worked "in collective gangs at such tasks as clearing land and digging canals,"[81] under primitive living conditions with little food and rampant disease —it is easy to see why a sense of despair soon settled over the country. Truong Nhu Tang: "The fact is that today Communism has been rejected by the people and that even many party members are questioning their faith. Members of the former resistance, their sympathizers and those who supported the Vietcong are disgusted and filled with bitterness. These innocent people swear openly that had they another chance their choice would be very different. The common heard expression is: 'I would give them not even a grain of rice, I pull them out of their hiding holes and denounce them to the authorities.' " [82]

The Buddhist human-rights appeal conveyed much the same impression: "Since the liberation thousands have committed suicide out of despair. Thousands have fled the country in small boats. Hospitals are reserved for cadres; civilians hardly have a chance to be hospitalized in case of sickness, while more than 200 doctors remain in detention. Schoolchildren under fourteen have been assigned to collect pieces of scrap material in big garbage heaps and other places during the summer vacation. . . . A country that used to export rice has no rice to eat, even though the number of 'laborers' has now increased about ten times." The government, the appeal went on to say, prohibits "creative thinking and participation of independent groups. Totalitarianism destroys all possibility of genuine national reconciliation and concord." [83]

Some years after these words were written, a great and angry dispute broke out in the United States over the question of whether there was any practical validity or moral point in the distinction between authoritarianism and totalitarianism. Not surprisingly, those who dismissed the distinction as academic were in general veterans of the antiwar movement, who still refused to see that (as Gershman said in 1978) "for the Vietnamese, the distinction between a society that is authoritarian . . . and one that is totalitarian" turned out to be anything but academic. [84]

Peter L. Berger, one of the few former members of the antiwar movement who recognizes that "the transformation of Saigon into Ho Chi Minh City now offers a crystal-clear illustration of the difference between authoritarianism and totalitarianism, both in terms of political science and political morality," expresses amazement at "the persistent incapacity of even American professors to grasp a difference understood by every taxi driver in

Prague." He believes that this incapacity derives in large part from a strong ideological interest in hiding "the fact that totalitarianism today is limited to socialist societies"—a fact that "flies in the face of the socialist dream that haunts the intellectual imagination of the West. . . ."[85]

I have no doubt that Berger is right about this. But where Vietnam in particular is concerned, there is a strong interest not only in protecting the socialist dream in general but, more specifically, in holding on to the sense of having been on the morally superior side in opposing the American struggle to prevent the replacement of an authoritarian regime in the South with a totalitarian system. The truth is that the antiwar movement bears a certain measure of responsibility for the horrors that have overtaken the people of Vietnam; and so long as those who participated in that movement are unwilling to acknowledge this, they will go on trying to discredit the idea that there is a distinction between authoritarianism and totalitarianism. For to recognize the distinction is to recognize that in making a contribution to the conquest of South Vietnam by the Communists of the North, they were siding with an evil system against something much better from every political and moral point of view.

Some veterans of the antiwar movement have protected themselves from any such acknowledgment of guilt by the simple expedient of denying that there is any truth in the reports by refugees like Toai, Coan, and Tang or journalists like Lacouture. Noam Chomsky, for example, speaks of "the extreme unreliability" of these reports,[86] and he is echoed by William Kunstler, Dave Dellinger, and other inveterate apologists for the Vietnamese Communists. Peter Berger compares such people to "individuals who deny the facts of the Holocaust" and rightly considers them "outside the boundaries of rational discourse."[87]

There are, however, others—like the editors of the Socialist magazine *Dissent,* Irving Howe and Michael Walzer—who are fully aware of the horrors that have followed the American withdrawal and the Communist conquest, and who are at least willing to ask, "Were We Wrong About Vietnam?" But of course their answer to this question is No. They were right because they were against both Saigon *and* Hanoi; they were right "in refusing to support the imperial backers of both." What then did they support? "Some of us . . . hoped for the emergence of a Vietnamese 'third force' capable of rallying the people in a progressive direction by enacting land reforms and defending civil liberties." But since, as they admit, there was very little chance of any such alternative, to have thrown their energies into opposing the American effort was tantamount to working for the Communist victory they say they did not want. Nevertheless, they still congratulate themselves on being against the evils on both sides of the war: "Those of us who opposed American intervention yet did not want a Communist victory were in the difficult position of having no happy ending to offer—for the sad reason that no happy ending was possible any longer, if ever it had been. And we were in the difficult position of urging a relatively complex argument at a moment when most Americans, pro- and antiwar, wanted blinding simplicities." [88] This is not moral choice; this is moral evasion—irresponsible utopianism disguised as moral realism. Given the actual alternatives that existed, what did the urging of "a relatively complex argument" avail for any purpose other than to make those who urged it feel pleased with themselves? If it served any purpose at all for the people of South Vietnam, it was to help deliver them over to the "blinding simplicities" of the totalitarianism Howe and Walzer so piously deplore and whose hideous workings they are now happy to denounce and protest against, even though there is no one in Ho Chi Minh City or Hanoi to listen or to hear.

Another veteran of the antiwar movement, Professor Stanley Hoffmann of Harvard, who also sees "no reason not to protest the massacres, arbitrary arrests, and persecutions perpetrated by the regimes that have taken over after our exit," nevertheless urges "those who condemned the war . . . to resist all attempts to make them feel guilty for the stand they took against the war." It was not, says Hoffmann, the antiwar movement that contributed to these horrors, but rather the people (led by Nixon and Kissinger) who were supposedly fighting to prevent them. True as this was of Vietnam—where "a monstrously disproportionate and self-destructive campaign" only added "to the crimes and degradation of eventual Communist victory"—it was even truer of Cambodia. "All those who, somehow, believe that the sufferings inflicted on the Cambodian people, first by the Pol Pot regime, and now by the Vietnamese, retrospectively justify America's attempt to save Phnom Penh from the Reds" were instructed by Hoffmann in 1979 to read a new book "showing that the monsters who decimated the Cambodian people were brought to power by Washington's policies."[89]

The book Hoffmann was referring to, *Sideshow: Kissinger, Nixon and the Destruction of Cambodia,* by the English journalist William Shawcross, sought to demonstrate that those Americans who fought to stop the Communists from coming to power in Cambodia were responsible for the crimes the Communists committed when the fight against them was lost. They can be held responsible, not as one might imagine because they did not fight as hard as they should have, or because in the end they deserted the field, but on the contrary because they entered the field in the first place. By attacking—first by bombing, then by invading—the North Vietnamese sanctuaries in Cambodia, the Americans (that is, Nixon and Kissinger) not only drove the Communists deeper into Cambodia, thereby bringing the war to areas that had previously been at peace. They also intensified the rage and bitterness of the Khmer Rouge (as the Cambodian Communists under Pol Pot were called), thereby turning them into perhaps the most murderous rulers ever seen on the face of the earth.

Sideshow is a brilliantly written and argued book. Indeed, not since Hannah Arendt's *Eichmann in Jerusalem*—which shifts a large measure of responsibility for the murder of six million Jews from the Nazis who committed the murders to the Jewish leaders who were trying to save as many of their people as they could—has there been so striking an illustration of the perverse moral and intellectual uses to which brilliance can be put.

There are, for example, the clever distortions and omissions that enable Shawcross to charge the Nixon Administration with having destabilized the neutral government of Prince Norodom

Sihanouk by bombing the sanctuaries (when in fact Sihanouk welcomed these attacks on the Communist military bases within his own country which he himself was not powerful enough to banish) and with causing large numbers of civilian casualties by the indiscriminate pattern of the bombing raids (when in fact care was taken to minimize civilian casualties). But what is fully on a par of perversity with Hannah Arendt's interpretation of the Jewish role in the genocidal program of the Nazis against them is the idea that Pol Pot and his followers needed the experience of American bombing and the "punishment" they subsequently suffered in the war against the anti-Communist forces of Cambodia to turn them into genocidal monsters.

This idea about the Khmer Rouge can easily enough be refuted by the simple facts of the case. Thus according to Kenneth Quinn, who conducted hundreds of interviews with refugees from Cambodia, the Khmer Rouge began instituting the totalitarian practices of their revolutionary program in areas they controlled as early as 1971.[90] So too Father François Ponchaud, who was in Phnom Penh when the Communists arrived and whose book *Cambodia: Year Zero* Shawcross himself calls "the best account of Khmer Rouge rule":[91] "The evacuation of Phnom Penh follows traditional Khmer revolutionary practice: ever since 1972 the guerrilla fighters had been sending all the inhabitants of the villages and towns they occupied into the forests to live, often burning their homes so they would have nothing to come back for."[92]

Indeed, as Shawcross himself points out, this revolutionary program was outlined in uncannily clear detail in the thesis written at the University of Paris in 1959 by Khieu Samphan, who would later become the Khmer Rouge commander in chief during the war and the head of state afterward. But Shawcross, in line with his own thesis that it was the war that made "the Khmer Rouge . . . more and more vicious,"[93] stresses that "the methods this twenty-eight-year-old Marxist prescribed in 1959 for the transformation of his country were essentially moderate."[94] In support of the same thesis, he quotes Quinn to the effect that "the first steps to change radically the nature of Khmer society" that the Khmer Rouge took in 1971 were "limited."[95]

What Shawcross fails or refuses to see is what Ponchaud understands about such moderate methods and limited steps—namely, that they remained moderate and limited only so long as the Khmer Rouge lacked the power to put them into practice. "Accusing foreigners cannot acquit the present leaders of Kampuchea," Ponchaud wrote (before the Vietnamese invaded Cambodia and replaced the Khmer Rouge Communists with a puppet Communist regime of their own); "their inflexible ideology has led them to invent a radically new kind of man in a radically new society." Or again: "On April 17, 1975, a society collapsed; another is now being born from the fierce drive of a revolution which is incontestably the most radical ever to take place in so short a time. It is a perfect example of the application of an ideology pushed to the furthest limits of its internal logic." [96]

The blindness to the power of ideas that prevents Shawcross from recognizing ideology as the source of the crimes committed against their own people by the Khmer Rouge is his greatest intellectual sin. It is a species of philistinism to which many contemporary intellectuals (who, as intellectuals, might be expected to attribute a disproportionate importance to the role of ideas) are paradoxically prone, and it takes the form of looking for material factors to account for historical developments even when, as in this case, the main causal element is clearly located in the realm of ideas.

But this sin is exceeded in seriousness by the moral implications of Shawcross's book. As Peter W. Rodman (who has been an aide to Henry Kissinger both in and out of government) says in concluding a devastating critique of Shawcross's scholarship: "By no stretch of moral logic can the crimes of mass murderers be ascribed to those who struggled to prevent their coming into power. One hopes that no craven sophistry will ever induce free peoples to accept the doctrine that Shawcross embodies: that resistance to totalitarianism is immoral." [97]

Yet it is just this "craven sophistry" that Stanley Hoffmann reaffirms in the very face of the horrors that have befallen the peoples of Indochina under Communist rule: "As Frances FitzGerald put it," he writes, "our mistake was in creating and building up 'the wrong side,' and we were led by that mistake to a course of devastation *and* defeat."[98] One can almost forgive Anthony Lewis for asking "What future possibility could be more terrible than the reality of what is happening to Cambodia now?"[99] since he asked this question before the Khmer Rouge took over. One can almost forgive the New York *Times* for the headline "Indochina Without Americans: For Most, A Better Life" on a piece from Phnom Penh by Sydney H. Schanberg[100] since it was written before the Khmer Rouge had begun evacuating the city and instituting a regime that led to the death of nearly half the population of the country. Such writers should have known enough about the history of Communism to know better, and they should now be ashamed of their naivete and of the contribution they made to the victory of forces they had a moral duty to oppose. Nevertheless, they were not yet aware of what Hoffmann already knew when he *still* described the Communists as the right side in Indochina and still denounced those who resisted them as immoral and even criminal. This is almost impossible to forgive.

In May 1977, two full years after the Communist takeover, President Jimmy Carter—a repentant hawk, like many members of his cabinet, including his Secretary of State and his Secretary of Defense—spoke of "the intellectual and moral poverty" of the policy that had led us into Vietnam and had kept us there for so long. When Ronald Reagan, an unrepentant hawk, called the war "a noble cause" in the course of his ultimately successful campaign to replace Carter in the White House, he was accused of having made a "gaffe." Fully, painfully aware as I am that the American effort to save Vietnam from Communism was indeed beyond our intellectual and moral capabilities, I believe the story shows that Reagan's "gaffe" was closer to the truth of why we were in Vietnam and what we did there, at least until the very end, than Carter's denigration of an act of imprudent idealism whose moral soundness has been so overwhelmingly vindicated by the hideous consequences of our defeat.

POSTSCRIPT TO THE TOUCHSTONE EDITION:

THE ISSUE OF "FULL DISCLOSURE"

IN THE EARLY drafts of this book, there was a short section describing the evolution of my own position on Vietnam. In the end, however, I eliminated this section as well as several other personal references that had been scattered throughout the manuscript. The main reason I did so was that whenever I made an appearance as a character in the story, the tone seemed to go off, and no matter how much I fiddled with the prose, these personal references remained jarring and incongruous. As an alternative, I considered putting them into the Notes at the back of the book, or writing a special preface or an appendix. But resorting to mechanical devices did not solve the problem of propriety. The fact was that to introduce autobiographical material was to violate the impersonal character of the book I had written, and so I cut it out.

Anyone in the least familiar with my work will know that I have never been shy in talking about myself in print; indeed, as a writer

I have made something of a notorious specialty of using my own experience as a way into the discussion of large public issues. In addition to several such essays, I have written two books in this autobiographical or confessional mode, *Making It* (1967) and *Breaking Ranks* (1979). Both of these books were available in paperback when the original edition of *Why We Were in Vietnam* was published. Therefore I concluded that there was really no need to cover the same ground again, especially as *Breaking Ranks,* which goes into great detail on how I felt about Vietnam from beginning to end, had come out so recently that it would still be fresh in the memory of any interested party.

Since I am now reverting to the confessional mode, I might as well go the whole way and admit that I had another reason for cutting out those personal references. This was my wish to escape the charge, so frequently made against me in the past, that I was incapable of writing about any subject without bringing myself into it. In editing and revising the early drafts of this book, which still contained the personal material, I concluded that if the charge were to be made against me *this* time, it might for once be justified.

Instead, the main and often the only charge made against the book by hostile reviewers was that I had left myself out of it. The reason, they alleged, was that I was trying to cover up my own record of opposition to the war. Having been warned by several early readers of the manuscript that this would happen unless I put myself back into the book, I suppose I had no business being amazed when it did; nevertheless I was, and still am.

Amazed or not, however, and convinced though I remained that cutting myself out of this book had been the right thing to do from the point of view of literary and intellectual propriety, there could be no question that it had been a serious political error. I do not doubt that hostile critics would have derided me for excessive preoccupation with self if I had brought my own record in. On the other hand, it would have been harder for them to divert attention from the questions I raised about Vietnam and to focus the discussion instead on the issue of my character.

Be that as it may, in the hope of disposing of that issue, and so freeing this book to serve the purpose for which it was written in the first place, I have decided to add an account of where I stood on the war to this new Touchstone edition.

2.

I first became seriously interested in Vietnam in 1961, and from the start, I was skeptical about the wisdom of American military intervention. In the beginning this skepticism mainly expressed itself indirectly—through the articles I commissioned or chose to publish in *Commentary* (of which I had become the editor in 1960). The first such article, referred to on page 18 above, was written by Joseph J. Zasloff shortly after the Taylor mission of 1961 had recommended an expansion of the American military commitment. While stipulating that "aggressive and flexible military measures" by the South Vietnamese "were necessary to eliminate the guerrillas," Zasloff emphasized that "force alone cannot solve the problem," and he strongly suggested that even in combination with "the right political, economic, and social policies," only a very large American military commitment had any chance of being effective. Not only did I agree with this analysis; in later years, I often pointed proudly to the Zasloff article as an indication that *Commentary*—in the phrase George McGovern once used of himself—had been "right from the start" on Vietnam.

It was, however, with even greater pride that I later pointed to an article by Hans J. Morgenthau entitled "Vietnam—Another Korea?" that I featured as the lead piece in the May 1962 issue of *Commentary*. Morgenthau was even more prescient than Zasloff in predicting that "the present primarily military approach" was dragging us into a war that "cannot be won quickly, if it can be won at all," and that it was bound to have "a profound impact upon the political health of the nation."

From that point on—and with the exception of two dissenting pieces in defense of the war by Oscar Gass—I ran article after article in *Commentary* criticizing American policy. I did not, of course, agree with every word of these articles, but I certainly shared in the general perspective from which they were mainly written: that Vietnam was, in the familiar slogan, "the wrong war at the wrong time and in the wrong place." Wrong not morally but from a prudential point of view. Wrong not because the Communists were a benevolent force against whom we had no right to fight, but because we would be unable to win such a war in such a place at acceptable cost. Wrong because in any event the issue in Vietnam was fundamentally "political" and could not be resolved by military means.

Unlike Morgenthau, who gradually departed from this position in favor of the highly moralizing stance exemplified in some of the statements quoted above (e.g., pages 105, 185, and 188), I stuck with it on the whole until the bitter end, and even beyond. If Morgenthau had not broken with *Commentary* in 1964 over a different matter, we would undoubtedly have broken over Vietnam. For even as early as the mid-sixties, I found myself increasingly repelled by the hysterical denunciations of the United States for immorality and criminality that were becoming the standard rhetoric of the antiwar movement in general and that Morgenthau was uncritically endorsing. In *Making It,* published in December 1967 but written in 1965–66, at a time when I was still on intimately friendly terms with the editors of *The New York Review of Books,* I criticized them for "a stance of opposition to the Vietnam war which . . . was mainly serving the objective of proving how dreadful the United States was." *Commentary,* by contrast,

> had been publishing articles severely critical of American policy in Vietnam since 1961 . . . and although the magazine was so far from [its] old hard anti-Communist position as to incur the suspicion in certain quarters of having gone soft on Communism, it was still anti-Communist enough to be out of phase with a climate of opinion which, as Norman Thomas put it, loved the Vietcong more than it loved peace.

I wrote very little in the last years of the sixties, but I remained actively engaged in opposition to the war through my association with Negotiation Now (see pages 88 and 103 above), and through my work as editor of *Commentary*. Among the pieces on Vietnam I published in that period, Theodore Draper's were probably the most important, and if I had any serious disagreements with anything he said at the time, I do not recall what they were. By this point, Draper—like everyone else, including me—was growing more and more exasperated with the war, and this showed in his tone and in occasional moralistic outbursts. But neither he nor any other contributor to *Commentary* accused the United States of genocide and similar crimes, nor suggested that a Communist victory would be good for Vietnam.

In those days, the antiwar position with which I associated myself was calling for a negotiated settlement, and we all tended to believe that the United States rather than Hanoi was the main obstacle to such a settlement. By 1969, however, I had come to the conclusion that the war was lost, that a negotiated settlement was impossible, and that an immediate American withdrawal, although undesirable, was the least bad of the alternatives now before us. I said all this in a speech I delivered at a mass demonstration in New York in the fall of that year.

Then, in May 1971, I wrote a piece for *Commentary* entitled "A Note on Vietnamization" in which I repeated the call for an immediate withdrawal. Summarizing my previous feelings about Vietnamization, I said that Nixon's determination

> to move out in stages and in such a way as to give the South Vietnamese a fighting chance to defend themselves against a Communist takeover after the last American was gone . . . was not the policy I would have wanted him to follow, but to me it seemed a plausible enough path for the United States to take in getting itself out of the war. Having opposed the American military intervention in Vietnam from the beginning but never having seen any reason to rejoice over the prospect of a Communist victory, I saw no reason now to oppose a policy of American disengagement which might still prevent a Communist victory from occurring, *provided that policy did not entail continued American military participation in the war, whether on the ground or in the air* [italics in the original].

After taking issue with those who thought that Nixon's real intention was to widen the war, I went on to say that he was much more likely

> to proceed with a policy he will persist in calling Vietnamization but which will in fact amount not to an American withdrawal from the war and a transfer of the responsibility for the defense of their own country to the South Vietnamese themselves, but only an American withdrawal from *combat operations on the ground*. . . . If Vietnamization originally seemed to mean turning the war over to the South Vietnamese to fight as best they could by themselves, it has now apparently come to mean turning only the war on the ground over to the South Vietnamese while we go on bombing South Vietnam, North Vietnam, Laos, and Cambodia at a rate which continues to defy comprehension, so great is it and so disproportionate in its destructiveness to any conceivable objective.

The conclusion that followed inexorably from this analysis was, I said, a source of "embarrassment" to me. Yet I could see no way out of it:

> As one who has never believed that anything good would ever come for us or for the world from an unambiguous American defeat, I now find myself . . . unhappily moving to the side of those who would prefer just such an American defeat to a "Vietnamization" of the war which calls for the indefinite and unlimited bombardment by American pilots in American planes of every country in that already devastated region. Vietnamization once appeared to be a plausible alternative to a complete and immediate American withdrawal. Today a complete American withdrawal—from the air as well as the ground—may be the only way of bringing a policy of Vietnamization, as the President himself once seemed to define it, truly and seriously into play.

In embracing the idea that "an unambiguous American defeat" was the lesser evil as compared with an indefinite American military commitment, I was certainly more candid than most of my political friends who went on pretending, to themselves as well as to others, that there was an escape from this grim trap. But I later came to see that I had also been facile in failing to take the full measure of what an American defeat would cost. In 1976, when the consequences of that defeat had begun to become apparent, I wrote a long article for *Commentary* entitled "Making the World Safe for Communism" which began with the words:

> At the height of the opposition to the Vietnam War, government officials frequently warned that should the American effort be defeated there, the result would be a right-wing backlash at home and a lapse into isolationism. Obviously the right-wing backlash never materialized, but just as obviously an isolationist mood *has* taken hold of the country since we left Vietnam.

After trying to show that an American withdrawal from the struggle to contain the spread of Soviet power in particular and Communism in general would lead to a Soviet-dominated world, I concluded that 1976 article with the following statement about Vietnam:

> . . . Vietnam was the wrong war in the wrong place at the wrong time. . . . When we were losing we said we were winning, and in a desperate effort to win, we applied military force in ways that were at once brutal and inhibited and that inspired widespread repugnance at home. But wrong as the war the United States fought in Vietnam was in all these respects, it was not wrong in the purposes for which it was fought. Those purposes were to check the spread of Communism into a country which, though not free, still enjoyed more liberty than any Communist regime allows (and certainly more than it has enjoyed since falling to the Communists), and by so doing, to discourage further Communist aggressions against other countries in which liberty already existed or at least had a chance to develop. That the American military intervention in Vietnam ended in failure, and worse than failure, is an argument not against those purposes but against the lack of wisdom with which they were in that instance pursued.

3.

No one who had read those words had any reason to be surprised by *Why We Were In Vietnam* when it came out six years later. Indeed, by 1982, I had already written *Breaking Ranks,* in which at least fifty pages were devoted to the development of my ideas about Vietnam, and *The Present Danger* (1980), in which those ideas were developed further in the light of Iran and Afghanistan. On top of all that, I had also run a series of articles in *Commentary* by such writers as Guenter Lewy, Peter Berger, and Charles Horner, all of which helped to shape my own thinking and were consistent with the analysis offered in the pages above.

Nevertheless, and in spite of so highly visible and easily available a public record, one reviewer of this book after another accused me of trying to keep it "a secret from the reader" that I too had been an opponent of the war. To accuse me of reticence about myself or of lacking candor about my ideas does at least have the virtue of novelty, but that is the only virtue which can be ascribed to it. Why, then .did this preposterous charge not only recur over and over again but become the main issue in the response to the book?

The answer, of course, is that smearing the character of the author was the only way to discredit the argument of the book. For all efforts to impugn that argument on scholarly grounds simply failed. Thus some reviewers asserted that I had made serious errors of fact, but in every instance these putative "errors" turned out to be either illusory or only differences of opinion over the interpretation of facts correctly stated in the book itself. Similarly with the charge that I relied only on secondary sources. Even if true, this would have been irrelevant to the question of accuracy. But it was in any event false, since I had used such primary sources as the memoirs of the principals and The Pentagon Papers, and whenever I relied on secondary sources, I was careful to cite them in the Notes.*

---

*Usually authors are aggrieved if they are not given credit when their work is cited by others; in this case, however, Theodore Draper, whose work I credited a number of times, complained in a lengthy review that I had used him as an "unpaid researcher"—a farcical complaint made all the more comical by the fact that as the editor of *Commentary*, where most of his writings on Vietnam originally appeared, I *did* pay him for his researches.

With nothing substantial to go on, then, the reviewers resorted to the "sneers, libels, [and] parrot phrases" that George Orwell long ago identified as the main weapons with which the Left tries to discredit anyone who criticizes its orthodoxies. In particular, they all parroted Theodore Draper's allegation that I was "smug and sanctimonious" in "lashing out" at those with whom I had "essentially agreed only yesterday." Now, I well remember how I felt when I was writing this book: sometimes indignant, sometimes disgusted, sometimes heartbroken, but never satisfied either with myself or with anyone else. Yet (as with the business of secondary and primary sources) even if this book *were* smug and sanctimonious, how would that affect the truth or falsity of the story it tells and the argument it makes?

I will, however, now risk being accused of sanctimoniousness once again by saying that unlike most of those with whom I "essentially agreed only yesterday," I have been willing to reexamine my position (and theirs) in the light of the consequences that have flowed from the American defeat that all of us, whether explicitly or implicitly, favored. As a result of that reexamination, I have come to the conclusion—spelled out in the pages above— that some of the things we once thought were right and some were wrong, horribly wrong. It is a major and continuing scandal that so many members of the intellectual community should persist in their refusal to engage in a similar reassessment. But what is even worse, what amounts to a true *trahison des clercs,* is that they should use every weapon in their polemical arsenals, up to and including misrepresentation and defamation, to prevent others from reopening the debate. Those of us who believe that a new look at "the lessons of Vietnam" is absolutely essential to the political health of the United States must not allow this—shall we call it?—preemptive strike to succeed.

NOTES

CHAPTER ONE

1. Quoted in Arthur M. Schlesinger, Jr., *The Bitter Heritage*. Boston: Houghton Mifflin Co., 1967, p. 70.
2. Jean-Paul Sartre, quoted in Guenter Lewy, *America in Vietnam*. New York: Oxford University Press, 1978, p. 299.
3. Frances FitzGerald, *Fire in the Lake*. Boston: Atlantic–Little, Brown, 1972, p. 375.
4. Digby Diehl, "Looking at Forty," *Esquire,* Mar. 1981.
5. Quoted by John Vinocur, "Anti-Americanism in West Germany Appears in Many Guises," New York *Times,* July 5, 1981.

CHAPTER TWO

1. Theodore Draper, *Abuse of Power*. New York: The Viking Press, 1967, p. 54.
2. David Halberstam, *The Best and the Brightest*. New York: Random House, 1972, p. 212.

3. Arthur M. Schlesinger, Jr., *A Thousand Days*. Boston: Houghton Mifflin Co., 1965, p. 322.
4. Arthur M. Schlesinger, Jr., *The Bitter Heritage*. Boston: Houghton Mifflin Co., 1967, p. 8.
5. *A Thousand Days*, pp. 538, 547.
6. *The Bitter Heritage*, pp. 23–24.
7. New York *Times*, Apr. 17, 1962.
8. Joseph J. Zasloff, "The Problem of South Vietnam," *Commentary*, Feb. 1962.
9. Quoted in Guenter Lewy, *America in Vietnam*. New York: Oxford University Press, 1978, pp. 12–13.
10. Hans J. Morgenthau, "The 1954 Geneva Conference: An Assessment," in *America's Stake in Vietnam*. New York: American Friends of Vietnam, 1956, p. 69. Quoted in *America in Vietnam*, p. 8.
11. Harry S. Truman, *Memoirs*, Vol. II: *Years of Trial and Hope*. New York: Doubleday & Co., 1956, p. 106.
12. George F. Kennan, *American Diplomacy: 1900–1950*. London: Secker & Warburg, 1952, pp. 117–18, 114.
13. Dean Acheson, speech to National Press Club, June 12, 1950, quoted in Richard H. Rovere and Arthur M. Schlesinger, Jr., *The MacArthur Controversy*. New York: Farrar, Straus & Giroux, 1951, p. 100.
14. *Years of Trial and Hope*, p. 339.
15. *Ibid.*, p. 463.
16. *Ibid.*, p. 339–40.
17. *Ibid.*, p. 340.
18. *Ibid.*, pp. 338, 371.
19. *Ibid.*, p. 345.
20. *Ibid.*
21. Thomas Powers, *The Man Who Kept the Secrets*. New York: Pocket Books, 1981, p. 36.
22. *Years of Trial and Hope*, p. 241.
23. *Ibid.*, p. 339.
24. *Ibid.*, p. 380.
25. *Ibid.*, p. 420.
26. *Ibid.*, pp. 341, 360.
27. *Ibid.*, p. 441.
28. *Ibid.*, p. 446.
29. William Manchester, *American Caesar*. New York: Dell Publishing Co., 1979, p. 696.

30. *Ibid.*, p. 798.
31. *RN: The Memoirs of Richard Nixon.* New York: Grosset & Dunlap, 1978, p. 110.
32. *Ibid.*, pp. 126, 128.
33. Quoted in *America in Vietnam*, p. 6.
34. *RN*, p. 152.
35. Marcus G. Raskin and Bernard B. Fall, eds., *The Viet-Nam Reader.* New York: Random House, 1965, p. 61.
36. *Public Papers of the Presidents of the United States: Dwight D. Eisenhower, 1954,* 1960, p. 383. Quoted in *America in Vietnam*, p. 6.
37. *RN*, p. 150.
38. *Ibid.*, p. 155.
39. *The Pentagon Papers*, Senator Gravel ed., Boston: Beacon Press, 1971, I:387.
40. *The Best and the Brightest*, pp. 113, 103.
41. *Years of Trial and Hope*, pp. 402–3.
42. *The Best and the Brightest*, p. 114.
43. *America in Vietnam*, p. 5.
44. *RN*, p. 152.
45. *The Memoirs of Sir Anthony Eden: Full Circle.* London: Cassell & Co. Ltd., 1960, p. 97.
46. *RN*, p. 152.
47. *Ibid.*, pp. 152–53.
48. *Abuse of Power*, p. 32.
49. *RN*, p. 152; John Foster Dulles, quoted in *Abuse of Power*, p. 28.
50. *Abuse of Power*, p. 27.
51. *Full Circle*, p. 97.
52. First draft of Eisenhower's memoirs, quoted in Stephen E. Ambrose, "The Ike Age," *New Republic*, May 9, 1981.
53. *The Pentagon Papers*, Gravel ed., I:378.
54. *Abuse of Power*, p. 26.
55. *RN*, pp. 152, 154.
56. *Ibid.*, p. 151.
57. Chalmers M. Roberts, "The Day We Didn't Go to War," in *The Viet-Nam Reader*, pp. 65–66.
58. *RN*, p. 151.
59. *Abuse of Power*, p. 34.
60. *The Pentagon Papers*, New York *Times* ed. New York: Bantam Books, 1971, p. 44.
61. *RN*, p. 154.

62. *Full Circle*, p. 97.
63. Quoted in Ambrose, *New Republic*, May 9, 1981.
64. Quoted in *Abuse of Power*, p. 34.
65. *RN*, p. 155.
66. *The Pentagon Papers*, New York *Times* ed., p. 16.
67. *Ibid.*, p. 14.
68. Emmet John Hughes, *The Ordeal of Power*. New York: Dell Publishing Co., 1964, p. 182. Quoted in *Abuse of Power*, p. 223.
69. *Eisenhower Papers 1954*, p. 949. Quoted in *America in Vietnam*, p. 11.
70. *Pentagon Papers*, *NYT* ed., p. 22.
71. Quoted in *America in Vietnam*, p. 13.
72. Dwight D. Eisenhower, *Mandate for Change*. New York: Doubleday & Co., 1963, p. 372.
73. *Abuse of Power*, p. 40.
74. See note 9 above.
75. See note 69 above.
76. Quoted in *America in Vietnam*, p. 13.
77. *Ibid.*, p. 12.
78. David Halberstam, *The Making of a Quagmire*. New York: Random House, 1965, p. 42.
79. *America in Vietnam*, p. 10.
80. *Ibid.*, p. 16.
81. *A Thousand Days*, p. 539.
82. *America in Vietnam*, p. 15.
83. Jean Lacouture, "A Bittersweet Journey to Vietnam," New York *Times*, August 23, 1976.
84. *America in Vietnam*, pp. 23–24.
85. Quoted in *A Thousand Days*, p. 548.
86. *America in Vietnam*, p. 6.
87. Quoted in Daniel Ellsberg, *Papers on the War*. New York: Simon and Schuster, 1972, pp. 80–81.
88. Quoted in *A Thousand Days*, p. 544.
89. *Papers on the War*, p. 28.
90. "Cincinnatus" (Cecil B. Currey), *Self-Destruction*. New York: W. W. Norton & Co., 1981, p. 34.
91. *Abuse of Power*, p. 50.
92. *A Thousand Days*, pp. 85, 84, 537.
93. *RN*, p. 152.

94. *The Best and the Brightest*, p. 56.
95. Richard Lowenthal, "The Sino-Soviet Dispute," *Commentary*, May 1961.
96. *A Thousand Days*, pp. 351, 415.
97. *Abuse of Power*, p. 142.
98. Lyndon Baines Johnson, *The Vantage Point*. New York: Holt, Rinehart & Winston, 1971, p. 53.
99. Quoted in Norman Podhoretz, *Breaking Ranks*. New York: Harper & Row, 1979, p. 185.
100. John F. Kennedy, inaugural address, Jan. 20, 1961.
101. Quoted in *Papers on the War*, p. 127.
102. *A Thousand Days*, pp. 364, 374.
103. *Ibid.*, p. 769.
104. *The Best and the Brightest*, pp. 129–30.
105. *The Pentagon Papers*, Gravel ed., II:119.
106. Quoted in Peter Braestrup, *Big Story*. Boulder, Col.: Westview Press, 1977, Vol. I, p. 3.
107. *RN*, p. 151.
108. *A Thousand Days*, pp. 307, 311.
109. Quoted in *The Best and the Brightest*, p. 130.
110. *The Pentagon Papers*, Gravel ed., II:653.
111. *Ibid.*, p. 109.
112. *Ibid.*, p. 111.
113. *Ibid.*, p. 109.
114. *RN*, pp. 151–52.
115. New York *Times*, Apr. 9, 1961.
116. *Ibid.*, Dec. 10, 1961.
117. *Ibid.*, Dec. 22, 1961.
118. *Breaking Ranks*, pp. 181–83.
119. Theodore C. Sorensen, *Kennedy*. New York: Harper & Row, 1965, p. 653.
120. *Abuse of Power*, p. 52.
121. *Kennedy*, pp. 654–55.
122. *America in Vietnam*, p. 24.
123. *Pentagon Papers*, Gravel ed., II:79.
124. *Ibid.*, II:109.
125. *Papers on the War*, p. 111.
126. Quoted in *The Vantage Point*, p. 58.
127. Oscar Gass, "The New Frontier Fulfilled," *Commentary*, Dec. 1961.

128. *The Best and the Brightest,* p. 136.
129. W. W. Rostow, "Guerrilla Warfare in Underdeveloped Areas," in *The Viet-Nam Reader,* p. 115.
130. *America in Vietnam,* p. 28.
131. *The Best and the Brightest,* p. 135.
132. *America in Vietnam,* p. 28.
133. Dennis J. Duncanson, quoted in *America in Vietnam,* p. 28.
134. *Pentagon Papers,* Gravel ed., II:108.
135. *Papers on the War,* p. 61.
136. Sir Robert Thompson, in Richard M. Pfeffer, *No More Vietnams?.* New York: Harper & Row, 1968, p. 166.
137. Albert Wohlstetter, in *No More Vietnams?,* p. 4.
138. *Self-Destruction,* pp. 9–10.
139. *Abuse of Power,* p. 54.
140. Quoted in *Papers on the War,* p. 82.

CHAPTER THREE

1. Lyndon Baines Johnson, *The Vantage Point.* New York: Holt, Rinehart & Winston, 1971, pp. 42, 45.
2. *Ibid.,* p. 46.
3. *Ibid.,* pp. 47–48.
4. *Ibid.,* p. 573.
5. *Ibid.,* p. 53.
6. *Ibid.,* p. 48.
7. Quoted in Guenter Lewy, *America in Vietnam.* New York: Oxford University Press, 1978, p. 10.
8. Chalmers M. Roberts, in Marcus G. Raskin and Bernard B. Fall, eds., *The Viet-Nam Reader.* New York: Random House, 1965, p. 59.
9. Quoted in Theodore Draper, *Abuse of Power.* New York: The Viking Press, 1967, p. 33.
10. *The Vantage Point,* p. 54.
11. Quoted in Arthur M. Schlesinger, Jr., *A Thousand Days.* Boston: Houghton Mifflin Co., 1965, p. 542.
12. *The Vantage Point,* p. 54.
13. Quoted in *A Thousand Days,* p. 542.
14. *The Pentagon Papers,* Senator Gravel ed., Boston: Beacon Press, III:494.

15. *The Vantage Point*, p. 63.
16. Quoted in Peter Braestrup, *Big Story*, Boulder, Col.: Westview Press, Vol. I, p. 7.
17. Quoted in *America in Vietnam*, p. 33.
18. *Ibid.*, p. 35.
19. This evidence is summed up in *America in Vietnam*, pp. 35–36. For evidence that Johnson and his people believed that the attack had taken place, see George C. Herring, "The War in Vietnam," in Robert A. Divine, ed., *Exploring the Johnson Years*. Austin: University of Texas Press, 1981, pp. 36, 56.
20. Tom Wicker, "Lyndon Johnson vs. The Ghost of Jack Kennedy," *Esquire*, Nov. 1965.
21. The play was Barbara Garson's *MacBird!*
22. *The Vantage Point*, p. 115.
23. Richard N. Goodwin, *Triumph or Tragedy*. New York: Random House, 1966, p. 32.
24. *Big Story*, Vol. I., p. 8.
25. Quoted in *Abuse of Power*, p. 67.
26. *Ibid.*, pp. 67–68.
27. *Ibid.*, p. 67.
28. David Riesman and Michael Maccoby, "The American Crisis," *Commentary*, June 1960.
29. *The Vantage Point*, p. 68.
30. William Manchester, *American Caesar*. New York: Dell Publishing Co., 1978, p. 833.
31. *The Vantage Point*, p. 131.
32. "Department of State White Paper: Aggression from the North," in *The Viet-Nam Reader*, pp. 143–55.
33. I. F. Stone, "A Reply to the White Paper," *I. F. Stone's Weekly*, Mar. 8, 1965.
34. Quoted in *Abuse of Power*, pp. 96–97.
35. *Abuse of Power*, pp. 73–82.
36. *America in Vietnam*, p. 40.
37. Theodore Draper, "Ghosts of Vietnam," *Dissent*, winter 1979.
38. *America in Vietnam*, pp. 40–41.
39. *Abuse of Power*, pp. 86–87.
40. *America in Vietnam*, p. 41.
41. Quoted in *America in Vietnam*, p. 40.
42. *The Vantage Point*, p. 145.
43. *Ibid.*, p. 132.

44. *Ibid.*, pp. 144–46.
45. *Ibid.*, pp. 151–52.
46. *Ibid.*, pp. 152–53.
47. *Ibid.*, p. 153.
48. *America in Vietnam*, p. 146.
49. *The Vantage Point*, p. 153.
50. *Ibid.*, p. 149.
51. Rowland Evans & Robert Novak, *Lyndon B. Johnson: The Exercise of Power.* New York: The New American Library, 1966, pp. 550–52.
52. *Ibid.*, p. 551.
53. *Ibid.*, p. 559.
54. Quoted in Harry G. Summers, Jr., *On Strategy.* Carlisle Barracks, Pa.: Strategic Studies Institute, U.S. Army War College, 1981, pp. 7–8.
55. *Ibid.*, p. 11.
56. Quoted in *Lyndon B. Johnson: The Exercise of Power*, p. 552.
57. New York *Times*, Apr. 6, 1965.
58. David Halberstam, *The Making of a Quagmire.* New York: Random House, 1965, p. 319.
59. *Big Story*, Vol. I, p. 50.
60. *Ibid.*, pp. 45–46.
61. *Lyndon B. Johnson: The Exercise of Power*, p. 563.
62. "Containing China," *Commentary*, May 1966.
63. New York *Times*, Apr. 6, 1965.
64. *Ibid.*, Feb. 10, 1965.
65. *Big Story*, Vol. I, p. 46.
66. *Lyndon B. Johnson: The Exercise of Power*, p. 537.
67. *Ibid.*, p. 539.
68. *Ibid.*, p. 562.
69. Leslie H. Gelb (with Richard K. Betts), *The Irony of Vietnam.* Washington, D.C.: The Brookings Institution, 1979, p. 158.
70. Quoted in *Lyndon B. Johnson: The Exercise of Power*, p. 538.
71. New York *Times*, Oct. 16, 1965.
72. *The Irony of Vietnam*, pp. 129–30.
73. New York *Post*, Jan. 17, 1966.
74. Quoted in Norman Podhoretz, *Breaking Ranks.* New York: Harper & Row, 1979, p. 188.
75. "Attention All Military Personnel," in Paul Jacobs and Saul Lan-

dau, *The New Radicals*. New York: Vintage Books, 1966, pp. 253–56.

76. "The U.S. Government Has Deceived Us," in *The New Radicals*, p. 251.
77. Susan Sontag, *Trip to Hanoi*. New York: Farrar, Straus & Giroux, 1968, p. 72.
78. *Ibid.*, pp. 26, 46, 63, 26, 76, 67.
79. *Ibid.*, pp. 67–68.
80. *Ibid.*, pp. 36, 71.
81. *Ibid.*, pp. 72–74.
82. *Ibid.*, pp. 75–76.
83. Mary McCarthy, "Hanoi," in *The Seventeenth Degree*. New York: Harcourt Brace Jovanovich, 1974, pp. 272, 208.
84. *Ibid.*, p. 272.
85. *Trip to Hanoi*, p. 17.
86. *The Seventeenth Degree*, p. 283.
87. *Ibid.*, p. 312.
88. *Ibid.*, pp. 215, 222.
89. *Ibid.*, pp. 236, 238.
90. *Ibid.*, pp. 278, 302–3.
91. *Ibid.*, pp. 276, 314–15.
92. *Ibid.*, pp. 316, 230–31.
93. *Ibid.*, pp. 297, 299, 277, 298–99.
94. *Ibid.*, p. 277.
95. *Ibid.*, pp. 303, 318, 307.
96. *Ibid.*, p. 318.
97. Frances FitzGerald, *Fire in the Lake*. Boston: Atlantic-Little, Brown, 1972, p. 169.
98. *Ibid.*, pp. 170–71, 173–74.
99. *America in Vietnam*, p. 273.
100. Edward Lansdale, in W. Scott Thompson and Donaldson D. Frizzell, eds., *The Lessons of Vietnam*. New York: Crane, Russak & Co., 1977, p. 44.
101. *Fire in the Lake*, p. 177.
102. *Ibid.*, pp. 194, 177, 196.
103. *Ibid.*, pp. 226–27.
104. Quoted by Dennis H. Wrong in "Liberal Anti-Communism Revisited," *Commentary*, Sept. 1967.
105. Diana Trilling, in "Liberal Anti-Communism Revisited," *Commentary*, Sept. 1967.

106. Michael Harrington, in "Liberal Anti-Communism Revisited," *Commentary*, Sept. 1967.
107. Richard H. Rovere, in "Liberal Anti-Communism Revisited," *Commentary*, Sept. 1967.
108. Arthur M. Schlesinger, Jr., in "Liberal Anti-Communism Revisited," *Commentary*, Sept. 1967.
109. Dwight Macdonald, in "Liberal Anti-Communism Revisited," *Commentary*, Sept. 1967.
110. Lewis A. Coser, in "Liberal Anti-Communism Revisited," *Commentary*, Sept. 1967.
111. William Phillips, in "Liberal Anti-Communism Revisited," *Commentary*, Sept. 1967.
112. Philip Rahv, in "Liberal Anti-Communism Revisited," *Commentary*, Sept. 1967.
113. Harold Rosenberg, in "Liberal Anti-Communism Revisited," *Commentary*, Sept. 1967.
114. Richard H. Rovere, in "Liberal Anti-Communism Revisited," *Commentary*, Sept. 1967.
115. Quoted in *American Caesar*, p. 808.
116. Robert Pickus, in "Liberal Anti-Communism Revisited," *Commentary*, Sept. 1967.
117. Noam Chomsky, *American Power and the New Mandarins*. New York: Pantheon Books, 1967, pp. 399–400.
118. *Ibid.*, pp. 221, 9, 16.
119. *Ibid.*, pp. 10, 16.
120. *Ibid.*, pp. 261–62.
121. Daniel Ellsberg, *Papers on the War*. New York: Simon and Schuster, 1972, p. 33.
122. Richard A. Falk, in Erwin Knoll and Judith Nies McFadden, eds., *War Crimes and the American Conscience*. New York: Holt, Rinehart & Winston, 1970, p. 32.
123. Hans J. Morgenthau, in *War Crimes and the American Conscience*, p. 15.
124. Guenter Lewy, "Vietnam: New Light on the Question of American Guilt," *Commentary*, Feb. 1978.
125. Quoted in *Breaking Ranks*, p. 232.
126. McGeorge Bundy, "End of Either/Or," *Foreign Affairs*, Jan. 1967.
127. Chester L. Cooper, quoted in *America in Vietnam*, p. 50.
128. *The Pentagon Papers*, New York *Times* ed. New York: Bantam Books, 1971, p. 516.

129. *America in Vietnam,* pp. 430–31.
130. Richard H. Rovere, in "Liberal Anti-Communism Revisited," *Commentary,* Sept. 1967.
131. Charles F. Kriete, "The Moral Dimension of Strategy," *Parameters,* No. 2, 1977.
132. Edward Lansdale, in *The Lessons of Vietnam,* p. 114.
133. *The Pentagon Papers,* Gravel ed., III:644.
134. Quoted in Arthur M. Schlesinger, Jr., *The Bitter Heritage.* Boston: Houghton Mifflin Co., 1967, p. 66.
135. See Robert W. Tucker, *Nation or Empire?* Baltimore: Johns Hopkins Press, 1968.
136. *The Seventeenth Degree,* p. 322.
137. Norman Mailer, *The Armies of the Night.* New York: The New American Library, 1968, p. 184.
138. *The Irony of Vietnam,* p. 335.
139. *The Armies of the Night,* p. 184.
140. *The Irony of Vietnam,* p. 217.
141. *The Bitter Heritage,* p. 76.
142. *The Irony of Vietnam,* pp. 141–42, 153.
143. *Ibid.,* pp. 140, 142.
144. *Ibid.,* p. 338.
145. *The Vantage Point,* p. 371.
146. *The Irony of Vietnam,* p. 338.
147. *Ibid.,* p. 340.
148. *The Vantage Point,* pp. 250, 255.
149. *The Irony of Vietnam,* p. 339.
150. *The Irony of Vietnam,* pp. 217–18.
151. William C. Westmoreland, quoted in "Cincinnatus" (Cecil B. Currey), *Self-Destruction.* New York: W. W. Norton & Co., 1981, pp. 21–22, 65.
152. *Self-Destruction,* pp. 9–10.
153. Edward N. Luttwak, "A New Arms Race?," *Commentary,* Sept. 1980.
154. Henry A. Kissinger, *White House Years.* Boston: Little, Brown & Co., 1979, pp. 1004–5.
155. *Self-Destruction,* p. 44.
156. *Ibid.,* p. 124.
157. *Wall Street Journal,* Dec. 5, 1969.
158. Robert W. Chandler, *War of Ideas.* Boulder, Col.: Westview Press, 1981, p. 34.

159. *Ibid.*, pp. 164–67.

160. *Ibid.*, pp. 199–201.

161. Fred C. Weyand, quoted in *On Strategy*, pp. 49–50.

162. *The Irony of Vietnam*, p. 328.

163. *Fire in the Lake*, p. 398.

164. Don Oberdorfer, *Tet!* New York: Doubleday & Co., 1971, pp. 329–30.

165. *America in Vietnam*, p. 199.

166. David Halberstam, "Getting the Story in Vietnam," *Commentary*, Jan. 1965.

167. Leonard Sussman, in *Big Story*, Vol. I. p. xxix.

168. *America in Vietnam*, pp. 400–401.

169. Lewy provides a parallel-column comparison in *America in Vietnam*, pp. 402–03.

170. Tom Wolfe, *Mauve Gloves & Madmen, Clutter & Vine*. New York: Farrar, Straus & Giroux, 1976, pp. 42–44.

171. *America in Vietnam*, p. 401.

172. *The Pentagon Papers*, Gravel ed., IV: 261.

173. *America in Vietnam*, pp. 404, 403.

174. *The Irony of Vietnam*, p. 320.

175. *Papers on the War*, p. 277.

176. Edward Jay Epstein, *Between Fact and Fiction*. New York: Vintage Books, 1975, pp. 81–82.

177. *Ibid.*, pp. 88, 91.

178. Martin F. Herz, *The Prestige Press and the Christmas Bombing, 1972*. Washington, D.C.: Ethics and Public Policy Center, 1980, p. 2.

179. *Ibid.*, p. 32.

180. *America in Vietnam*, p. 413.

181. *The Prestige Press*, pp. 57–60. Anthony Lewis quoted, p. 47.

182. *The Irony of Vietnam*, p. 105.

183. Walter LaFeber, "The Last War, the Next War, and the New Revisionists," *democracy*, I:1, 1980.

184. *White House Years*, p. 298.

185. William Small, quoted in *Between Fact and Fiction*, p. 213.

186. George A. Bailey, quoted in *Between Fact and Fiction*, p. 218.

187. *Between Fact and Fiction*, pp. 215, 223.

188. *Ibid.*, p. 225.

189. *Big Story*, Vol. I., pp. 620–21.

190. *Ibid.*, pp. 619–20, 629.

191. *Ibid.*, pp. 628–29.

192. *The Vantage Point*, p. 418.
193. Quoted in *Big Story*, Vol. I., pp. 624–25.
194. *Big Story*, Vol. I., pp. 61, 60.
195. *Ibid.*, p. 56.
196. *The Vantage Point*, p. 379.
197. *Big Story*, Vol. I., p. 54.
198. *The Vantage Point*, p. 530.
199. *The Irony of Vietnam*, p. 332.
200. *White House Years*, p. 1019; see also pp. 1169–70.

CHAPTER FOUR

1. *RN: The Memoirs of Richard Nixon*. New York: Grosset & Dunlap, 1978, p. 256.
2. *Ibid.*, pp. 256–58.
3. David Halberstam, *The Best and the Brightest*. New York: Random House, 1972, p. 661.
4. *RN*, p. 348.
5. Quoted in William Shawcross, *Sideshow*. New York: Pocket Books, 1979, p. 86.
6. Nathan Glazer, "Vietnam: The Case for Immediate Withdrawal," *Commentary*, May 1971.
7. *RN*, p. 348.
8. *Ibid.*, p. 348.
9. Henry A. Kissinger, *White House Years*. Boston: Little, Brown and Co., 1979, p. 287.
10. *RN*, pp. 348–49.
11. *Ibid.*, p. 347.
12. *Ibid.*, p. 347.
13. *Ibid.*, pp. 347–48.
14. Sir Robert Thompson in Richard M. Pfeffer, ed., *No More Vietnams?* New York: Harper & Row, 1968, p. 168.
15. *White House Years*, p. 1032.
16. *RN*, pp. 404–5.
17. Kennedy and Johnson, both quoted in Guenter Lewy, *America in Vietnam*. New York: Oxford U. Press, 1978, p. 162.
18. *Ibid.*, p. 162.
19. Lyndon Baines Johnson, *The Vantage Point*. New York: Holt, Rinehart & Winston, 1971, p. 423.
20. *RN*, p. 409.

21. *White House Years*, p. 277.
22. *Ibid.*, pp. 281–82.
23. *Ibid.*, pp. 281–82.
24. *Ibid.*, pp. 287–88.
25. *Ibid.*, p. 294.
26. *Ibid.*, pp. 295, 446.
27. Quoted in *White House Years*, p. 510.
28. *RN*, pp. 451–52.
29. Muskie and Mondale quoted in *RN*, p. 453.
30. *White House Years*, p. 508.
31. Quoted in *RN*, p. 453.
32. *RN*, p. 594.
33. *White House Years*, p. 444.
34. *America in Vietnam*, p. 147.
35. *RN*, p. 499.
36. *White House Years*, pp. 992, 1009–10.
37. *RN*, p. 499.
38. *Ibid.*, p. 409.
39. *Ibid.*, pp. 586–87.
40. *White House Years*, p. 1109.
41. *RN*, p. 587.
42. *White House Years*, pp. 1038, 1109.
43. *Ibid.*, p. 1109.
44. Boston *Globe*, May 10, 1972.
45. *America in Vietnam*, pp. 200–201.
46. *Ibid.*, p. 201.
47. Tad Szulc, "Behind the Vietnam Cease-Fire Agreement," *Foreign Policy*, summer 1974.
48. *White House Years*, p. 1329.
49. *Ibid.*, p. 1362.
50. *RN*, p. 700.
51. *White House Years*, p. 1385.
52. *RN*, p. 734.
53. *America in Vietnam*, p. 415.
54. "Behind the Vietnam Cease-Fire Agreement," *Foreign Policy*, summer 1974.
55. *White House Years*, p. 1467.
56. "Behind the Vietnam Cease-Fire Agreement," *Foreign Policy*, summer 1974.
57. Martin F. Herz, *The Prestige Press and the Christmas Bombing,*

1972. Washington, D.C.: Ethics and Public Policy Center, 1980, p. 2.

58. *RN,* pp. 736–37.
59. *White House Years,* p. 1459.
60. *The Prestige Press,* pp. 67, 69.
61. Sir Robert Thompson, in W. Scott Thompson and Donaldson D. Frizzell, *The Lessons of Vietnam.* New York: Crane, Russak & Co., 1977, p. 105.
62. *America in Vietnam,* p. 413.
63. George McGovern, NBC interview, Dec. 26, 1972, quoted in *The Prestige Press,* p. 42.
64. Harold Hughes, quoted in *The Prestige Press,* p. 42.
65. Anthony Lewis, New York *Times,* Dec. 23, 1972, quoted in *The Prestige Press,* p. 47.
66. Washington *Post,* Dec. 28, 1972, quoted in *The Prestige Press,* p. 49.
67. See note 63 above.
68. Mike Mansfield, quoted in *The Prestige Press,* p. 42.
69. Jacob Javits, quoted in *The Prestige Press,* pp. 42–43.
70. "Behind the Vietnam Cease-Fire Agreement," *Foreign Policy,* summer 1974.
71. Brigadier F. P. Serong, quoted in *America in Vietnam,* p. 202.
72. Sir Robert Thompson, quoted in *America in Vietnam,* p. 202.
73. Sir Robert Thompson, in *The Lessons of Vietnam,* p. 105.
74. Daniel Ellsberg, *Papers on the War.* New York: Simon and Schuster, 1972, p. 261.
75. Earl C. Ravenal, *Never Again.* Philadelphia: Temple University Press, 1978, p. 126.
76. *RN,* p. 697.
77. *White House Years,* p. 1359.
78. *Ibid.,* p. 1345.
79. *RN,* p. 691.
80. *Ibid.,* p. 692.
81. *White House Years,* pp. 1366, 1353.
82. *RN,* pp. 696, 707, 702.
83. *White House Years,* pp. 1376–77.
84. *RN,* p. 741.
85. *Ibid.,* p. 690.
86. *White House Years,* p. 1435.
87. *RN,* p. 718.

88. *White House Years*, p. 1462.
89. *RN*, p. 737.
90. *White House Years*, pp. 1460, 1470.
91. *Ibid.*, p. 1473.
92. Richard Nixon, quoted in *America in Vietnam*, p. 203.
93. *RN*, p. 888.
94. Quoted in *America in Vietnam*, p. 204.
95. *America in Vietnam*, p. 205.
96. *Ibid.*, p. 207.
97. General Van Tien Dong, quoted in *America in Vietnam*, p. 208.
98. *White House Years*, p. 1470.
99. *Ibid.*, p. 1373.
100. McGeorge Bundy, "Vietnam, Watergate and Presidential Powers," *Foreign Affairs*, winter 1979/80.
101. *White House Years*, p. 1373.
102. *RN*, p. 607.
103. "Vietnam, Watergate and Presidential Powers," *Foreign Affairs*, winter 1979/80.
104. *RN*, p. 452.
105. *Ibid.*, p. 395.
106. Robert Shaplen, quoted in *America in Vietnam*, p. 221.
107. Doan Van Toai, "A Lament for Vietnam," New York *Times Magazine*, Mar. 29, 1981.

CHAPTER FIVE

1. Doan Van Toai, "A Lament for Vietnam," New York *Times Magazine*, Mar. 29, 1981.
2. General Fred C. Weyand, quoted in Harry G. Summers, Jr., *On Strategy*. Carlisle Barracks, Pa: U.S. Army War College, Strategic Studies Institute, 1981, p. 61.
3. S. Rajaratnam, *Wall Street Journal*, June 1, 1981.
4. Lyndon Baines Johnson, *The Vantage Point*. New York: Holt, Rinehart & Winston, 1971, p. 151.
5. Jimmy Carter, speech at Notre Dame, May 1977.
6. *The Vantage Point*, p. 152.
7. *On Strategy*, p. 7.
8. Alan Wolfe, "Jeane's Designs," *Nation*, Feb. 7, 1981.
9. *RN: The Memoirs of Richard Nixon*. New York: Grosset & Dunlap, 1978, p. 740.

10. Guenter Lewy, *America in Vietnam*. New York: Oxford University Press, 1978, p. 224.

11. Richard A. Falk, in Erwin Knoll and Judith Nies McFadden, eds., *War Crimes and the American Conscience*. New York: Holt, Rinehart & Winston, 1970, p. 6.

12. Erwin Knoll and Judith Nies McFadden, in *War Crimes and the American Conscience*, p. vii.

13. Bertrand Russell, quoted in *America in Vietnam*, p. 312.

14. *America in Vietnam*, p. 224.

15. Richard A. Falk, quoted in *America in Vietnam*, p. 312.

16. *America in Vietnam*, p. 317.

17. Quoted in *America in Vietnam*, p. 227.

18. Geneva Convention Relative to the Protection of Civilian Persons in Time of War, Aug. 12, 1949, in "Treaties Governing Land Warfare," Air Force pamphlet, July 21, 1958, p. 150. Quoted in *America in Vietnam*, p. 227.

19. International Committee of the Red Cross, *Draft Rules for the Limitation of Dangers Incurred by the Civilian Population in Time of War*. Geneva: 1956, Article 11. Quoted in *America in Vietnam*, p. 229.

20. Quoted in *America in Vietnam*, p. 229.

21. Richard A. Falk, quoted in *America in Vietnam*, p. 230.

22. Clergy and Laymen Concerned About Vietnam, quoted in *America in Vietnam*, p. 230.

23. Geneva Convention, Aug. 12, 1949, Art. 28, p. 145. Quoted in *America in Vietnam*, pp. 230–31.

24. Richard A. Falk, ed., *The Vietnam War and International Law*. Princeton, N.J.: Princeton U. Press, 1969, Vol. II, p. 240. Quoted in *America in Vietnam*, pp. 271–72.

25. Gabriel Kolko, in *War Crimes and the American Conscience*, p. 99.

26. Hans J. Morgenthau, in *War Crimes and the American Conscience*, p. 15.

27. Geneva Convention, Aug. 12, 1949, Art. 19, p. 141. Quoted in *America in Vietnam*, p. 231.

28. Quoted in *America in Vietnam*, p. 232.

29. Paul H. Nitze, in W. Scott Thompson and Donaldson D. Frizzell, eds., *The Lessons of Vietnam*. New York: Crane, Russak & Co., 1977, p. 199.

30. Jonathan Schell, in *War Crimes and the American Conscience*, p. 68.

31. Daniel Ellsberg, in *War Crimes and the American Conscience*, p. 83.
32. *America in Vietnam*, p. 301.
33. *Ibid.*, p. 304.
34. *Ibid.*, p. 448.
35. *Ibid.*, p. 326.
36. Robert Jay Lifton, in *War Crimes and the American Conscience*, p. 104.
37. Edward M. Opton, Jr., Nevitt Sanford, and Robert Duckles, in *War Crimes and the American Conscience*, pp. 113–14.
38. Hans J. Morgenthau, in *War Crimes and the American Conscience*, p. 110.
39. Telford Taylor, *Nuremberg and Vietnam*. New York: Bantam Books, 1971, p. 139.
40. Daniel Ellsberg, in *War Crimes and the American Conscience*, p. 130.
41. Edward M. Opton, Jr., Nevitt Sanford, and Robert Duckles, in *War Crimes and the American Conscience*, pp. 117–18.
42. Robert Jay Lifton, in "Questions of Guilt," *Partisan Review*, fall 1972.
43. Terry Nardin and Jerome Slater, "Vietnam Revisited," *World Politics*, Apr. 1981.
44. Michael Walzer, Review of *America in Vietnam*, *New Republic*, Nov. 11, 1978.
45. Theodore Draper, "Ghosts of Vietnam," *Dissent*, winter 1979.
46. Review of *America in Vietnam*, *New Republic*, Nov. 11, 1978.
47. "Ghosts of Vietnam," *Dissent*, winter 1979; Review of *America in Vietnam*, *New Republic*, Nov. 11, 1978.
48. Quoted in Walzer, *New Republic*, Nov. 11, 1978.
49. *America in Vietnam*, p. 269.
50. Review of *America in Vietnam*, *New Republic*, Nov. 11, 1978.
51. "Vietnam Revisited," *World Politics*, Apr. 1981.
52. Roger Hilsman, *To Move a Nation*. New York: Doubleday & Co., 1967, p. 444. Quoted in *America in Vietnam*, p. 303.
53. Barry Goldwater, quoted in *America in Vietnam*, p. 303.
54. Daniel Ellsberg, in *War Crimes and the American Conscience*, p. 82.
55. Peter L. Berger, "Indochina and the American Conscience," *Commentary*, Feb. 1980.
56. *America in Vietnam*, p. 223.

57. Richard H. Rovere, in "Liberal Anti-Communism Revisited," *Commentary*, Sept. 1967.

58. Richard H. Rovere, quoted in William Manchester, *American Caesar*. New York: Dell Publishing Co., 1979, p. 808.

59. Richard H. Rovere, in "Liberal Anti-Communism Revisited," *Commentary*, Sept. 1967.

60. Jason Epstein, "The CIA and the Intellectuals," *New York Review of Books*, Apr. 20, 1967.

61. Robert L. Heilbroner, "Counterrevolutionary America," *Commentary*, Apr. 1967.

62. "Indochina and the American Conscience," *Commentary*, Feb. 1980.

63. Tom Wicker, New York *Times*, July 8, 1979. Quoted in Charles Horner, "America Five Years After Defeat," *Commentary*, Apr. 1980.

64. Carl Gershman, "After the Dominoes Fell," *Commentary*, May 1978.

65. Nguyen Cong Hoan, Hearings Before the Subcommittee on International Organizations of the House Committee on International Relations, July 26, 1977, pp. 145–67.

66. Truong Nhu Tang, "Vietnam, the Myth of a Liberation," unpublished ms., 1981.

67. See note 65 above.

68. Doan Van Toai, "A Lament for Vietnam," New York *Times Magazine*, Mar. 29, 1981.

69. Jean Lacouture, interview with François Fejto, in *Il Giornale Nuovo* (Milan), quoted in Michael Ledeen, "Europe—The Good News and the Bad," *Commentary*, Apr. 1979.

70. Jean Lacouture, quoted in "After the Dominoes Fell," *Commentary*, May 1978.

71. "A Lament for Vietnam," New York *Times Magazine*, Mar. 29, 1981.

72. *Ibid.*

73. Quoted in "A Lament for Vietnam," New York *Times Magazine*, Mar. 29, 1981.

74. "A Lament for Vietnam," New York *Times Magazine*, Mar. 29, 1981; "After the Dominoes Fell," *Commentary*, May 1978.

75. Truong Nhu Tang, "Vietnam, the Myth of a Liberation," unpublished ms., 1981.

76. *Foreign Report*, July 16, 1981.

77. To Huu, quoted in "A Lament for Vietnam," New York *Times Magazine*, Mar. 29, 1981.

78. "A Lament for Vietnam," New York *Times Magazine*, Mar. 29, 1981.

79. "After the Dominoes Fell," *Commentary*, May 1978.

80. Quoted in "After the Dominoes Fell," *Commentary*, May 1978.

81. "After the Dominoes Fell," *Commentary*, May 1978.

82. Truong Nhu Tang, "Vietnam, the Myth of a Liberation," unpublished ms., 1981.

83. Quoted in "After the Dominoes Fell," *Commentary*, May 1978.

84. "After the Dominoes Fell," *Commentary*, May 1978.

85. "Indochina and the American Conscience," *Commentary*, Feb. 1980.

86. Quoted in "After the Dominoes Fell," *Commentary*, May 1978.

87. "Indochina and the American Conscience," *Commentary*, Feb. 1980.

88. Irving Howe and Michael Walzer, "Were We Wrong About Vietnam?," *New Republic*, Aug. 18, 1979.

89. Stanley Hoffmann, "The Crime of Cambodia," *New York Review of Books*, June 28, 1979.

90. Peter W. Rodman, "Sideswipe," *American Spectator*, Mar. 1981.

91. William Shawcross, "Shawcross Swipes Again," *American Spectator*, July 1981.

92. François Ponchaud, *Cambodia: Year Zero*. New York: Holt, Rinehart & Winston, 1978, p. 21. Quoted in "Sideswipe," *American Spectator*, Mar. 1981.

93. "Shawcross Swipes Again," *American Spectator*, July 1981.

94. William Shawcross, *Sideshow*. New York: Pocket Books, 1979, p. 243.

95. Kenneth Quinn, quoted in "Shawcross Swipes Again," *American Spectator*, July 1981.

96. *Cambodia: Year Zero*, pp. xvi, 192. Quoted in "Sideswipe," *American Spectator*, Mar. 1981.

97. "Sideswipe," *American Spectator*, Mar. 1981.

98. "The Crime of Cambodia," *New York Review of Books*, June 28, 1979.

99. Anthony Lewis, New York *Times*, Mar. 17, 1975. Quoted in "Sideswipe," *American Spectator*, Mar. 1981.

100. New York *Times*, Apr. 13, 1975. Quoted in "Sideswipe," *American Spectator*, Mar. 1981.

INDEX

Acheson, Dean, 22–23, 29, 30, 33, 34, 63, 112, 127, 134
Algerian war, 136–37
Alsop, Joseph, 82
Americans for Democratic Action (ADA), 101–2, 106
"America's Stake in Vietnam" (Kennedy), 19–20, 40
Angola, Soviet-backed intervention in, 176, 178
antiwar movement, 9–11, 13–15, 82–112, 123–39, 145, 167
anti-Americanism in, 13, 88, 103–5
anti-anti-Communism and, 88, 99–103
Cambodian operations and, 146–47
in Congress, 82–83, 84, 86, 124, 126–27, 147, 152, 154

election of 1968 and, 131–32, 137
favorable depictions of North Vietnam and, 90–99
horrors in Vietnam as responsibility of, 205–7
Johnson's mishandling of, 86–87, 105–9, 110–12, 124, 127
McCarthyism ascribed to, 179–182
moral issues in, 85, 103–5, 106–108, 109, 124, 138, 190
negotiated settlement sought by moderates in, 109–12
Nixon and expectations of, 133, 135–37, 146
North Vietnamese perception of, 129–30
Paris agreement and, 158–59
in pre-1965 period, 55–56, 85

241

antiwar movement (*cont.*)
  pro-Communism in, 87–100
  radicalization of moderates in, 137–39
  tactical issues in, 83–84
  Tet offensive and, 123–27
  totalitarianism as viewed by, 204–5
  treasonable acts of, 85–86, 179, 180
  war crimes as charged by, 13–14, 103–5, 180–82, 190–91, 193
Arendt, Hannah, 120, 180, 194–195, 207, 208
Attlee, Clement, 33, 34
authoritarianism, 204–5

Baldwin, Hanson, 68
Ball, George, 60, 127
Basic Principles of Détente, 151, 164, 165, 170
Bay of Pigs, 50–51, 58
Berger, Peter L., 193, 197–98, 204
Berlin blockade (1947), 24
Berrigan, Daniel, 105
Betts, Richard K., 109–12
Bidault, Georges, 38
Bigart, Homer, 52
"boat people," 173, 198–99
"body counts," 191
Bradley, Omar, 29
Braestrup, Peter, 71, 82, 116, 123, 126, 129
Brezhnev, Leonid, 51
Brown, Harold, 119
Browne, Malcolm W., 122
Buddhists, 60, 200, 203, 204
Bundy, McGeorge, 48, 49, 52, 59, 60, 106, 120, 123, 127, 167, 168
Bundy, William P., 57

Calley, William, 189
Cambodia, 40, 134, 165, 176, 210
  Communist victory in, 207–9
  incursion into (1970), 146–49
  secret bombing of (1969), 146, 148
Cam Ne, burning of, 125
Carter, Jimmy, 171, 178, 179, 210
Central Intelligence Agency (CIA), 177–78, 179, 180
Chamberlain, Neville, 11, 46
Chiang Kai-shek, 21, 27, 31, 39, 52
China:
  Communist victory in, 21, 22, 27, 63
  lesson learned from "loss" of, 45–46
China, People's Republic of:
  expansionism ascribed to, 27–30, 50, 174
  revolutionary violence advocated by, 49–50
  Soviet relations with, 33–34, 48–49, 109, 170, 176
  as U.S. surrogate state, 170
Chomsky, Noam, 103–4, 205
Christmas bombing (1972), 148
  as distorted by media, 121–23, 180
  peace talks and, 154–56, 157
  U.S. public opinion on, 156–157
Church, Frank, 69, 82, 86
Churchill, Winston:
  Indochina war and, 34, 35, 36–37, 48
  Munich and, 11, 35, 47
"Cincinnatus," 47, 62, 113
Clark, Ramsey, 179
Cohen, Benjamin V., 180
Communism:
  anti-anti-, 99–103

Nazism related to, 11, 194–95
as Soviet-dominated
    movement, 20–22, 27, 33–34
support for, in antiwar
    movement, 87–100
as unpopular among
    Vietnamese, 172–73, 203–4
Congress, U.S., 68–69, 70, 79,
    149, 178, 179
aid to Indochina cut by, 164,
    165–67, 171–72
anti-Communist consensus and,
    33–34
as applied to Indochina, 31–40,
    49–53, 65–66, 105
British position vs., 34–35
containment policy, 21–31, 100,
    102, 130
doves in, 82–83, 84, 86, 124,
    126–27, 147, 152, 154
early successes of, 24
as global in scope, 21–24
hawks in, 86, 127
liberation (rollback) policy vs.,
    28–31, 50, 73, 169
new isolationism and, 12–13,
    177–78
Republican attacks on, 30–31
Soviet sphere of influence and,
    26–27
Vietnamization as retreat from,
    169–70
Coser, Lewis A., 101
Cronkite, Walter, 125
Czechoslovakia, Communist coup
    in (1948), 21, 26–27

Davies, John Patton, 33
De Gaulle, Charles, 48, 136–37
democracy:
South Vietnam as "proving
    ground" for, 19, 41–43, 51
U.S. commitment to, 42, 197

Diem, Ngo Dinh, 18, 19, 40, 41,
    55, 57, 68, 70, 138, 172, 203
coup against, 60, 61, 71, 142
first steps toward democracy
    taken by, 42–43
political authoritarianism of,
    43–44
U.S. pressure on, 45, 52
Dien Bien Phu, 31, 32, 34, 40, 54–
    55, 66, 117, 134
domino theory, 32, 168, 176–77
Dong, Pham Van, 96, 200, 202
Dong, Van Tien, 165
draft, 25, 65, 79
Draper, Theodore:
as source, 17, 36, 38, 42, 47, 50,
    63, 66
U.S. role in Vietnam criticized
    by, 75–76, 109, 190, 191
Dulles, John Foster, 30, 36, 42,
    50, 66, 130, 138
"calculated risks" of, 38–39
Geneva accords and, 39–40
on importance of Indochina, 31,
    34–35, 39
Durbrow, Elbridge, 52

Easter offensive (1972), 117, 148,
    150–52, 162, 167
Eden, Anthony, 34–35
Eisenhower, Dwight D., 17, 25,
    30–42, 48, 130, 132, 134
Diem regime and, 41, 42, 45
Geneva accords and, 39–40, 41
on importance of Indochina,
    31–33, 74
Kennedy compared with, 47,
    50–51, 54, 59, 62–63
Korean War and, 30–31, 71, 73,
    136
in refusal to enter Indochina
    war, 32, 35, 36–38, 59, 62–63
wars of national liberation and,
    52, 53

Ellsberg, Daniel, 46–47, 58, 61–62, 104–5, 120, 158–59, 186, 188, 193
Epstein, Edward Jay, 121, 125
Evans, Rowland, 82
"extermination of traitors," 43

Falk, Richard A., 105, 180–82, 184
Fern, Jack, 125
Finney, John, 126–27
FitzGerald, Frances, 14, 96–100, 116, 201, 209–10
Ford, Gerald, 166, 178
France, 21
    in Indochina war, 17, 19, 27, 31, 36–37, 45
"free-fire zones," 182–84, 191
Fulbright, J. William, 68–69, 127, 197

Galbraith, John Kenneth, 45, 53, 60, 61
Gass, Oscar, 58
Gavin, James M., 38
Gelb, Leslie H., 109–12, 120, 129
Geneva accords (1954), 19, 20, 39–40, 41, 43, 55, 66
Geneva Conventions, 183, 184, 185
Germany, Nazi, U.S. compared with, 13, 87, 88, 104
Germany, partition of, 20
Gershman, Carl, 202, 204
Geyelin, Philip, 84
Giac, Thich Manh, 203
Glazer, Nathan, 138–39
Goldwater, Barry, 192
    in election of 1964, 70–71, 73, 86, 142
Goodwin, Richard N., 16, 60, 70–71, 112
Grass, Guenter, 15
Great Society, 79–80, 110

Greece, Communist uprising in (1940s), 20, 24
Gruening, Ernest, 82, 83, 84

Haig, Alexander M., Jr., 160
Halberstam, David, 16, 17, 34, 43, 48, 52, 58, 59, 82, 135
Halleck, Charles, 35
Harriman, W. Averell, 24, 33, 46, 49
Harrington, Michael, 100
Hatfield, Mark, 182
Hayden, Tom, 100, 179
Heilbroner, Robert L., 196–97
Herz, Martin F., 155, 156
Hilsman, Roger, 75, 145, 192
Hiss, Alger, 133, 134
Hitler, Adolf, 11, 23, 104, 194–95
Hoan, Nguyen Cong, 198, 199
Ho Chi Minh, 19, 35–36, 41, 42, 66, 91, 96–97, 108, 111
    Marxism-Leninism of, 98–99
Hoffmann, Stanley, 206–7, 209, 210
Howe, Irving, 205–6
Hughes, Harold, 156–57
Humphrey, Hubert, 79, 101–2, 106, 132, 136, 137

imperialism, 196
"imperial Presidency," 177–78
Indochina war (1950s), 17, 19, 27, 31–40, 45, 48, 54–55
    containment policy as applied to, 31–40
    loss of, as threat to Southeast Asia, 34–35
    military victory impossible in, 38–39
    settlement of, see Geneva accords
    "taint of colonialism" in, 35–37, 40, 50
    U.S. planning for, 32

U.S. refusal to intervene in,
32–40, 59, 62–63, 66
International War Crimes
Tribunal, 180, 181–82
isolationism, 12–13, 25, 65, 86,
177–78

Javits, Jacob, 157
Johnson, Lyndon B., 10, 17, 49,
56, 61, 64–82, 140, 142, 168,
171, 178
antiwar movement and, 82–85,
86–87, 105–12, 123, 124, 127,
129, 133
bombing of North initiated by,
69–70, 72, 74–78
combat troops committed by,
77–79
containment policy advocated
by, 65–66, 73
deception ascribed to, 68–74,
117, 121, 128
in election of 1964, 70–74, 86,
142
in election of 1968, 131, 132
Kennedy compared with, 64–
66, 73, 80–81
large-scale deployment of
ground troops avoided by,
73–74, 76–78
Munich as symbol for, 65
peace initiatives and, 110–11,
143
wartime mobilization avoided
by, 79–81, 106, 130
as "wheeler-dealer," 73, 84–85

Kearns, Doris, 80
Kennan, George F., 22, 26
Kennedy, John F., 10, 16–20, 41,
44–63, 67, 68, 70, 74, 75, 83,
85, 134, 140, 142, 171
"America's Stake in Vietnam"
speech of, 19–20, 40

Bay of Pigs and, 50–51
containment policy advocated
by, 50–52, 53, 65, 73, 102
democracy in Vietnam as goal
of, 19, 42, 43, 51–52
Diem regime and, 44–45, 60
gradual intervention as policy
of, 56–59, 61–63, 77, 79
Johnson compared with, 64–66,
73, 80–81
loss of China and, 45–46
Munich as symbol for, 47–48,
65
as unenthusiastic about U.S.
commitment in Vietnam, 17–
19, 56
Kennedy, Robert, 58, 131, 132
Khmer Rouge, 146, 165, 207, 208–
209, 210
Khrushchev, Nikita, 49, 51, 52,
176
Kirkpatrick, Jeane, 179–80
Kissinger, Henry, 113–14, 124,
130, 139, 141, 168–69, 178
Cambodian operations and,
147, 207
enforcement of Paris agreement
and, 159, 164, 165–68
peace initiatives and, 143–44,
145, 150, 152–56, 157–63
Vietnamization and, 148, 149,
150–51
Korea, partition of, 20
Korean War, 22–26, 27–31, 50–
51, 102, 107, 130, 132, 187
brutality of, 193, 194–95
Chinese and Soviet aggression
in, 27–30, 48
containment policy defined
by, 21, 22–24, 27–31, 65–66,
73
international response to, 24
potential expansion of, 28–30,
71–72, 86

Korean War (*cont.*)
  settlement of, 30–31, 136
  support in U.S. for, 24–26, 35
Kriete, Charles F., 108

Lacouture, Jean, 199
LaFeber, Walter, 123–24
Laird, Melvin, 143
Lansdale, Edward G., 39, 108
Laos, 40, 70, 134, 176
  incursion into (1971), 148, 149–
    150
LeMay, Curtis, 86
Lewis, Anthony, 122, 157, 210
Lewy, Guenter:
  as source, 34, 43, 45, 61, 75,
    105, 106, 113, 118, 122, 142,
    148, 151–52, 155, 164, 165,
    180, 187, 190–91, 192, 193–94
Lifton, Robert Jay, 188, 189
Lodge, Henry Cabot, 70, 134–35
Lowell, Robert, 56
Lowenthal, Richard, 48
Luttwak, Edward N., 113
Lynd, Staughton, 100, 181

MacArthur, Douglas, 28–30, 71,
    73–74, 86, 113, 178
McCarthy, Eugene, 82, 86, 131
McCarthy, Joseph, 66, 133–34
McCarthy, Mary, 92–96, 99, 103,
    104, 109, 200, 201
McCarthyism, 26, 33, 178
  antiwar movement accused of,
    179–82
McCloskey, Pete, 135
Macdonald, Dwight, 56, 101
McGovern, George, 82, 83, 84,
    86, 131–32, 153, 156, 157, 177
McNamara, Robert S., 60, 61, 67,
    69, 76–77, 120, 126, 185–86
  firm initial commitment
    advocated by, 53–54, 57, 62,
    63

McNaughton, John, 110, 115–16
McPherson, Harry, 127–29
Mailer, Norman, 109–10
Mansfield, Mike, 43, 55, 83, 157
Mao Zedong, 21, 27, 52
"massive retaliation" doctrine, 53
media, 145, 146, 157
  antiwar stance of, 124, 125–26
  distortion ascribed to, 116–23,
    128, 180
  escalation criticized by, 83–84
  importance of Vietnam
    accepted by, 81–82
  in pre-1965 period, 18, 32, 55
Middleton, Drew, 122
Mohr, Charles, 117
Mondale, Walter, 147, 148
Morgenthau, Hans J., 20, 105,
    178, 180, 185, 188
Morse, Wayne, 81, 82, 83, 94
Munich conference (1938), as
    symbol, 11–13, 23, 35, 47–48,
    49, 65, 104
Muskie, Edmund, 147
My Lai massacre, 13, 187–89

Nam Dinh, bombing of, 118–19
Nardin, Terry, 190, 191, 192
National Liberation Front (NLF),
    44, 75, 199, 201
  FitzGerald's account of, 96–98
  as North Vietnamese proxy,
    174–75
National Security Council (NSC),
    37, 39–40, 41, 79, 108
Nazi Germany, *see* Germany,
    Nazi
Nazism, Communism related to,
    11, 194–95
Negotiation Now, 88, 103
Nelson, Gaylord, 82
New Left, 89–90, 96
New York *Times,* 55, 56, 81–82,

83, 117–18, 120–21, 122, 145,
146, 185, 210
Nixon, Richard M., 31, 36, 50, 52,
124, 133–63
as arch villain, 133–34, 135
Cambodian operations and,
146–48, 207–8
Christmas bombing and (1972),
121, 148, 154, 156, 180
containment policy attacked
by, 30, 134, 169
in election of 1968, 132, 137
in election of 1972, 152, 153,
177
enforcement of Paris agreement
and, 154, 162–63, 164, 165–
168
escalation options of, 140–42
first Indochina war and, 32, 35,
37, 48, 54–55, 134
immediate withdrawal expected
of, 133, 135–37, 146
Laotian operations and, 149–50
peace initiatives and, 143, 145,
150, 151, 152, 153, 155–56,
157–58, 159–63
saving of South Vietnam as
goal of, 139–40
on significance of Vietnam, 168
Vietnamization and, 143, 146–
151
will to power of, 167–68
withdrawal strategy of, 10, 168–
171
Nixon Doctrine, 169–71, 178
Nolting, Frederick E., Jr., 52, 53
North Atlantic Treaty
Organization (NATO), 21,
53, 66
Northshield, Robert J., 125
nuclear warfare, 32, 49, 53, 71

Oberdorfer, Don, 116
Opton, Edward M., Jr., 189

Paris peace talks and agreement,
140, 143–44, 151–68
Christmas bombing and, 154–
156, 157
congressional action and, 165–
167
"decent interval" theory and,
158–60, 161, 166, 168
enforcement issue in, 154, 159,
162–63, 164–68, 170–72
October 1972 proposals in, 151–
154, 157, 159–61
overthrow of Saigon
government demanded in,
144, 150, 151, 152, 157–58
as U.S. victory, 159–60
violations of, 163–65
"peaceful coexistence," 49, 51
Pentagon Papers, 41, 58, 69, 119–
121, 129
People's Revolutionary Party
(PRP), 98
Phillips, William, 101, 102
Pickus, Robert, 103
Pleiku incident (1965), 123
Pol Pot, 207, 208
Ponchaud, François, 208, 209
press, see media
Provisional Revolutionary
Government (PRG), 175, 199

Quinn, Kenneth, 208

Radford, Arthur W., 31, 32, 34,
35, 37
Rahv, Philip, 101, 102
Ravenal, Earl C., 159
Reagan, Ronald, 179, 180, 210
"re-education camps," 199–201
Ridgway, Matthew B., 38, 127
Roberts, Chalmers M., 37
Roche, John P., 106
Rodman, Peter W., 209
Rosenberg, Harold, 101

Rostow, Walt W., 59–60, 128, 178
Rovere, Richard H., 100, 101–102, 107, 195
rules of engagement (ROE), 192–193
Rusk, Dean, 11, 48, 49, 54, 69, 110, 178
Russell, Bertrand, 13, 180, 181
Russell, Richard B., 35

Safer, Morley, 125
Salisbury, Harrison, 117–19, 120
Sartre, Jean-Paul, 13, 181
Schanberg, Sydney H., 210
Schell, Jonathan, 185–86
Schlesinger, Arthur, Jr., 43, 46, 53, 60
    on anti-Communism, 100–101, 102
    as source, 16, 17–18, 19, 48, 57
    as war critic, 109, 110, 112
Service, John Stewart, 33
Shaplen, Robert, 173
Shawcross, William, 207–9
Sihanouk, Norodom, prince of Cambodia, 207–8
Slater, Jerome, 190, 191, 192
Sontag, Susan, 90–93, 94, 95, 96, 99, 103, 201–2
Sorensen, Theodore, 16, 17, 56, 58
Southeast Asia Treaty Organization (SEATO), 66
Soviet Union:
    Chinese relations with, 33–34, 48–49, 109, 170, 176
    Communist expansionism and, 20–22, 27, 28, 176–77, 178
    North Vietnamese relations with, 151, 152, 164–65, 170, 175–76
Stalin, Joseph, 91, 92, 195, 201–2
Stennis, John, 35

Stevenson, Adlai, 30, 49–50, 132, 134
Stilwell, Joseph W., 52
Stone, I. F., 75
Suez War (1956), 39
surrogate state system, 170
Szulc, Tad, 152, 155, 156, 157–58, 163

Tang, Truong Nhu, 198–99, 201, 203–4
Taylor, Maxwell, 53, 54, 56, 57, 69, 72, 127
Taylor, Telford, 120, 180, 188
Tet offensive (1968), 116–17, 120, 138, 142, 168, 172, 175
    as antiwar "streetcar," 123–27
    distorted reporting of, 116–17, 120, 123
    predictions of, 128–29
Thieu, Nguyen Van, 77, 138, 139, 144–45, 165, 172–73, 200–201, 202
    peace talks and, 144, 152–54, 155–56, 157, 159, 160–61, 162–63, 164, 166, 167
Tho, Le Duc, 143, 148, 152
Thomas, Norman, 88
Thompson, Sir Robert, 62, 141–142, 151, 156, 158
Thuy, Xuan, 143
Toai, Doan Van, 173, 175, 199–200, 201
Tonkin Gulf resolution, 68–70, 81, 82
    pretext for, 69, 70, 121
totalitarianism, 194–95, 204–5
Trilling, Diana, 100
Truman, Harry S., 33, 46, 130, 131, 132
    Czechoslovakia and, 26, 27
    Indochina and, 17, 27–28, 36, 40

Korean War and, 23–26, 27–29,
30, 65, 71–72, 73, 86, 107
Truman Doctrine, 21, 22, 24, 65,
169, 171
see also containment policy
Tuong, Ho Huu, 201
Tuyen, Tran Van, 200–201

United Nations, 24, 183–84

Vietcong (VC), 18, 44, 76–77,
114, 115, 116, 119, 134, 138,
172, 182, 186, 187, 199, 204
FitzGerald's account of, 96–98
as North Vietnamese proxy,
174–75
war crimes of, 184–85
Vietminh, 18, 27, 41, 43
as Communist vs. anti-
colonialist forces, 35–36
Vietnam:
partition of, 19, 20, 43, 173
U.S. ignorance on, 46–47, 114
Vietnam, Democratic Republic of
(North Vietnam):
air strikes initiated against, 54,
57, 69–70, 71, 72, 74–78, 84,
121, 123
bombing of nonmilitary targets
in, 117–19
Christmas bombing of (1972),
121–23, 148, 154–57, 180
as depicted by U.S. writers,
90–99
elections in (1960), 42
mining of harbors in ,151, 152,
167, 168
population statistics for, 186–87
South Vietnam invaded by
(1975), 44, 76, 172–73
Soviet relations with, 151, 152,
164–65, 170, 175–76

subversion in South ascribed
to, 44–45, 48, 55, 68, 74–76
Vietnam, Republic of (South
Vietnam):
army of, 41, 62 (*see also*
Vietnamization)
Communism unpopular in, 172–
173
containment policy extended
to, 40, 49–53, 65–66, 105
free elections proposed for
(1956), 19, 20, 41–42
nature of Communist
insurgency in, 43–44, 76
North Vietnamese invasion of
(1975), 44, 76, 172–73
population statistics for, 186–87
as "proving ground for
democracy," 19, 41–43, 51
reduction of U.S. aid to, 164,
165–66, 171–72
U.S. covert operations in, 39
Vietnam, Socialist Republic of,
198–205
disillusionment with
Communism in, 203–4
executions in, 198
freedoms eliminated in, 201,
202–3
political prisoners in, 199–201
refugees from, 173, 198–99
Stalinism in, 201–2
as totalitarian regime, 204–5
Vietnamization, 145–51, 158, 164
Cambodian operations and,
146–49
Easter invasion and (1972),
150–51
Laos operation and, 149–50
origins of, 142–43
as retreat from containment
policy, 169–70
Vietnam Veterans Against the
War (VVAW), 182

Vietnam war:
bloodbath predicted after loss of, 138–39, 198
civilian casualties in, 118–19, 184–87, 192
as civil war vs. foreign invasion, 44, 74–76, 104–5, 172–73, 175, 183
consequences for U.S. of defeat in, 12–13, 34, 54, 78, 109, 168, 177–78, 195–96
containment of China as goal of, 27–28, 48, 108–9, 174
credibility gap in, 67–74, 117, 120, 126
failures of U.S. leadership in, 171
gradual buildup vs. firm initial commitment in, 56–59, 61–63, 77
as guerrilla war, 47, 59, 62, 113, 184–85
historical perspective on brutality in, 193–95
lessons of, 12–14
political vs. military approaches to, 45–46, 60
POWs in, 91, 95, 166
selfish motive ascribed to U.S. in, 196–97
shortcomings of U.S. military in, 112–16
Soviet role in, 175–76
U.S. casualties in, 79, 148–49, 195
U.S. forces introduced into, 53–57
U.S. public opinion on, 54–56, 71, 81, 87 (*see also* antiwar movement)
U.S. troop strength in, 57, 61–62, 77, 78–79
U.S. vs. North Vietnamese escalation of, 74–76
victory as possibility in, 54, 84
war of ideas in, 114–15
Vincent, John Carter, 33, 34
Vinh, Nguyen Van, 164

Wallace, Henry, 25–26, 73, 131–132
Walzer, Michael, 190, 191, 192, 205–6
war crimes, 103–5, 120, 180–93
forcible relocations as, 182–84
genocide charged as, 13–14, 186–87
indiscriminate use of firepower as, 184–87
"legalistic" analyses of, 190–91
massacres as, 187–89, 191
minimization of U.S. casualties and, 191–93
tribunals and conferences on, 120, 180–82, 186
of Vietcong, 184–85
Washington *Post,* 16, 82, 84, 122–123, 157
Watergate, 166, 167, 177
Westmoreland, William C., 61–62, 70, 78, 112–13, 117, 126, 128, 168–69, 178
Weyand, Fred C., 115, 175
Wheeler, Earle G., 128
White, Theodore H., 46
Wicker, Tom, 70, 198
Wiggins, J. Russell, 82, 84
Wise Men, 127, 129
Wohlstetter, Albert, 62
Wolfe, Tom, 118
World War II, 23, 25, 65, 187, 193–94

Young, Stephen, 82, 86

Zasloff, Joseph J., 18